My Very Good, Very Bad Cat

Chicken Soup for the Soul: My Very Good, Very Bad Cat
101 Heartwarming Stories about Our Happy, Heroic & Hilarious Pets
Amy Newmark. Foreword by Robin Ganzert.

Published by Chicken Soup for the Soul Publishing, LLC www.chickensoup.com
Copyright ©2016 by Chicken Soup for the Soul Publishing, LLC. All Rights Reserved.

The publisher gratefully acknowledges the many publishers and individuals who
granted Chicken Soup for the Soul permission to reprint the cited material.

Front cover artwork courtesy of iStockphoto.com/ WebSubstance (©WebSubstance)
Back cover photo of cat with rope courtesy of iStockphoto.com/Astakhova (©Astakhova)
Back cover photo of striped cat courtesy of iStockphoto.com/Azallya (©Azallaya)
Interior cat illustrations courtesy of iStockphoto.com/andale (©andale)
Interior photos of cats courtesy of Chicken Soup for the Soul employees
Photo of Amy Newmark courtesy of Susan Morrow at SwickPix
Photo of Robin Ganzert courtesy of Michael Price

Cover and Interior by Daniel Zaccari

Distributed to the booktrade by Simon & Schuster. SAN: 200-2442

Publisher's Cataloging-In-Publication Data
(Prepared by The Donohue Group, Inc.)

Chicken soup for the soul : my very good, very bad cat : 101 heartwarming
   stories about our happy, heroic & hilarious pets / [compiled by] Amy
   Newmark ; foreword by Robin Ganzert.

   pages : illustrations ; cm

   ISBN: 978-1-61159-955-8

   1. Cats--Behavior--Literary collections. 2. Cats--Behavior--
Anecdotes. 3. Cat owners--Literary collections. 4. Cat owners--
Anecdotes. 5. Human-animal relationships--Literary collections. 6.
Human-animal relationships--Anecdotes. 7. Anecdotes. I. Newmark, Amy.
II. Ganzert, Robin. III. Title: My very good, very bad cat : 101
heartwarming stories about our happy, heroic & hilarious pets

SF445.5 .C45 2016
636.8/02   2015956063

PRINTED IN THE UNITED STATES OF AMERICA
on acid∞free paper

25 24 23 22 21 20 19 18 17 16   01 02 03 04 05 06 07 08 09 10 11

My Very Good, Very Bad Cat

101 Heartwarming Stories about Our Happy, Heroic & Hilarious Pets

Amy Newmark

Foreword by Robin Ganzert

President and CEO, American Humane Association

CSS

Chicken Soup for the Soul Publishing, LLC
Cos Cob, CT

Chicken Soup for the Soul

Changing lives one story at a time®
www.chickensoup.com

Contents

❸

~My Healer Cat~

❹

~My Surprising Cat~

5

~My Endearing Cat~

6

~My Clever Cat~

❼
~My Therapist Cat~

❽
~My Hunter Cat~

9
~My Nanny Cat~

10
~My Heroic Cat~

Foreword

I just love cats. They're ornery, goofy, surprising, clever, endearing and absolutely adorable. Fascinating, independent, hilarious and precious, they are great hunters, therapists, healers and heroes in our lives. From the meows to the purrs to the scratches, those of us who love cats know that every day is *Caturday*!

Our feline friends have long enriched our human lives. Even Winston Churchill commented about the personalities of cats in relation to us humans, saying, "I am fond of pigs. Dogs look up to us. Cats look down on us. Pigs treat us as equals." I just love the cat-attitude!

If you love cat-attitude, humorous antics and heartwarming adventures, then be prepared to fall in love with these stories. We love the way that Chicken Soup for the Soul features rescued cats in their stories, and the way they highlight the merits of black cats and senior cats, the ones that are often left behind at the shelters. We appreciate that royalties from this book will help support the work that American Humane Association is doing, to promote cat adoption and animal welfare.

You'll read about "ornery cats" in Chapter 1, including Junior, an adorable little white cat who becomes a fierce warrior whenever a dog happens by. It's amazing how often we hear about big dogs that are terrified of little fluffy cats, isn't it? Who's running things around here, anyway? Oh yes… that would be the cats.

I loved the "goofy cat" stories in Chapter 2, including the one about Scooter, a three-legged cat who finally overcomes his fear of the dreaded vacuum, attacks it while it's off, and never runs away from it again.

Cats are wonderful healers for their human charges as well, and you'll read all about those "healer cats" in Chapter 3. I can't stop thinking about a little stray named Lion who was rescued by a mentally ill girl and then stopped the girl from killing herself.

Chapter 4 is filled with stories about "surprising cats." You won't believe all the different ways that cats manage to confound their humans. I chuckled when I read about the woman who was cat sitting for a friend and didn't realize she had inadvertently welcomed an interloper into the group. Two months later, she got to share in the kittens that resulted from that confusion.

We all know people who don't want cats and then fall madly, reluctantly in love with them. You'll feast on those "I-told-you-so" stories in Chapter 5, all about those "endearing cats" who turned unsuspecting non-consenting adults into cat lovers. One husband even gave up his fishing season when an adopted stray cat had her kittens in his beloved boat.

"Clever cats" abound in Chapter 6. I got a kick out of King Murphy, a big Maine Coon rescue who performs amazing feats, including playing board games with a little girl, even using the spinner and then wearing the jewelry he wins.

Sometimes cats have a bad reputation for being aloof, and that's just not right. Chapter 7 is all about those intuitive, friendly "therapist cats" who seem to know just what their humans need. You'll be wowed by the story of a stray kitten who attaches himself to a man dying of cancer, not leaving his side for one moment, and who then disappears, never to be seen again, as soon as the man passes on.

I think every cat owner knows about that famous hunting instinct, and Chapter 8, about "hunter cats," shares stories about all the ways that cats have channeled that instinct in non-harmful ways. I loved the story about the cat family that went so far as to put an easel at the end of their driveway to display all the items their cat stole from the neighbors, so that everyone could reclaim their possessions.

Cats can be amazing nurturers as well, often mothering puppies or human babies. Those "nanny cats" are the subject of the stories in Chapter 9. One mom even reports that she learned some good parenting strategies from watching how her momma cat cared for her new human baby.

And finally, we read about "heroic cats" in Chapter 10, because, surprisingly, cats often save people and other animals. In the story "We Rescued Each Other," a man with Asperger's and stuttering rescues a black cat because they are both "not wanted." The cat has therapeutic value, and helps the man become happier, more outgoing, and more assertive.

I recognized all these cat attributes as I read these stories, because cats have always been a big part of my life. One of my first pets was Daisy, a stray kitty that found her way into our home in Arkansas. Daisy was with us for many years enjoying our family's weekly spaghetti night. She was my best friend while I was growing up. Ms. Kitty was another favorite feline in our home, as was Mercedes while I was in college. Years later, Annie and her litter of kittens showed up on our doorstep in Winston-Salem, North Carolina. My husband and I spent many hours helping Annie feed her new babies. Happily, we found forever loving homes for all of Annie's kittens.

Now, our family is the home to three felines who provide us with constant love, humor and joy. And just recently, my husband rescued two precious stray kitties, delivering them to my retired parents who love their new furry best friends.

While cats make purr-fect pets for some people, it's important to remember that though they appear to be very independent, cats are actually dependent on us humans for their needs, including food, water, medical attention, shelter and companionship. But our furry friends provide us with years of unconditional love and devotion that far outweigh the daily responsibilities.

If you wish to have a feline join your family, remember to consider the following… Do you want a kitten or an adult cat? Kittens need a lot of attention and will have to be house-trained. On the plus side, they do adapt well to their new home and surroundings. For many people, especially those who work outside the home, an adult cat is a wise choice for a loving pet.

Do you want a long- or short-haired cat? Long-haired cats require daily brushing to keep their fur from matting, so be prepared to spend time grooming your new feline best friend.

Do you want a male or female? Both male and female felines can be equally playful and affectionate! Gender is purely a personal preference.

You may be the purr-fect cat owner if you…

- Believe caring for a pet for fifteen to eighteen years does not seem like a lifetime
- Look forward to having your ankles rubbed by an affectionate, loving creature
- Don't mind sharing your house with someone who sheds
- Don't mind sharing your house with someone who will never clean up after him or herself
- Love a housemate who will randomly and regularly entertain you with outrageous and silly antics, at his whim, not yours!

You can set the stage for a life filled with love and companionship by adopting a cat from your local shelter today. American Humane Association created Adopt-a-Cat Month® in 1983, and during every June since then we have encouraged adoptions from local animal shelters. But those of us who know how much fun it is to have cats in our lives know that every day is *Caturday*, and every month is Adopt-a-Cat month!

Once you adopt a feline friend, be sure to care for your cat by remembering the following:

- Twice is nice. Visit your veterinarian twice a year to keep your kitty healthy and happy.
- No tubby tabbies! Lower the risk of obesity by feeding the right food and providing exercise. Ask your veterinarian about the right diet for your cat based on his age and activity.
- Don't bug your cat! It's easy to prevent parasites with year-round protection.
- Lost and found. Be sure to get your feline micro-chipped!

- Cleanliness counts. Use proper sized litter boxes for better cleanliness.
- Play for prey. Cats need exercise and play, so be sure to provide toys and activities.
- The more the merrier! Cats are social, and adopting two or more provides for a loving home.

As you make your way through this wonderful collection, be sure to look at the photos at the beginning of each chapter. You'll meet ten adorable cats who are part of the Chicken Soup for the Soul family — each one rescued off the streets or from a shelter.

So if inspiration strikes after enjoying these stories and looking at the photos, please visit your local shelter to adopt a new best friend. Remember, there is no greater love than that of a cat. And thank goodness they have nine lives for all that love they have to give you!

~Robin Ganzert, President and CEO, American Humane Association

Django

Chapter 1

My Very Good, Very Bad Cat

My Ornery Cat

Fun fact: The Internet sensation known as "Grumpy Cat" is actually a perfectly happy cat named Tardar Sauce, and her grumpy appearance may be the result of feline dwarfism and an underbite.

The Great Escape

*Fun fact: It is believed that in ancient Egypt killing
a cat incurred the death penalty because cats were
viewed as sacred beings.*

y best friend from kindergarten had become a flight attendant and lived in Boston. We were on the phone one night when she complained that she would have to work a three-day trip to Paris.

"What a problem!" I said. "I'd love to be able to get away for a few days!"

"Then come here," she said. "Bring Kathy with you, enjoy Boston, and feed my cat. I'll leave the key with David next door." I wondered if it could really be that simple. My husband told me to go and enjoy myself, and my sister Kathy said her bags could be packed in an instant. We were about to have an adventure!

We had a very easy drive to Boston and felt that was a good omen. We arrived at Dave's apartment a half-hour early, and he was waiting for us — another good omen. But he had this little smirk on his face and, as he handed us the key, he said, "Lots a luck!"

"What do you mean?" we asked.

"I mean good luck with that cat. Jackie's my friend," Dave said, "but I wouldn't go in there if my life depended on it. Here's the list of instructions and some treats. You'll need them just to get in." He chuckled, shook his head and closed his door.

Kathy and I looked at each other. Neither one of us cares much for cats, but that's partially due to allergies. We had taken our antihistamines. We'd be fine.

We walked next door reading Jackie's list. She didn't mention the cat's name, so we returned to Dave's apartment.

"What's the cat's name?" I asked.

"Jackie calls him Simon," he said. "I call him Psycho."

Kathy and I tentatively approached Jackie's door, reassuring each other that Dave was a nut. We put our ears to the door and heard nothing. We put the key in the lock, and then we heard him. The cat was purring, but very loudly. In fact, it was more of a growl than a purr. I was afraid to open the door, but Kathy urged me on. "Come on! It's only a cat...."

We opened the door, and as the cat bounded toward us, the treats came in handy! I threw them as far as I could across the room, and the cat ran after them. I saw on a table next to the door a bag labeled in big letters: "READ THIS!" I grabbed it and slammed the door.

Inside the bag was another note along with a jar of pennies and a spray bottle of water. The note said that if Simon was acting up, we could shake the jar of coins or spray him with the water. This was not a good omen, so instead of going into the apartment, we took our bags back to the car and went to dinner.

We ordered wine immediately. I told Kathy about my last visit to Jackie's, pre-Simon. She has a beautiful studio apartment. Every surface is covered with whimsical treasures gathered as she travels the world. The studio has an open living/dining area. Her bedroom is in an alcove with louvered, bi-fold doors that seal off the bedroom from the rest of the apartment.

We also talked about Simon's (or Psycho's) behavior. What we had seen in our very brief encounter was that the cat was a big ball of white fur and would have been considered pretty if not for its evil countenance and its size. I am no judge of cats, but I think this one weighed about thirty pounds. In any case, he was big. Fat. Huge. He had a furrowed brow, probably from frowning so much, and red eyes that made him look possessed.

Over a second glass of wine, we decided that when we returned to the apartment, Kathy would throw more treats at the cat, I would make sure his dish was full, and we would sequester ourselves in the bedroom.

We got back to the apartment armed for battle. Kathy held the jar of coins, and I had the spray bottle. We would be brave. I opened the door, and the cat leapt at us with a hiss that could be heard throughout Boston. Kathy shook her coins frantically. I held my water bottle aloft, waiting for an opportune time to spray. Kathy threw the treats as far as she could. I checked on the cat food, and we ran to the bedroom, slamming those louvered doors. The lock was a hook-and-eye, and I latched it as fast as my trembling fingers allowed.

We could hear Psycho eating as we got into our pajamas, laughing nervously about how silly we were. Kathy looked around, admiring Jackie's souvenirs. She also noted long, silky hair pretty much everywhere. As we got into bed, we saw the hair on the spread and the pillow. Oh my God, I thought, Psycho must sleep in this bed. We each gulped another pill— without water, of course, because we dared not go to the kitchen.

We told each other to relax and get some sleep, but as our heads hit the pillows we heard the first whump. Psycho wanted in and was throwing himself at the door. Thank God there was a door! Whump again. And again. And now a yowl, a cat sound somewhere between a screech and a wail. How long could he keep that up? Long enough for Dave to knock on the wall and say, "I warned you."

But then it stopped. Psycho had given up. It was quiet out there. So quiet that I could hear Kathy's asthmatic breathing along with my own.

Then a new sound. Glass tinkling and what I knew to be treasures being knocked off the cocktail table, the desk, the TV stand, and the bookcase as Psycho rose higher and higher and nearer to the bedroom door. Then an explosion! The hook and eye gave way against the tremendous thirty-pound force. The louvered doors blew open, and Psycho flew into the room like a Super Cat, a demon, and landed on our bed. We jumped up screaming. I used my water spray to keep him back. Kathy grabbed the bags, and we ran into the living room. I pulled an ottoman in front of the bedroom door, knowing it would never hold back the behemoth. We grabbed the key and, still in our pajamas, fled the apartment.

Passing by Dave's door, we dropped the key in his mailbox, and I swear I heard him chuckling. We got to the car and figured we could get back home by 2:00 a.m. I could see the apartment from the parking lot. We had left on the bedroom lights, but we didn't care. I worried briefly about Psycho's food, but figured he could live on his fat for a month. Besides, Jackie would be home in two days. I stepped on the gas and looked back to see the outline of a big, hairy cat sitting on the windowsill.

Adventure? You can have it. Next vacation, Motel 6.

~Eileen Melia Hession

Catflexing

*Fun fact: A cat's back is extremely flexible because it
has up to fifty-three loosely fitting vertebrae. Humans
only have thirty-four.*

Years ago, I had the great fortune to work as a literary publicist for a small non-fiction publishing house in Berkeley, California. For reasons that were never quite explained to me, if a manuscript was odd, quirky, or in any way bizarre, the editors would immediately assign the project to me. Apparently, they felt my personality and talents were best suited for this kind of fare. Looking back, I have to admit, I did seem to have a penchant and sincere love for the stuff.

During my tenure I successfully promoted everything from cookbooks for bug-eaters to coffee-table books featuring cats that paint. In keeping with the twisted/quirky/oddball theme, I began working with one particular author, Stephanie Jackson, whose book focused on an untapped feline fitness frenzy she lovingly invented and appropriately coined as "Catflexing."

Stephanie first penned this brilliant "exercise how-to" as an inside joke. She created a colorful calendar full of photos of her performing a variety of exercises with her two cats as if they were barbells. In all of the pictures the cats look as blissful as she does — perfectly Zenned out in this owner-cat bonding experience. Stephanie gave the calendars to her family and friends as a gift and inside joke. But it wasn't long before the joke was on her because everyone she knew said it was too good, too hilarious and too "what-the-world-needs-now" to be kept hidden from the public one minute longer. So, reluctantly, at first, the author brought her idea to our publishing house and instantly we knew we had a hit on our hands. And voila — *Catflexing* was born!

Created with the body-conscious cat-lover in mind, *Catflexing* fused the athletic and feline fanatical worlds while simultaneously answering the burning age-old question, "How can I maintain my fitness regime without sacrificing quality time with my cat?"

On one particular sunny summer day in San Francisco, I was charged with the task of finding a suitable stunt cat to "stand in" for the author's own beloved feline. We were doing a live satellite feed for *Good Morning Australia* (the Aussie version of *Good Morning America*) and unfortunately Stephanie's own cat, with whom she had Catflexed for many years, could not travel to the set that day.

Luckily, at the last minute, a co-worker of mine came to the rescue by volunteering his own beloved kitty as "guest star" for the job. Frankly, I was relieved to cross that off my to-do list.

What my dear colleague failed to mention was that his "little puddy tat" was in fact a healthy twenty-nine-pound Maine Coon behemoth that blocked out the sun. (Also, being a rather strange-looking, overweight, angry, drooling, red-eyed sort of cat.) But beggars can't be choosers. This wasn't "America's Next Top Feline Model." So we would just have to make do.

Of course, Stephanie's own cat at home was a seasoned *Catflexing* pro. And by way of drastic comparison, it floated into the ring at a lithe seven pounds — quite a departure from the wretched Chewbacca cat on set that day. (And lest I forget to mention it, it is important to note that at this point in time Stephanie, though incredibly fit, was about eight months pregnant, and utterly bursting at the seams.) The poor unsuspecting woman was about to appear on live television wearing a Spandex maternity leotard and go right into a routine of dead lifting and bench pressing with a ginormous Wookie Cat.

The stunt-double cat and Stephanie had never had the pleasure of meeting, let alone "Catflexing" together before. We were running way behind, the director was already counting us down and there was no time for me to warn Stephanie. Stephanie had not even caught a glance of this disturbing fur-squatch (who appeared to be suffering a touch of IBS or similar ailment.).

We barely got into the studio before "Action!" was called. Peeking out from behind the camera, I crossed my fingers and toes, held my breath and said a silent Hail Mary.

Being a literary publicist had its ups and downs, but I never expected those to include watching an extremely pregnant client try to heft a behemoth cat up and down on live television! I wondered if there was an Aussie word for "sheer panic."

All I could do was watch in horror as the creature screeched, scratched, clawed, spat, drooled and generally pulled some truly ungrateful faces as Stephanie blithely performed her trademark sit-ups and squats, deep knee-bends and over-the-head kitty-cat crunches. It was clear that things were not going to end well, but Stephanie struggled on. The fitness instructor-turned-author-turned scratching post bravely and gracefully stretched her arms and bent down and lifted the irritated, wild-eyed animal behind her neck, onto her stomach and way, way up in the air… all with an almost Zen-like perma-grin plastered on her face.

It was not until months later, looking back at this moment, that I realized Stephanie's smile was not so much "beauty queen poise" as it was "I am going to kill the moron who did this to me." I didn't even realize that I (and probably most of the crew) had stopped breathing until at last the tortured beast broke free from the workout and escaped in a billowing tornado of dust, dander and fur.

Silence fell on the studio as the kitty clouds settled. Stephanie, ever the stalwart professional, having realized we were still rolling, looked straight into the camera, smiled and managed to calmly say, "Well… it's not for *every* cat."

Cut to still-store of the book cover. Cue graphics, with store details, fade out. Cue music, fade to black, and we're out!

The book, to no one's great surprise, met with great success. I pitched Stephanie as a guest to various TV segment producers, landing her on some major network programs including *The Rosie O'Donnell Show* and several Animal Planet programs. My ultimate goal was achieved when I booked Stephanie on Comedy Central's *The Daily Show*. I thought it would be perfect for them (and an amazing promotional opportunity for Stephanie's book — a total win-win). And not only did they agree to do the show, the producers (including Steve Colbert) flew out to San Francisco and did a hilarious in-depth feature segment with Stephanie, her book and her exercising felines.

We were inundated with calls from all over the world. I remember media people from England calling me and saying, with their sweet British accents, "Brilliant! You know, I rather think one could do this with quite small dogs, as well."

By the way, I found out (after the fact, of course), that the Maine Coon cat we borrowed for the Australian satellite feed? Her name was Monster.

Brilliant indeed.

It all goes to show you what incredible, amazing, unpredictable and, yes, sometimes even quirky creatures cats can be. And I am so very glad they are.

~Erika Whitmore

Bootsie's Pick-Me-Up

*Fun fact: Just like humans, animals react to
medications differently, so how your cat reacts after
having anesthesia may be hard to predict.*

"Bootsie survived the surgery! The vet says she's ready for pickup, but I'm swamped. I'll be tied to my desk for the rest of the afternoon. Could you please take her home for me and get her settled?"

While I'd never met my boss's precious cat, we'd spoken of little else that morning. Well known for her nocturnal spats with the neighborhood cats, Bootsie had come home with a nasty gaping wound above her left eye. It had required immediate suturing.

Of course, I'd take the little darling home. Just two months into my job as the assistant to Sue, the charter bus company's director of marketing, I welcomed any opportunity to prove myself to my new boss.

I pulled up to the door of the clinic not thirty minutes later. Smoothing down the front of my new navy skirt, I tossed back my hair and breezed into the lobby, the picture of administrative efficiency.

"But where's Bootsie's crate?"

Excuse me? Sue hadn't said anything about a crate.

The weary receptionist sighed and jerked her thumb in the direction of a teetering pile of flattened cardboard.

"She'll have to go home in one of our temporary ones. There'll be an extra charge, of course."

No problem; I was confident money wasn't an issue when it came to sweet Bootsie.

Brandishing a fully constructed sturdy pet carrier, the white-coated vet also handed over a small medicine vial.

"Here she is! She's still sleepy from the anesthetic. But Sue told you about the pill, right?"

Not wanting to get my crate-challenged boss into yet more trouble, I nodded.

"Okay. So, half as soon as you get her home. No more, no less. Half. For the alertness, to help her wake up."

I hefted the surprisingly heavy crate under one arm and headed for the car after stealing a quick peek through the nearest air hole. What an angel. Much larger than I'd expected, the ginger gem was curled into a slumbering ball. Poor poppet. She'd apparently escaped blindness by a whisker's breadth. Her sutured wound was a virulent, angry pucker just above her left eye.

Time to get this girl home.

How odd. Halfway up the final hill, just fifteen minutes from our destination, the car began to unexpectedly decelerate. I pumped the gas pedal frantically. The vehicle responded by stubbornly shuddering to a halt in the middle of the curb lane. With the fuel indicator hovering beyond empty and the engine refusing to turn over, I had to accept that I'd run out of gas.

Muffled rustles emanated from inside the crate; the patient was stirring. I couldn't abandon my charge, could I? No. But I had to. She was too heavy to carry. Surely, no one would steal her in the short amount of time it would take to schlep down the road to the gas station. I popped open the hood to alert other drivers to the situation and locked the doors.

As I lurched back up the hill some fifteen minutes later, shifting the gurgling and cumbersome gas container between my increasingly aching hands, my eyes were drawn to a curious image. A tangerine bundle of fury was hissing maniacally while frenetically hurling itself to the top of the driver's side window and, paws outstretched, sliding in slow motion to the bottom. Over and over. Bootsie. Possessed. How did she get free? The answer came quickly. Bits of shredded cardboard were strewn throughout the interior.

Time was running out. That requisite half pill was calling. The poor dear was probably scared out of her mind at awakening with a thumping headache in an enclosed box in a strange vehicle. Surely my calming presence would soon reassure her and restore her good nature. I'd have her home in a jiffy.

I hefted the container to the thirsty tank and quickly poured. Carelessly, as it turned out. Multiple gas droplets splayed onto my skirt and shoes. My head now thick with the gaseous fumes, I opted for the closest door. Startled out of her obsessive leaping, Sue's darling streaked for the gas pedal, neatly wedging herself underneath. There she remained, resolutely lodged, a virtual hissing machine. Acknowledging that this wasn't terribly conducive to driving, I summoned the courage to inch into the driver's seat, tuck my knees up under my chin and begin crooning her name. These gestures proved woefully ineffective; the hissing morphed into plaintive screeches. I took scant comfort in the observation that her stitches remained intact despite the exhaustive escape efforts and subsequent acrobatics.

Five deafening minutes passed. Then ten. Just as I began to think I'd have to risk serious finger shredding as a result of dragging her out from under the pedal, the little minx suddenly stretched, eased herself out and gracefully leapt up onto the seat beside me. She proceeded to settle in as if this was our normal routine.

The blessed reprieve was quickly replaced by a horrid reality. The carrier transport option was toast. How was I going to get this hellion into her house? I'd have to wrap her up in something. Naturally, the only solution was my cherished woolen jacket that just moments ago had paired nicely with my now ruined skirt. As I reluctantly eased it off my shoulders, her eyes snapped open. I'd have to be quick.

She wasn't pleased. Clutching the now impossibly twisting, hissing and spitting bundle, I stumbled to the front door. After shakily inserting the key, I wrenched it open. Once I carefully lowered the jacket to the floor, the little creature shot out, tore over the carpet and vanished up the stairs.

My overwhelming relief was once again short-lived. Bootsie still needed her pill.

It was teensy, the size of a grain of rice. The vet mentioned it had to be cut in half. Was he kidding? No, he'd stressed it quite clearly. Dumping my now repulsively fur-lined, saliva-soaked jacket in the hallway, I headed for the kitchen.

A quick perusal revealed only butcher's knives. Wielding the least lethal-looking one of the bunch, I firmly cleaved the pill in two, then watched in disbelief as both halves plopped off the cutting board onto the floor and began rolling merrily along the tiles before disappearing under the fridge.

Enough. I was done. Time to call for backup. I rang the office and asked for my boss.

"Hi, Kelly. No, Sue's gone for coffee. She said she'd be back in an hour or so."

Gone for coffee for an hour or so while I was alone with Bootsie?

Bootsie zoomed into the kitchen, took one look at me and darted back out. I was dismissed.

And the note I left next to the empty pill bottle?

"Bootsie's here. Somewhere. No worries — she's more than alert. Trust your coffee break was good. Should you require yet another pick-me-up, you can happily find it under your fridge."

~Kelly L. McKenzie

Karmic Lessons from the Cat

Not-so-fun fact: Thirty percent of older cats develop kidney disease.

What do you do when you are stepmother to a cat that despises you? Even worse, how do you come to terms with that hatred when the feline is named Karma? This was my dilemma years ago. It felt too ominous to say, "Karma hates me," so I made it my mission to win over the cat and get Karma on my side.

Karma was a street kitten that decided to follow my boyfriend Andrew home. That same night, Andrew had found fifty dollars on the street and had discussed his views on kindness and karma with a co-worker. He decided the evening was fated and named the cat Karma. Initially, Karma was wild, tearing up the apartment Andrew kept meticulously clean with his sister, with whom he lived at the time. Karma would bounce off the walls, a crazed ball of hair that leaped like a ninja and yowled like a banshee.

Karma's love for Andrew was intense. Of all the humans on the street, he had recognized something special in him. He would lie on Andrew's chest, relentlessly licking his shirt until it was soaked, no matter how many times Andrew pushed him off. He followed him like a shadow and leaped into his arms to nestle in like a baby, adoring and possessive. It was a love story for the ages.

When Andrew's sister realized she was allergic to cats, I adopted Karma. Naively, I thought it was a perfect solution. I could have a handsome cat as a pet, and he and Andrew could still see each other. Little did I know that Karma's love was exclusive, reserved solely for his savior. He was a one-human cat, and anyone else was an interloper, an intruder, an unwelcome competitor for Andrew's affections. I was instantly public enemy number one.

Karma despised me with an all-consuming hatred that no amount of kitty treats and catnip would appease. He would sit on top of my bookshelves and swat me on the head every time I passed by. I could see him visibly cringe every time he heard my voice. Friends were startled by the way the cat glared at me with a look of pure contempt.

Karma would regularly chase me around my apartment and wrap around my ankle, biting and scratching until he drew blood. More than once, I would cower in the bathroom like Shelley Duvall from *The Shining* and see a furry paw clawing under the bathroom door. It was a reign of terror administered by a seven-pound mound of fluff. Of course, when Andrew would come to visit, Karma would leap into his arms and gaze adoringly at him. Between purrs, he would throw a sideways glance in my direction as if to say, "See? I am capable of great love. Just not for you. Ever."

Despite Karma finding me despicable, I found him irresistible. He had emerald eyes, a pink nose, and a magnificent tail he held like a flag. He sported puffy tufts of fur around his legs so he looked like he was wearing bloomers. What woman hasn't gone through a phase of loving a handsome bad boy, convincing herself that if only she loved him enough, he would change his ways?

Once Andrew and I married, I hoped that Karma would soften his stance against me. After all, we were a family now. He and Andrew were under the same roof again, and I could no longer be blamed for taking him away from his love.

No such luck. Karma reluctantly accepted me as his servant, but nothing more. He would wake me up in the morning by slapping my face with his paw and demanding his breakfast. He decided that water bowls were beneath him and instead took to waking me up in the middle of the night so that he could have a fountain drink from the bathroom sink. More often than not, he would finish slurping and then chase me back to bed, biting my ankles. I began to suspect that these late-night rituals were a sinister plot to exhaust me and hasten my demise. He was obviously playing the long game, and I had to grudgingly admire his persistence and cunning. I knew that if he ever learned how to operate a can opener, my days would be numbered.

"If something happens to me, it was Karma," I warned a friend who happened to have Karma lounging on her lap at the time.

"Of course, it's Karma. Karma will get us all. That is the beauty of the karmic wheel," she replied, scratching Karma's ears as he purred.

"No. I mean if I am snuffed out, it was the cat," I insisted, pointing at Karma. "He'll make it look like an accident, but I know it'll be him. Remember this conversation if something happens to me."

My friend scoffed and looked at the cat, who was innocently licking his paws, pretending he hadn't just flashed me a dirty look moments before.

Perhaps I could be considered pathetic, continuing to hope that one day Karma would find it in his heart to love me, just a little. I tried to convince myself that I had enough love for the two of us. I grasped at any crumb he would toss my way: a look that was indifferent rather than pure loathing, the times that he let his paws touch my lap on his way to Andrew, his acknowledgment of my presence while he was waiting for me to fill his food dish. I still believed that I could win him over in time.

When Karma was around seventeen years old, he developed kidney problems. He became skinny and listless, his bony body feeling more like a fragile bird than a cat. I could hold his frail body on my chest and stroke his head, and he wouldn't try to escape. That's when I knew he was really sick. At that point, I would have given anything for him to give me a vicious scratch or bite. When we took him to the vet for his final injection, Andrew and I stayed with him, crying and stroking his fluffy bloomers until he closed his eyes.

It may seem strange that I could be broken hearted by the loss of a cat that never liked me. I still expect to see him trotting toward me when I use a can opener or wait to feel his sharp little teeth attacking my ankles when I get up in the middle of the night. At the time, a friend suggested that maybe I was heartbroken because now I knew I would never have a chance to win over the cat. I don't think it was that. I think I finally understood that it was possible to love a crabby cat for who he was, not who I wished he could be. Our ability to love is bigger than we realize. Karma taught me that I could love without ego or expecting anything in return. Perhaps this was my Karmic lesson to learn, delivered in the form of a grudge-holding, glaring cat.

~Kristine Groskaufmanis

Junior

Fun fact: Some people believe that if you dream about a white cat, you'll have good luck.

A white ball of fur, nails, and teeth was thrashing on top of the young dog that had foolishly wandered into our garage. My father tried to pry her off the poor canine, but all he got was scratches on his shoes and one on his leg. Junior wanted that dog gone right away. The dog managed to break free, blindly running out of the garage and across the road. He frantically disregarded any car that might have been driving on the asphalt because that danger was nothing compared to the white ball of insanity threatening to destroy him.

We had gotten the tiny, delicate kitten from a friend of my sister, who had commented that she looked just like her mother. This characteristic caused someone in my family to suggest we name her Junior, and the name stuck.

Junior grew to be a little smaller than an average cat, but her personality was that of a tiger. She hated dogs and only barely tolerated the two we had. Once in a while, she would attack the larger dog, and he would turn his face away and just try to get out of her way.

Whenever she saw a stranger dog, things got very interesting. She would sneak up and slowly make her way to the unsuspecting beast. She would then puff herself up until she looked five times her normal size. Then she would spring into action, and all we would see was a white flash of nails and teeth. When she was attacking a dog, she was unrecognizable as a cat. She looked like something out of this world, and that was her weapon. How can a dog fight something that looks like it was sent by the devil?

One time a client came by in his truck. As my father was talking to the man, his Blue Heeler jumped out of the cab and wandered about the yard. Junior spotted the dog. We saw her approaching and doing her dance, moving sideways and arching her back.

My father advised the man: "Watch out, that cat attacks dogs."

The man responded, "Nah, my dog eats cats for breakfast."

Just then, Junior sprang toward the dog and attacked. The poor dog did not know what to make of this white blur scratching at his face. He frantically escaped and retreated to the cab of the truck. Disappointed, the man exclaimed, "You big chicken!" Junior walked away to the back of the garage, still furious but proud of her accomplishment. The dog waited patiently in the truck while the client talked business with my father.

This happened several times to different dogs. Junior even attacked a blind dog. No kidding. Junior had no remorse for dogs that came into her territory.

She was also a next-level mouse hunter. When regular mice became too easy, too boring, she started bringing home prairie dogs. A prairie dog is prone to a ferocious self-defense, but once in a while, Junior would drag one of these guys home and offer it to us.

Not surprisingly, Junior had muscle tone that I have never seen on a cat. We noticed her muscles as she climbed the stairs, and my brother nicknamed her Sarah Connor after the fierce, muscular heroine in the *Terminator* movie we had recently watched.

Junior was not spayed. Despite Bob Barker's efforts, no one I knew had their pets fixed in the rural southwest. I did not even know where a veterinarian could be found. Junior had a few litters and we managed to find homes for all of them. As her kittens grew into adulthood, we began to receive reports of those cats attacking dogs. She taught her kids well, and they became warriors in their own battles against the dog invasion force.

Although Junior was a vicious fighter, she was soft and gentle when interacting with her human friends. She loved to be petted, and she would occasionally sleep on my bed at night. When she was around, I felt strangely protected. When we played in the back yard, Junior was usually around but at a distance, as though she was watching over us.

We lost Junior during our family's big move. She hated car rides, and halfway to our destination, she finally had enough. She broke free from her crate and squeezed out of my old pickup's vent window as we slept in a motel room. The next morning, we walked around the neighborhood next to the motel calling her. If she was there, she was not coming to our calls. After a few hours, my father decided that we needed to press on and let Junior be.

Two decades later, we still talk about Junior when the family conversation turns toward our furry friends. We remember her victories, we acknowledge her influence, we regret our separation far too soon, and we wonder how she made out in her new home. Maybe there is a family of dog-attacking warrior cats near that motel right now.

~Dan C.

Road Trip

Fun fact: Cats can make more than a hundred different sounds; dogs can only make about ten sounds.

After having nineteen cats over thirty-five years, we were done. No more cats. No more scooping, feeding, and feline traumas. Besides, we were going to winter in the sunny South. And you don't want to drag a cat on a 1,200-mile car trip. We would be free as birds. On the trip to South Carolina we would talk about how cute our grandkids were, plot vacation escapades, and listen to quiet music or maybe a book on CD.

Then an orange-and-white stray cat trotted into our yard. For a few days, he meowed from a distance. So we left food out, which must have tasted better than dead mice because he wound around our ankles and let us pet him. In a week, he owned us.

The more we did for him — worming, de-fleaing and vaccinating — the more affectionate he became. Tucker even shrugged off being neutered. Instead of resenting us, he seemed to think we had rescued him from the man in the white smock. The only thing he hated was the car ride to the vet. During those fifteen minutes, he howled and tore at the cage like a Tasmanian devil.

Otherwise, Tucker was a baby. He cuddled on the couch with us and turned belly-up for stroking while he purred deeply with his eyes rolled back.

We advertised in the paper and begged friends and family to adopt this beautiful, housebroken, affectionate buddy who had all his medical bills pre-paid. We were leaving for three months and we needed to find him a home. But there were no takers, and we reluctantly admitted that we were embarking on cat number twenty.

When we left upstate New York for South Carolina at 5:00 a.m., it was dark, snowing and fifteen degrees. Tucker was in a huge cage that filled most of the back seat of our SUV. He would be fine with that much space, we told ourselves. He'd cry a bit, then settle down and sleep.

Not exactly. He howled; he gargled; he moaned. He clawed at the cage mesh and pushed his face into it until his nose was raw. The roads were slippery and snow was building up. We told him everything was okay. He didn't buy it.

A half-hour later, he scratched at the small litter pan at one end of the cage, yanking it around. Kitty litter sprayed the back of my head. He squatted ten times and shifted targets. For ten miles, he fought for position. Finally, he was quiet. "That's better," I said.

Then the aroma hit. The car was really packed, so there was not much air inside, and most of that no longer qualified as air. "We've got to do something!" my wife pleaded. "I can't breathe."

I grunted so I didn't have to open my mouth, but we were on a highway in blinding snow. It would be dangerous to park on the shoulder, so we slogged another seven miles at thirty-five miles per hour until the next exit. No services were open yet. In a parking lot, we discovered that Tucker had scattered kitty litter over everything except what it was supposed to cover, and that had, of course, missed the pan. The cage was a mess, and he had poo on his belly, tail and paws. While I clutched the frightened cat to my chest in the snow and wind, Carol cleaned him using paper towels and snow. Tucker's tail was between his legs.

"He's ashamed," Carol said. "Poor thing!" When she finished with him, she worked on the cage, scraping what little litter was left to barely cover the bottom of the pan. Finally, she cleaned me up. "You better let me register at the hotel," she said.

I returned him to the cage. "There can't be any more in him," I said. Wrong. "He can't miss again." Wrong. Between episodes, he dug at the cage and yowled, and somehow caught a claw in the back of the zipper and pulled it open. We didn't know it until his head poked between us, eyes wide. "Let's try him out of the cage," I said. "It can't be any worse."

It wasn't worse, just different. The howling subsided into meows. He roamed restlessly, shedding hair, crouching each time a tree whizzed past (and Kentucky has a lot of trees). He tried to leave through the windshield fifty times. He tried to push out through the passenger window. That worked out well because he stepped on the window-opening button so the glass slid down with a whoosh just as a semi passed us in six lanes of traffic. We all flinched at the sudden roar and rush of air. I fumbled to raise the glass. Luckily, the noise scared Tucker, who dove for the back seat.

We were congratulating ourselves on a close one when a window behind us whizzed down. He'd done it again! Carol lunged for him, grabbing his tail to keep him from jumping out while I pulled up the window button, unable to see where he was and afraid I might decapitate him. I set the childproof window locks and then the door locks for good measure. How could I be so out of practice? I thought fondly of the days we crammed our back seat full of children for vacations and only had to deal with feet kicking our backs and voices whining, "Are we there yet?"

"Are we there yet?" Carol asked.

By southern Kentucky, he began to calm down. Oh, he still shed furiously, so we breathed an atmosphere that consisted of oxygen and fur soup. All three of us sneezed our way through Tennessee. But he began to nap between escape attempts. Eventually, he sat upright on the console between Carol and me and stared ahead like a regular passenger. I think he decided we had all been abducted by this four-wheeled beast, and we'd all escape together somehow. He stared at us and made gentle meows as if to ask if we had figured out a plan yet.

Finally, he curled his fifteen-pound body on my lap for a long, undisturbed pet and nap. You know how draining long drives are, how dopey they make you? Not this one. By the time we arrived, I was ready to climb a mountain or dig the Panama Canal. The clock said it took us eighteen hours instead of our usual sixteen. But the time had rocketed past like a two-hour action movie. It was a good thing we had three months before the return trip.

~Garrett Bauman

Little Monsters

Fun fact: A cat's hissing often sounds like a snake, and some researchers believe cats may have developed this distinct sound by imitating snakes they encountered in the wild.

I was a Navy brat growing up, which meant my father was assigned to a new duty station every few years. Until the age of five, my younger brother and I lived in the suburbs. When our dad was sent to a rural area in upstate Maine, our parents were determined to show us what country living was about.

Dad searched high and low for the perfect house, but was unable to find one that met his "countrified" requirements. Then, purely by accident, he came across an old farmhouse set on several acres of land with a barn, a huge garden plot, and a pond.

We were in our new home a few months when Dad came home from work one day with a cardboard box in his hands. We could hear mewling sounds coming from inside the box.

"What in the world have you brought home?" my mother asked.

My father, lover of all things lost and forgotten, told us how a co-worker's cat had given birth to a litter of kittens. She found homes for all of them except two and was on her way to take the final pair to the local pound when Dad offered to adopt them.

One look inside the box was all it took for my brother and me to instantly fall in love. The kittens were adorable. One was pure black with four white socks, and the other was a mixture of black, browns, and grays. I chose the black one and named her, predictably, Fluffy. My brother chose the other and named him, of all names, Dirty Face.

Mom was not as thrilled, but we begged, and the cats stayed.

And so began the love-hate relationship between the cats and our mother. It was as if those two critters could sense her initial reluctance at them being there, and they made sure she knew they never forgot it.

It started out innocently enough. The wooden legs on the kitchen table became their scratching posts, and they had that dining set looking like something from a salvage yard in no time. They also shredded two sets of sheer drapes my mother made for the living room.

When they got older, they would leave little treasures for her on the back stoop, things like dead mice and moles and small birds. Fluffy and Dirty Face were not easily deterred, however. If they couldn't find any prey outside, they would take easy pickings from inside the house.

As a special treat for our dad's birthday, Mom was defrosting a pair of T-bone steaks and a couple of lobsters in the kitchen sink. That afternoon, we ran errands with her. When we got back, the steaks and lobsters were gone. We searched everywhere for the missing birthday menu items, but couldn't find them. We couldn't find the cats either. A few hours later, my brother yelled from upstairs that he had found Fluffy and Dirty Face. They were stretched out under my brother's bed on the hardwood floor, their bellies swollen to an alarming size with the remains of their stolen booty scattered around them. Apparently, the T-bones were not to their liking. The lobsters were a different story. To this day, I have never seen a pair of lobsters picked so clean.

While both cats seemed to take particular delight in terrorizing our mother, Fluffy was the more aggressive. About the worst Dirty Face would do was pounce from dark corners and scare her, but Fluffy clearly had a more adventurous streak.

The final straw came one evening when my mother drew a hot bubble bath and told us not to disturb her. Apparently, Fluffy didn't get the memo. Mom was soaking in the tub, unaware the cat had somehow managed to climb the outside trellis and squeeze in through the open bathroom window holding a small green snake, still alive, in its mouth. My mother heard a soft plop and opened her eyes to find

Fluffy perched on the rim of the tub.

"How did you get in here?"

Then she looked down.

I will never forget the blood-curdling scream from that bathroom. We watched as our mother, covered in bubbles and wearing only a towel, came racing down the stairs yelling for our dad.

"Those cats hate me!" she cried.

The following week, Dad took them to a neighbor's farm several miles away, where they quickly adapted to their new surroundings as barn cats, playing amongst the horses and hay and tall clover in the back pasture. We visited them often that last summer before we moved. On one of our last visits, the farmer came over to the barn and told us about a strange occurrence that happened a few days prior.

"Those two cats are wrapped in mischief."

"What do you mean?" Dad asked.

He pointed to Dirty Face.

"That one there ain't so bad. Just likes to jump out from behind the barn door and scare the dickens out of my wife when she goes to collect eggs from the hens.

"But that one there," he said, pointing at Fluffy, "is pure devil. We don't know how in the world she got in the house, but the other morning while we were eating breakfast, she jumped up onto the kitchen table and dropped a live baby copperhead onto my wife's plate. Can you believe that?"

Our dad tilted his head back and laughed. "Doesn't surprise me in the least."

~Cheryll Snow

The Prodigal Cat

*Fun fact: Cat food left outdoors may encourage hungry
coyotes to eat it (and your cat), too.*

Our decade-old gray Tabby, Augie, whose ancestry must have included Attila the Hun and Genghis Kahn, had escaped. It was a crisp Christmas morning and my husband wanted a fire. Augie was snoozing in his secluded corner, fifteen feet from the door, so my husband slipped out for firewood. Coming in, his arms full of wood, he became aware of a quick furry exit.

Augie had recently been in a skirmish that reduced half his face to hamburger. The vet had sent him home with antibiotics and the dreaded head cone, to be worn at least until mid-January. He was not supposed to go outside wearing that thing.

When Augie didn't show up that night for dinner (despite our calling "Here, kitty kitty, turkey trimmings"), we decided the prodigal would surely return the next day. After all, if The Cone impaired his ability to slurp down his usual canned food, how would he manage with four-legged food that could run away?

Three days later, I was trudging through the snow, leaving "lost cat" notes at every home on the block. A "lost pet" ad with photo went in the paper. But by the end of the week, concluding he was gone for good, I washed his sleeping pad and dishes.

Our life with Augie had begun one blistering August afternoon. While I sweated in the kitchen preparing dinner, my husband and son left in search of shade. They ended up at a local riverside park legendary for unauthorized animal disposal. Unwanted bunnies and kittens and native groundhogs roamed its thick landscaping shrubs. Coyotes in the adjacent hill considered the park their private restaurant.

Enter tender-hearted husband and son, who heard a weak meow from a drainage culvert. The tiny one, who couldn't resist a chicken nugget plucked from the trash, found himself wrapped in an old towel and headed for a new future.

"He will be an outdoor cat," my husband assured me, rummaging in the cupboard for some tuna. My asthma had limited pets to those swimming in a fish bowl. Augie, so named for being found in August, would break the household furry-pet ban.

The "outdoor cat only" promise was forgotten as winter came. I vacuumed twice as much and went to the doctor for stronger asthma medicine. When Aug became the Handsome Hunk for local fertile female felines, I shuffled him off to the vet for The Operation. Of course, the bill got padded: "Animal Control laws require a rabies shot." And that led to a notice from Animal Control that he needed a pet license to dangle off his flea collar.

Life with Augie soon settled into a rhythm of cat food and catting around. Not wanting to install a pet door (the neighborhood had raccoons), we resigned ourselves to increased use of the back door for his "duty" and "recreation," the latter requiring at least annual trips to the vet for his relapses into warfare.

Despite doting human care, some cats have no moral conscience for taking care of their keepers in old age. And thus, our prodigal felt compelled to escape that Christmas morning, liberating him to revel in the riotous living curtailed by his convalescence.

Three weeks later, I was fixing dinner one frigid January night when my husband came in after teaching school, holding a familiar gray-striped animal. "He was sitting in the garage when I raised the door," he said. The Prodigal had returned — skinnier, filthy, and still wearing the dreaded head cone. We peeled it off, retrieved his food dish and opened a remaining can of cat food. Augie ate seconds and thirds. When picked up, he pushed his head into the crook of an elbow, unwilling to look at us. If cats could talk, he might have said, "I have sinned against thee. I am no longer worthy to be called your pet cat. Please accord me a corner of the garage for duties in catching mice." His repentance speech included a recital of extra-loud purring. For a week, he refused to leave the house.

That was three years ago. His Christmas adventure didn't cure him of the occasional need for vet trips and recovery cones. But never again has he taken such an extended vacation from his human family. Life is too good when you don't have to worry where your next meal is coming from. Especially when Christmas might mean some turkey trimmings.

~Jeanne Zornes

Never Name a Cat After Dylan Thomas

Fun fact: Ancient sailors thought it brought on trouble to say a cat's name, even though cats were welcomed on board to keep rodents under control.

My first mistake was probably in naming him after Dylan Thomas. My orange cat, named after the poet who had authored "Do Not Go Gentle into That Dark Night," took the message of that poem just a little too seriously. As my friend so perfectly put it: "That cat isn't going anywhere gently."

To be fair, I couldn't have known what was coming. When I first met Dylan, he was cowering in the back of a cage at the local animal shelter. His name at the time was Armand. A friend had seen his ad in the paper and, knowing that I was looking for a cat and was partial to orange kitties, had suggested I go see him. He wasn't exactly what I was looking for — I'd wanted a young kitten, preferably a female. Dylan was almost two years old, male, and afraid of everything. His ad had stated that he would need some "time to warm up" in his new home.

Meeting him at the shelter, though, I was warned that he would need quite a bit of time to be left alone to explore his new home on his own terms. His previous owners had abandoned him, simply putting him outside in December in New England and then moving away. A neighbor had seen him and kept him on his porch for a week before bringing him to the shelter.

There wasn't an open room for me to visit with him at the shelter, and this grand orange cat curled himself into the far corner of his cage, watching me. From another cage, a calico threw herself against the bars, trying to get me to pat her. She purred relentlessly, walking back and forth against my hand and her cage door so much that she built up static electricity and began to shock herself. Still, she purred and reached her paws out, literally grabbing for my attention. Dylan curled himself away from me and went to sleep.

I brought Dylan home. It took the shelter employees an unsettling amount of time to get him into the cat carrier, and by the time they brought him out to me, I was a bundle of nervous energy, wondering if I was making the right move. Dylan yowled for the first ten minutes of the drive, but then pressed himself in the back of the carrier and remained silent.

Once we were home, I let him out, and he quickly investigated my Netherland Dwarf rabbit. I got my first good look at Dylan as he raced for the safety of my bed; I hadn't been able to fully see into the cage at the shelter. He was impressively big and had beautiful orange stripes down his legs. The tip of his tail was white. Once he disappeared under my bed, I assumed I wouldn't see him for days, as I'd been warned.

That night, I woke up to Dylan climbing on me as I lay in bed. I didn't touch him or even dare to move; I just let him explore my bed in the safety of the darkness. I was elated that he was feeling confident enough to venture out already.

And that was when the adventure started. Not only was Dylan confident enough to roam throughout my apartment, he assumed that everything in it was his.

Within a few days, he had shredded entire rolls of toilet paper while I slept. He punctured a tube of toothpaste and a bottle of spray-in hair conditioner with his teeth. He carried a plush dog, larger than his head, throughout the apartment, frequently bringing it up to my bed. He stole rolls of paper towels and decorated the kitchen in confetti. In less than thirty seconds, he chewed a hole in a brand-new bag of cat litter. He stole a tray of a dozen cupcakes that I had purchased from the store and chewed through the bottoms. He chewed off the corners of my unopened mail, tore pages out of my notebooks, and dog-eared (or should it be cat-eared?) the corners of too many paperbacks. He climbed up onto the back of the toilet tank, picked up the full box of tissues with his mouth, and dragged it into the living room where he proceeded to pull out the tissues and shred them. (He's done this multiple times, along with his toilet-paper and paper-towel tricks.)

In one of his more stellar stunts, Dylan bit into a glass Christmas tree light before carrying it around the apartment in his mouth. His vet almost didn't believe me when I called after that incident.

And that's not to say that he was neglected — far from it. I began investing in every type of cat toy on the market. Dylan had piles of toys that he loved — he just thought my things were more fun.

In less than six months, my exasperated status updates on Facebook prompted a friend to suggest that maybe Dylan was lonely. I had to admit that she was probably right. Dylan came dashing into the room any time I played a YouTube video with cats in it; he would search for the cats, talking to them all the while.

And so, questioning my sanity, I went back to the shelter and adopted another cat, a young female calico. Dylan was determined they would be instant friends, though the female, whom I named Cara didn't agree at first.

In time, Cara came around, and Dylan had his buddy. His destructive behavior stopped almost immediately, though I still have to guard my toilet paper and paper towels. Now I'm lucky to watch these two play games of tag throughout my apartment. Having two cats wasn't in my plan, but I'm learning that life often takes turns that you never see coming. Now these two are my buddies, and I wouldn't trade them for the world.

Dylan still has a few tricks up his sleeve — he opens my kitchen cabinets every night, and carries the rubber stopper from the bathroom sink throughout the house. He recently ate half a paper towel that he got out of the covered trash, prompting an unusual call to the vet. But for the most part, he's settled, content to play with Cara. I still keep the toilet paper stored up high, though — with him, you just never know.

~Paige Cerulli

My Boy, George

Fun fact: Adult cats have thirty teeth. Kittens have twenty-six baby teeth, which they lose when they're about six months old.

rush my cat's teeth? I'd do better poking hot needles into my eyes. We'd just returned from a health-and-wellness checkup, and the veterinarian said my cat had tartar and redness along the gum line. She recommended a dental-food diet and encouraged me to brush his teeth. The items on my kitchen counter seemed innocent enough — salmon-flavored paste and a nubby rubber thimble.

The vet's advice was correct, but I knew my cat. Taking out extra life insurance seemed like a really good plan before venturing forth. Don't get me wrong, I love my boy, and I'd do anything for him, but this seemed like a recipe for disaster.

***

It was Mother's Day, and cats were on sale at the Humane Society. George had been found outdoors by a concerned cat lover who'd kept him a few days before turning him in. The sign on the cage said, "Approximately one year old. George doesn't like to be picked up." That should have been my first clue.

He prowled and howled, scratching at the door as if to say, "Get me out of here." There was nothing about his attitude that said, "Please take me home. I'll be a nice little kitty."

I knew George was different, but then again so was I. This cat strummed my heartstrings like a well-tuned banjo. Huge, staring green eyes and the most gorgeous face you could imagine. It didn't matter that he was a black cat. I didn't believe the superstition.

After I answered a million questions to prove I would be a responsible owner, I was handed George in a cardboard box. Fortunately, I'd brought a friend and cat lover with me. Tammy was a foster mom for the SPCA when she worked in Texas, and was an expert when it came to cats. Thank God, she was with me.

On the expressway, George burst out of the cardboard box and found his way under the clutch. Shifting gears was out of the question. With the car in neutral in the centre lane, cars passed and honked on both sides. I would have raised my middle finger at them, my own brand of instant messaging, but my hands had a death grip on the steering wheel.

My friend managed to get George into the back seat, and I was relieved to get the little black bundle home. We showed him his litter box, he did some scratching, and then proceeded to explore. For the most part, he seemed docile. George had a new home!

The honeymoon was soon over. Three days after his adoption, I had a call from Public Health indicating he'd bitten the person who rescued him. A representative would follow up. Yikes, my cat had a criminal record!

By then, I knew George was prone to scratching and biting. His demeanor in the cage was manifesting itself. He'd sometimes follow me down the hallway and nip at the back of my legs. I presumed it was all about power and control and adjusting to his new surroundings. As a registered nurse, I'd worked in psychiatry for ten out of the last forty years. I understood behavior and took the time to look at cause and effect. I could forgive his actions. When the investigator from Public Health arrived, she said, "I'm not really a cat lover." It was a brief visit, and fortunately George refrained from biting her.

**

George continued to be a bit of a nasty boy. Never a lap cat, he only wanted affection when it suited him. I understood and respected his wishes. He'd still nip and sometimes let me know when enough was enough. A cat just acts the way it feels!

The second year I had him, he escaped through my daughter's bedroom window, two floors up in a condo. She'd taken the panels out to clean them, not thinking he'd see it as an escape route. She was in tears, and so was I.

My heart was broken, and that's when I realized how attached I'd become to him, even though he mostly behaved badly. I posted pictures and notices on all the local signposts, knocked on neighbors' doors, searched relentlessly, prowled the neighborhood late at night and walked around shaking a treat bag. I didn't care if I looked like an idiot. I just wanted him back.

After seventy-two hours, I was devastated. It was time for one final look around. At 11:00 p.m., I ran into my neighbor walking her dog. By then, I was resigned to the fact that George was gone. The neighbor gave me a hug, and I walked across the street to my condo entrance. As I approached the front door, a little black devil rushed toward me from under the shrubs. I'd like to think he jumped into my arms, but that's not his style. He did, however, allow me to pick him up and take him inside. There was only a slight "nip" in the elevator. I presumed it meant he was happy to see me.

* * *

George is now seven years old and a tad more complacent. It took three years for him to lie beside me on the couch for a whole fifteen minutes, and another two years before I could actually pick him up for three minutes without him biting me. This was progress.

But that whole brushing the cat's teeth thing had me stymied. I knew the vet was right, but I also understood my cat. Just getting George into a cage to visit the vet was a challenge. Usually, it involved a bit of hissing, retrieval from under the bed and a chase down the hallway.

At the vet's, he always makes a liar out of me. "He's not necessarily a friendly cat," I say, but when they open the carrier door, out pops a docile black cat. He explores the counter and waits patiently for shots. They open his mouth, check his teeth and gums, and even trim his nails, with no bloodshed.

George and I have a peaceful co-existence and I love him dearly, but that toothbrush and paste seemed akin to raising a red flag in front of a bull. I looked at him and shook my head.

I left the sample toothbrush and paste in the community laundry room. It was safer there, and so was I.

His favorite diversion at the moment is a long piece of thick red string. He plays with it, takes it in his mouth and bites down while I pull it through. At my next veterinarian's visit, I will assure her I'm flossing my cat's teeth. That's almost like brushing, isn't it?

~Connie Cook

Reprinted by permission of www.offthemark.com

11

What Are We Going to Do About Watson?

*Not-so-fun fact: "Kitten season," when animal shelters
usually have an overabundance of kittens, occurs in
the late summer and early fall.*

s there truly such a thing as a bad cat? Yes, I think so. His name is Watson. And I think his mother might even agree.

I know thousands of cats on a very personal level — as personal as you can get, a cat might tell you. Sticking my fingers in their ears and their mouths and sometimes other places they won't admit, I try to remember I am trespassing on the feline's sense of dignity each time I examine a cat within the four walls of my veterinary exam room. But even there, where some lash out in fear, some climb the walls, and others will not be trespassed upon, I cannot say I've met a bad cat. Until Watson.

His wily mother had evaded capture for years and is responsible for thousands of cats being born, generations and generations of cats, all in the abandoned and crumbling barn of a patch of farmland, parceled into smaller and smaller lots until all that was left was her barn surrounded by a crop of red brick houses. I often wonder why she finally gave herself up. Whatever the reason, she surrendered quite easily in the end, with Watson squirming and dangling from her mouth. We celebrated the capture of this last feral female along with her last litter from that old, rotting barn. She seemed to make peace with it and was placed in a home, where she seemed to enjoy kibble and an indoor life sitting on a cushion by the window. The kittens, one by one, also found loving homes — all, that is, except Watson.

As kittenhood — where much is forgiven — became adulthood, what to do about Watson became the daily question. He was a bad seed, my staff said. But not in the hissy, scratching, bitey kind of way — though under certain circumstances, he would judge that sort of response to be appropriate. He was bad in the "I-know-it's-bad-and-I'm-doing-it-anyway" sort of way.

"He could just live here forever…" I said tentatively, knowing that it was my turn to take the unadoptable cat home.

"Yes, but he's so disrespectful."

"He's not disrespectful; he's just young," I countered. But it was true. Our other clinic cats, well into their teens and prized for their respectfulness, were tired of this now two-year-old pushing them out of their resting spots only to get up himself seconds later. They were tired of him attacking their tails, stealing their toys and kicking litter everywhere. And the office staff was tired of him hanging up on clients, deleting computer entries as they typed, taking their pens, breaking open bags of food and treats, knocking things on the floor, and ripping up books and paper. He ran full throttle to the sound of a printer in action, to the door at each tinkle of the bell, to the phone when it rang, and to the water running in the sink.

He seemed to be everywhere all at once, and so skilled as a climber and thief, it was impossible to completely Watson-proof the clinic, already proofed as it was for cats. And I will admit I was tired of tripping over him, which I did at least six times a day. I was tired of him clinging around my leg as I headed to my next appointment. I could not remember the last time I'd worn a skirt or dress to work.

"Did you know he's fond of socks?" someone said.

"Yes, he tries to pull them off me when I sit at my desk," I said.

"He steals them from my gym bag."

"Oh. Is that your sports bra on the floor there?" I asked.

"Oh, yes, he likes those, too."

"What else has he got there?" I asked.

"Never mind. Watson, give me that. Stop running. Give it up."

I will not say we did not love Watson, just that he was far too involved for a clinic cat.

So Watson came home with me. And this opened up a whole new set of possibilities for Watson to hone his badness, and particularly his skill as a thief.

At first, there was a settling-in period when my two resident cats, Merry and Gus, and two large dogs, Penny and Dan, had to get used to Watson's presence and wildness, his burgeoning and undeniable superiority.

They'd look at me one after the other as though to ask, "Mom, what are we going to do about Watson?"

Once all had agreed upon his top cat/dog status, which took surprisingly little time to establish, he began to systematically take over every prime resource available, and then he began to scout for items worth thieving.

Pens continue to be a favorite, and he especially loves the sound they make rolling down the hall in the middle of the night. Penny, our yellow Lab, loves to present us with a dishtowel tugged off the stove door or a shoe when we come home. And this may be how Watson became interested in towels, slippers and even the odd shoe. Why pull pink fiberglass out of the walls in the basement when all these other delectable items are scattered about a house full of kids?

The kids would ask me one after the other when they could not find a pair of socks or mitts between them: "What are we going to do about Watson?"

When the dolls and toys were put away for good, he began to steal jewelry and underclothing. And once again they asked, "What are we going to do about Watson?"

It's been interesting living with a cat like Watson. The kids learned to keep their doors shut. Gus escaped and ran away. And then Louis, a gray Tabby, moved in, and Watson loves him, so they co-cat this house. He has taught Louis how to open doors and to thieve. Louis's favorite find is a cloth doll with long black wool hair or any large, damp towel that he can drag down the stairs. Watson's is, of course, any pair of socks. Over the years, these two partners in crime have grown old together and are more likely to be found curled up in a gray-and-white-spotted swirl than stealing pens, socks or earrings. And nobody asks, "What are we going to do about Watson?" They can usually be found in their spot on the couch, sleeping with Louis's doll and Watson's socks.

~Carol Teed

Our Family Christmas Card

*Fun fact: In Icelandic folklore, a person who doesn't
have at least one new item of clothing for Christmas
will be taken by a horrible Yule Cat.*

Last year, Art and I decided to dress in matching holiday sweaters and, along with our three cats, snap a "family" Christmas picture. Mailing it out as a Christmas card to relatives and friends sounded like fun, especially considering all the kids' pictures we've received over the years. We'd accumulated many cute cards to display along with hideous ones of babies, animals and people. This card, including our feline family, would be payback. It was a good idea, but not so easy to pull off.

Our first challenge was finding two identical holiday sweaters we both liked and would wear while taking our picture. We shopped in the men's department of a large store for a better selection of colors and patterns, and because Art wouldn't be caught dead in women's clothes.

The first sweater to catch my eye was navy blue, trimmed in white, displaying a beautiful wintry snow scene. It was a frontrunner. We continued our search, looking for something more colorful. The next one we liked was a white cable turtleneck sweater. Not colorful at all, but a perfect winter sweater. The final sweater in the running consisted of a red background with two white reindeer on the front, surrounded by a swirling snowflake design. We agreed this was the one.

Now the search for our sizes began. There were many in large sizes, less in medium and very few in small. After looking through hundreds of sweaters, I couldn't believe we found a small petite in the men's department for me. "A Christmas miracle!" I shouted loudly. Embarrassed, I hid behind a stack of sweaters.

Next, I stopped at the Dollar Store and picked up three red bows. I planned to tie them around our cats' necks as bowties. It would be easier than trying to keep small Santa hats on their active heads.

Picture day finally arrived. Art set up his camera and timer in front of our living room couch, while I corralled the three cats into the room. We wore our matching sweaters; the cats wore their red bows. If only it were this simple. Art held Daisy, our youngest striped kitten, on his lap while I held Oliver, a seven-year-old, gray-and-white male, and Ginger, a twenty-four-year-old tuxedo cat.

Daisy was the first cat to get fidgety and run away. While Art was chasing after her, the timing device went off. I was left sitting there with two cats on my lap in a firm grip with a surprised look on my face. Our second attempt was even worse. The camera didn't work, and when Art left the couch to fix the flash, it went off unexpectedly. This picture showed the tail and rear end of Daisy, and Art's crotch. Not a great family image for a Christmas card.

In the next shot, Oliver and Daisy had both run off, leaving me with poor old Ginger, who was happy to be sitting on my lap, or any lap, sleeping. By our seventh attempt, we decided to give up on the cats and take only our picture. We were both tired from the constant running back and forth chasing cats and adjusting cameras, and perfectly content sitting back and relaxing on the couch. I'm surprised we didn't fall asleep like Ginger.

Our final picture turned out well. We shot it holding photographs of our three cats. I was elated just to be smiling and not trying to restrain a runaway cat.

~Irene Maran

Figaro

Chapter 2

My Very Good, Very Bad Cat

My Goofy Cat

Fun fact: Cats, camels and giraffes are the only four-legged animals that walk "contralaterally." The right front leg and the left back leg move forward at the same time, and then the left front leg and the right hind leg move forward together.

Scooter Versus the Vacuum

*Fun fact: Some cats can be "desensitized" so they won't
be scared of the vacuum, but this type of training is
more successful if done when they're still kittens.*

Scooter was fearless. A three-legged calico, Scooter had to fight from birth just to make sure her mother didn't decide she was too injured to live.

She'd puff herself up enough to scare cats twice her size — including her big brother.

She'd challenge visiting dogs — and even though she couldn't outrun them, she'd outsmart them. She'd jump just beyond their reach, and then dangle a paw or tail to taunt them.

She'd look at the vet with a Clint Eastwood gaze that seemed to say, "That all you got? I lost a leg, bub. It was cut off by my mom's umbilical cord at birth. You think you can scare me with your feeble shots and banana-flavoured penicillin?"

Even car rides didn't faze her.

There was only one thing she was ever afraid of — the vacuum.

Other noises didn't bother her, even sudden noises. She'd cuddle while I watched hockey games and didn't flinch when I cheered for my Canucks. But the vacuum sent her scurrying for cover. Even when the vacuum wasn't anywhere near her, she'd hear it and hide. If she saw it coming out of the closet, she'd bolt into the next room.

If Scooter was Super Cat, the vacuum was her kryptonite. The vacuum was her arch-nemesis. She didn't just fear it; she loathed it.

When she was five or six, some days when it started, she'd watch the machine for a few moments before she ran to hide. As crazy as it seems, I began to suspect she was plotting its demise. Then, one afternoon, Scooter saw her big chance.

The vacuum was turned off, sitting at the foot of the stairs. Scooter was in my office. She poked her head out to look at it. When she saw that it wasn't moving — or hadn't noticed her — she slowly approached it, like she was stalking a bird. Then, without warning, she attacked. She took her paw and hit it once, twice, three times. I couldn't believe what I was seeing. She saw me watching and made sure I didn't miss her victory. She swatted the vacuum's base again and again and again. I wasn't sure whether to laugh or applaud.

If the vacuum had been a living creature — or a couch — her claws would have eviscerated it. But the vacuum was a vacuum and emerged unscathed.

This didn't lessen Scooter's triumph.

She circled again and sliced at it again — striking the metal base to make sure the vacuum got the message: "This is my house."

After I was sure Scooter had finished celebrating her victory, I finally turned on the machine. It roared to life. Scooter didn't budge. The three-legged, eight-pound calico looked at the vacuum with a homicidal gleam in her eyes that made one thing very clear: "I own you."

Scooter never ran from a vacuum again. Instead, whenever a vacuum appeared, she'd watch it carefully to make sure it never forgot for a moment that she was the boss.

~Mark Leiren-Young

14

More Fiber, Please

Fun fact: Cats that develop compulsive disorders, such as eating fabric, usually do so when they are less than two years old.

My cat Lilo and I are both fabric lovers: I'm an amateur seamstress, and Lilo devours cloth with as much gusto as if it's tuna.

The Roman shades I fashioned for my window, the duvet covers and pillowcases I sewed for my bed, the first quilt I ever made, my custom pair of yoga pants—all have fallen victim to Lilo's ravenous appetite. Once she started gnawing on a baby blanket while I was still guiding it through the sewing machine!

The first hints of Lilo's strange tastes came soon after I took her in. I'd found her in a parking lot on one of those steamy August afternoons when heat radiates in visible waves off the pavement. She was a young thing, probably three months old, and tiny—just three pounds of scrawny muscle. I lured her inside with kibble and then put up notices around the neighborhood and on Craigslist about a found kitten. No one came forward.

A few days later, Lilo was curled up in my lap, purring and licking the hem of my T-shirt. "Isn't that cute?" I thought. "She's trying to groom me." I petted her and returned my attention to the magazine I was reading.

When I looked back down, Lilo had eaten a nickel-sized hole in my shirt. "You are an odd little cat," I said, but shrugged off her behavior as bizarre kitten antics.

A week or so later, I gave Lilo a fabric mouse toy. You know the ones — filled with batting, with squiggly little tails to make them look more like the real thing.

I set the toy in front of her. She pounced, then sank her teeth in and started to wolf it down. When I realized that she was literally eating her toy, I tried to stop her. But she is a cat and will do what she wants. She bolted under the couch to finish her treat, her throat rumbling with that proud, possessive purr cats make when they successfully catch prey. In less than a minute, the mouse was gone.

That was the last time I gave Lilo a fabric toy.

The biggest shocker came when I walked in on Lilo disemboweling my throw pillow collection. The scene was similar to an all-you-can-eat buffet after several hungry high-school football teams have descended on it. She had swallowed a few square inches of cloth from each pillow before tearing out the stuffing and strewing it everywhere.

Each one of those pillows had been dear to me, as my mother and I had sewn them all. I blinked back tears.

Miraculously, "The Pillow Massacre of 2011" caused no harm to Lilo. Anything she was unable to digest, she spit up like hairballs on my carpet.

There were a lot of "hairballs" that week.

I talked to my vet. She said fabric-eating felines aren't common, but they're not unheard of, either. Kittens that do this usually grow out of it around one year of age. In the meantime, I should play more with Lilo to burn up some of her boundless energy, put her food in puzzle toys to keep her mind occupied, and add fiber to her diet in case she was eating fabric out of hunger.

Also, I should probably keep pillows out of reach for a while.

Alas, as soon as I hid one source of scrumptious textiles from her, she found another. For example, I had a bad habit of discarding my clothes on the floor instead of in the laundry hamper. Lilo took to grazing on them. Especially socks.

For a while, I kept count of how many socks she'd gobbled up. The tally reached seventeen, and then I lost track.

I learned to stop leaving my clothes on the floor.

Lilo grew into adulthood, but the problems continued. I tried to create a Lilo-proof house. My sewing projects — once strewn around — were corralled into a dedicated sewing room. I bought a coffee table with a removable top so I could stow pillows and blankets in safety whenever I left the living room. I got laundry hampers with lids and used them. During the day, I closed the bedroom door or kept my bed pillows in the closet.

Lilo was unfazed. If I was going to hide her favorite fabric from her, she'd find something else to dine on. She expanded her menu to the only textiles left within her reach: dishtowels, hand towels, and bath towels. If one had been left out to dry, she showed it no mercy.

I cried in frustration more than once. "I bet this is why your previous owners left you behind!" I would snap, then immediately feel guilty.

Unfazed, she'd walk over to me and rub against my leg, purring. She knew I could never let her go. Despite her strange habit, she'd grown on me. She was affectionate and kept my feet warm on winter nights. When she was excited about something, she chirped like a bird. And she was incredibly smart, able to do tricks like sitting on command and responding to whistles.

Still, I worried what all this fabric would do to Lilo's digestive system. So did my vet.

We decided to put her on medicine that has been shown to reduce peculiar cravings in cats with pica — the compulsion to eat things that aren't food.

A week later, a miracle occurred. I accidentally dropped a wool mitten from my coat pocket and left it on the living room floor without realizing it. An hour later, I returned to the living room. Lilo was resting on an ottoman, and the mitten was on the floor, untouched.

I was overjoyed.

Lilo occasionally slips up, but not often. I can now hang towels in the bathroom and kitchen without fretting. I can leave the bedroom door open without worrying she'll eat the sheets.

But I don't tempt fate. The sewing and laundry rooms are Lilo-free zones, and I never leave my clothes on the floor.

Lilo got me to finally learn the lesson my parents tried to teach me for years: pick up after yourself.

~Kathryn Kingsbury

Reprinted by permission of Bruce Robinson

The Cat Who Thought He Was a Goat

Fun fact: Goats have horizontal-shaped pupils, while
cats have vertical-shaped pupils.

"Is that a cat in with the goats?" the woman inquired as she and her daughter peered through the fence. "You shouldn't keep a cat in with your goats, at least not in close quarters like that," she informed me, shaking her head.

"He's not a cat," I laughed, as we watched Comet race up the ramp and on the play stand with the other goat kids. "He's a goat — at least he thinks he is."

The question was always the same. Every summer when we sold the kids, well-meaning goat experts arrived and informed us that unless you've got a huge barn with plenty of room, cats don't belong with goats. We had never heard of such nonsense.

Comet was a couple of years old when we rescued him from the pound and placed him with our miniature goats, hoping he'd do what cats do — keep the barn free from rodents. While the barn was tiny, the goats had an enclosed play yard fenced floor to ceiling, which kept them safe from dangerous critters.

Comet, with his mellow-golden eyes and his silky black-and-white fur, fit in perfectly with our three dwarf goats. On his first night in the barn, I checked on him, expecting to find him asleep in the loft. Instead, I found him nestled with Arby, our Nigerian dwarf, purring away. Not only did he cuddle with the goats, he played with them, ate their hay, nibbled their grains and drank from their water bucket instead of his bowl.

People had warned us the goats would butt him to death, but they didn't. We'd also heard that during kidding season, the mothers would attack him for fear he would hurt their babies. Nope. We'd even heard that with him around we should expect a reduced milk flow come milking time. Wrong again. In fact, it was the opposite. Comet's goat buddies trusted and loved him — after all, he seemed like a goat.

My husband had built a long wooden ramp that led to a double-tiered wooden play stand out in their play yard. Comet and the goats loved racing up the ramp as fast as they could, and jumping off the stand over and over. Sometimes, they had battles on the stand, butting each other as they played king of the hill. Comet held his own and fit right in.

Each spring, when the goats gave birth, Comet introduced the new babies to the wonderful racing and jumping game while the mother goats chewed their cud and got a much-needed break. At night, I'd often find him curled up with one of the kids instead of the mothers.

While I milked the goats, Comet patiently waited with the rest of the kids for his share of the warm, sweet milk they slurped out of the same pan. Inseparable, they had a great love for each other. Sadly, when a new set of kids got sold, Comet moped around with the mother goats that mourned their lost babies.

Throughout the years, we saved a lot of money milking and making cheese, and during those years the goats became our dear pets. Unfortunately, when the price of hay reached an all-time high, we couldn't afford our goats anymore.

Thankfully, my husband worked with someone who had a huge field where they could eat, roam, and live out the rest of their days in a happy, peaceful place. Not only did I cry when the goats left, but poor Comet was lost without his friends. For weeks after they had gone, he searched the barn, letting out a hauntingly mournful meow that broke our hearts.

We brought Comet indoors, but he would have none of that, and so he remained in the barn. Eventually, the crying stopped, and he adopted a routine of chasing mice, watching birds, and keeping me company while I gardened.

But Comet was never the same. He resumed being a cat. As if in continuous mourning, he never raced up the ramp again. Instead, he slowly waddled up it and flopped on the play stand where he rolled over and sunbathed, begging for a belly rub. Comet's racing days had ended.

Many years later on a sunny autumn day, Comet became ill. Suddenly too weak to walk or eat, or even lift his head, we had to carry him as the day wore on. He was going downhill quickly. With tears in my eyes, I said my final goodbyes to my old companion and thanked him for being such a wonderful friend.

As Comet struggled with his last breath, my sons arrived and said their farewells to this gentle soul who had graced our barn for so many years. None of us could imagine life without him.

After my sons finished, all eyes watched in awe as Comet raised his head, meowed, and raced up the ramp. Surrounded by love, he died on his play stand.

If humans can experience their deceased loved ones arriving and helping them transition through death, why not our sweet-spirited pets?

There is no doubt in my mind that Comet's loving goat buddies — who had passed away long ago — had arrived and raced Comet up the beloved ramp one last time as they escorted him across the great rainbow bridge. His life could not have ended in a more beautiful or meaningful way.

Although we hated losing him and will always miss him, we rejoiced knowing that Comet — who thought he was a goat — had joined his dear goat friends once more.

~Jill Burns

16

Nip's Throne

Fun fact: Cats instinctively cover their waste in the litter box to prevent predators from figuring out where they live.

I was in the back of the house folding laundry when I heard some tinkling noises in the big bathroom down the hall. As a mother, I knew where my kids were, and as a wife I knew where my husband was. And I knew they weren't home. Immediately, and with great apprehension, I peeked in the door. It was Nip, squatting on the toilet with his back to the door. I don't remember what I said or what noise I made, but I do remember Nip turned his head toward me, gave me his best look of aggravation, jumped down and ran out of the bathroom.

Of course, I wanted to talk to him about it, but he would have none of that. He meowed at the back door, so I let him out. But I wanted to know how he knew the toilet was the place to pee. He was in the bathroom a lot with me (mothers never go to the bathroom without someone hanging around), but I never told him what I was doing. And even if he heard the sound of tinkling water, how did he grasp what it was and why I was doing it?

I would have thought that training a cat to use the toilet would at least require a discussion on the merits of such behavior. And, as all cat-lovers know, training a cat is usually futile. They end up training you to give them treats for minimal exertion on their part.

I remember one night when my husband David was calling Nip

in for the night. I could hear him cajoling Nip with treats, a new toy mouse filled with catnip, and all manner of things. Nip just sat there on the other side of the driveway and stared at him. It was as if he had suddenly forgotten how to get from there to the back door.

Next thing I knew, David had gone out there, picked him up, and brought him into the house.

"You know you're going to be doing that from now on, don't you?" I asked.

"Not after just one time," David said confidently.

I never said "I told you so," but the cold, hard fact is that Nip never came to the door at bedtime again. He was instantly trained to wait for somebody to come and get him.

But I digress. Back to the toilet. Nip continued to use the toilet from then on, but he hated to be interrupted and would quickly jump down. I wanted to get a picture, so I would look for my camera when I heard him in there. It would have to be a quick shot, but I was determined to get at least one good picture.

Finally, I had to put my camera in the bathroom and leave it there. And it still took — no kidding — about a year before I finally got the shots I wanted. I got lucky — you can see the stream. Proof positive finally captured by my camera!

I had to have extras made. My mother framed one and showed it to everybody who came to her house for any reason. She called Nip her "grandcat."

I really miss old Nip. We've had a parade of cats over the years, but Nip was one of my favorites. He was sweet, loving, and smart. He loved to be kissed on the top of his head, which happens to be my favorite place to kiss a cat. He loved to sit in my lap, purring to beat the band. And, unlike the two human males living in the household, he never dribbled on the toilet seat.

You just can't ask for more than that from a cat, can you?

~Carol Weeks

17

Angel the Water Cat

*Fun fact: Most cats hate getting wet, but the Turkish
Van cat likes water because its ancestors in Turkey's
Lake Van region often cooled off in lakes during the
very hot summers there.*

Every cat has its little likes and dislikes, its own eccentricities. I grew up with cats; they were all completely different, and I loved each one for those differences. However, my current cat, Angel, a beautiful, white shorthaired cat, makes me laugh like no other cat I've known, due to her enjoyment of being soaked down.

It is often said that "dogs have masters, but cats have staff." I certainly feel that way every time I use a faucet in Angel's presence. She makes it clear, in no uncertain terms, that if the tap is turned on she must have her fair share of the water — not to drink, but to bathe in. She waits for me to wet my hand and then glide it down her body from her furry head to the tip of her tail, sometimes repeatedly, until she looks as if she has been in for a swim.

This peculiar habit started innocently enough. One day, in my kitchen, she was bathing herself with her tongue, as cats do, and I decided to help her out. Cats have a hard time reaching the top of their heads during their daily (hourly) bathing regimen, having to utilize the classic "wet side of paw, turn head, and slide dampened paw up and over ear" manoeuvre. It is fairly effective, with the added bonus of making them look totally adorable while executing this move (and don't they know it!). I figured if I put a bit of water between her ears, I could help the process. I hoped that she wouldn't dislike the added H_2O and bolt. To my delight, she seemed not only to like the addition of water to her ablutions, she even showed her appreciation by giving me a lick or two as I withdrew my hand. (This may have been a hint that I needed a bath, too, but I don't think so.)

Having seen that she didn't mind a friendly rub of water between the ears, I did it whenever I thought of it. Then I noticed that whenever I was at the kitchen sink, she seemed to appear out of nowhere. One day, in a hurry and deciding to dissuade her a bit from this baptism-like activity, I took a whole handful of water and rubbed it down her back. Far from discouraging her, this increased the vigour of her bathing as she tried to use up every drop before it dried, energetically licking herself on one side and then the other.

That's when things got out of hand. She discovered that I used the faucet in my bathroom even more frequently than the one in the kitchen — every morning, at the same time! One day, she arrived before I had soaked down my face for my morning shave, sat at my feet and watched expectantly. Not making any connection to past kitty water activity — humans can be so dense at times — I continued my shave until she let out a very loud "meow," clearly wanting something.

As she is a fairly quiet feline, I knew something was up. Was it the water? I decided to give her the old water pat-down to see if it would placate her. It worked like a charm. She moved away a foot or two and happily bathed as I shaved. After a few passes over my foamed-up, stubbly puss, I looked down to find my expectant pussycat back at my feet waiting for a second soak-down. I ignored her, believing that she was still "wet behind the ears," and continued my shaving. When she meowed again, I capitulated and gave her another soaking, stem to stern. Satisfied, she moved off and energetically went to work making the best use of the water. This continued until I had finished shaving.

This is now a daily ritual. Even if Angel is nowhere in sight when I turn on the bathroom faucet, I see the tip of her white tail in the bathroom mirror as she crosses hurriedly behind me to take her place at my side and wait for the first of many soak-downs, which she expects at regular intervals.

There has been one addition to this routine: She comes into the bathroom when I am in the shower and waits until I draw back the shower curtain. There is something very disconcerting about being naked and soaking wet and finding a cat waiting for you. Of course, I usually burst out laughing at the sight of my favourite feline anticipating my exit from the shower stall; it never gets old. And, of course, if I hesitate in the slightest before providing her with her customary watery pat-down, I hear about it. Loudly!

Cats have staff, and that staff better be quick about it!

~Kevin L. Dobson

18

Houdini's Ribbons and Bows

Fun fact: Try hanging lemon- or orange-scented air fresheners in your Christmas tree to deter your cat from climbing it.

"Not again," I grumbled as I watched our ten-month-old gray Tabby, Sergeant Tibbs, go through the heaving motions of coughing up a hairball. He'd padded out from beneath the Christmas tree to hunker down in front of me for the delivery of his gift. I groaned. Right on my family room carpet! Couldn't he do that outside?

But this particular present wasn't coming up easily, and Tibbs' body undulated more forcefully with each larger heave. "Hmm," I thought, growing nervous about his apparent difficulty.

Finally, after one last, huge contraction, our new family member managed to rid himself of the material causing his system so much distress. My mouth flew open and my eyes widened as Tibbs briefly investigated his undigested present: a golf-ball-sized wad of gleaming, partially chewed and salivated, multi-colored metallic Christmas ribbon.

"Oh, my! Chris, Parker, Cory!" I shrieked to my husband and sons as I bolted from my rocking chair to rescue the gooey gob from possible re-ingestion. The three sprinted to my side as I stared in shock at Tibbs, who gazed up at me with his innocent-looking, emerald eyes. Then he stood, licked his lips, quickly groomed his whiskers, and sauntered away.

"Look at this!" I demanded as I waved the ball in front of them. "This is what the cat just hacked up!" Three pairs of cornflower-blue eyes peered at the colorful, slimy wad, and three heads simultaneously snapped around to give me a horrified look. Then the raucous laughter started.

"It's not funny," I said. "He could have died!" Then I barked instructions. Within seconds, Chris, Parker and I were on our hands and knees, scouring the floors for every miniscule ribbon scrap, strip or curl. Cory rushed to his computer to do an Internet search on a cat's attraction to ribbons. Over a lifetime with five cats, I'd never had one eat ribbon. Yarn, yes. Ribbon, no. This was unfamiliar, dangerous territory.

I thought — hoped — it would be a single occurrence. But it wasn't. Tibbs kept munching. And he didn't need to see a decorated gift to know it existed. It could be carefully stashed on the other side of the house in a space he normally didn't visit. It seemed to call to him. "Here, kitty, kitty, kitty…" Even transparent tape became a meal.

The following Christmas, I tried again to decorate gifts with ribbons and bows. What was I thinking? Every package under the tree exhibited gnawed, punctured or shredded bows and nibbled corners. Tibbs hadn't left one present untouched. Even when I moved the packages to an area where I could keep an eye on them, he appeared like Houdini to chomp and devour. It escalated to a war of wills. No matter how much I bawled him out or flailed my arms to shoo him away, he persisted. I started imagining him plotting the destruction just to irritate me.

After bending over one day to inspect each package, and finding all of them taste-tested and damp, I plopped on the ground next to the mangled presents and heaved an exaggerated sigh. "Ah, Tibbs," I murmured. "Why do you have to undo all of the love and work I've put into these gifts?"

For me, this destruction was personal. I was an expert package wrapper and bow maker. As a teenager, I took pride in my elaborate creations. I painstakingly cut every paper sheet at a perfect ninety-degree angle and folded corners like a nurse folds, creases and tucks hospital bed sheets. Each piece of tape was carefully measured and placed. I spent hours crafting handmade bows. My mom even had me wrap my own presents. She first sealed each box and then had me clothe them in rich paper and shimmering tassels and bows. Now, I cringed on Christmas mornings when my husband and two young sons tore into their presents without first admiring them. All they seemed to care about was locating the prize encased in the wrapping, not the wrapping itself.

As I breathed another exasperated sigh, Tibbs unfurled himself from his napping hideaway under the tree, crept out from under the low-hanging branches, extended each limb in an elongated stretch, meowed a "hello" and plunked himself down in my lap. Then he looked up at me with those adoring green eyes and gave me that what-are-you-so-worried-about-when-life's-so-good look. I used my thumb and finger to massage the sweet spots between his ears, and his eyes dropped into contented slits. A light rumble vibrated his body.

As I massaged, my mind drifted to my storage closet, where reels of outdated ribbon languished. I cringed at the thought of the money wasted on unused supplies, even if they had been purchased on sale. I had to admit that I'd turned my talent and craft into an obsession.

"You're right, buddy," I said. "I do pour a lot of love into those wrappings, but it really is more about the joy the gift inside brings. The thrill I get when I see the boys' faces light up at the discovery." I hoisted him from my lap, laid him carefully on the floor and stood. "It looks as though my work-of-art-present days are over, my boy."

Off came the ribbons and bows, and I devised a way to seal the paper and successfully keep the tape away from Tibbs' searching nose. We happily delivered plainly wrapped, bowless, ribbonless gifts to our family and friends.

For ten Christmases, Tibbs delighted us as he boxed his way through and battled imaginary rivals hiding within discarded Christmas wrappings. He treated us to belly laughs when he hid in gift boxes and bags and stealthily appropriated our sixty-five-pound dog's Christmas gift: a humongous new bed. He stole our attention when he sat gazing — mesmerized — at the gold flame spikes dancing in the fireplace.

And he brought joy as he alighted on a lap to examine and approve of someone's newly opened present.

Then one miserable November day, our precious feline's too-short life ended. I imagined our beloved Sergeant Tibbs, who entertained and showered us with unconditional love, to be chewing ribbons and bows to his feline heart's content without reprimand or danger.

Four weeks later, I rummaged through the closet for the Christmas paper and bows. Shimmering wrapping, elaborate bow material and metallic ribbons caught my eye. "I can decorate to my heart's content now," I whispered to myself.

But I didn't. I put just enough love and flourish into the package wrappings to make them pretty, and thanked God for my little friend I missed so much. And I reminded myself that it's not the fancy wrapping covering the gifts, but the giving of them that fills my heart with joy.

~Andrea Arthur Owan

19

Zippee's Greatest Adventure

Not-so-fun fact: In the Middle Ages, black cats were severely persecuted. The church considered them witches' familiars or agents of the devil and believed they should be killed. Devil worshippers also sacrificed black cats to Satan.

His lithe body floated effortlessly through the air, sailing down the staircase and sticking his landing on the foyer floor. He could do the same thing in the opposite direction with just as much ease. This cat seemed to float on air. The fact that he had one eye didn't slow him down a bit.

He had been up for adoption at the local feed store where I bought cat food for our clan. Each visit entailed stopping at the cages and looking at the kittens available for adoption. I would place my standard contribution of five dollars in the donation box. It was Christmastime, and in the cage next to some cute, irresistible kittens was this solid black adult cat. It was hard to distinguish head from tail because he'd curled himself into such a tight ball. He lifted his head and greeted me with his one bright eye. My heart instantly connected with him, but my mind was reminding me why I couldn't bring this cat home. We were already a four-cat household.

The information card indicated he was a year old, recently fostered by a local cat-rescue group. He didn't even have a name. I whispered,

"If you are still here after Christmas, you will have a home."

Christmas came and I couldn't stop thinking about that poor cat with no name. I was haunted by the image of him spending Christmas alone in the feed store. I was positive that no one would want to adopt a year-old, one-eyed, black cat. I returned after Christmas and he was there, still curled up in his cage. He lifted his head and gave a scratchy meow when he saw me approach. Somehow, it was like he knew I had returned to keep my promise.

I inquired about the adoption fee and how this fellow had lost an eye. The manager explained the eye was removed due to an infection. The cat had been found abandoned and brought to the rescue group, which was asking half the normal adoption fee. I opened my envelope of gift money from my in-laws and paid the fee. I would thank them later for aiding in the expansion of their grandcat family.

I arrived home and was met with instant curiosity about the new cat in the carrier. Badger, our alpha cat, sat in front of the carrier and sniffed. He had proven in the past his compassion for new arrivals with our two younger cats, often referred to as "the babies." They had been a week old when I brought them home, and Badger had stepped up and become their protector. I was confident he would do the same for this cat. Callie, our most outspoken, took the new addition as an affront. The two babies, Squeeler and Bear, did not seem to mind having a new kid on the block. After the expected hisses, growls, and checking each other out, everyone, including my husband, began to adjust to the fact that our family had grown.

My husband and I discussed our new cat's name at length. We both agreed that the name should not refer to having one eye or being solid black. His name should reflect his personality. Once this cat was liberated from his cage, his first personality trait had become apparent. He loved running, leaping, and sailing through the air. We would call him Zippee.

I had become used to the sound of Zippee running and scampering through the house and the nightly "Pet Zippee Show." Then, one Saturday morning, Zippee's need for speed was almost his undoing. I was upstairs in the guest bedroom, enjoying the spring morning, with the window open. Zippee flew into the room, his normal airborne black streak. He landed dead center on the bed before springing toward the open window. To my horror, Zippee hit the window screen and burst right through it.

My first thought was that he was dead. My second thought was that cats might really have nine lives. I rushed to the window and found Zippee hanging on for dear life, his paws gripping the windowsill and his body dangling. His one eye expressed, "What the heck just happened?" and "Don't just stand there, do something!" Befuddled as to how this cat managed to turn around in mid-air and grasp the interior of the windowsill, I was thankful that he was unharmed. I lifted him back into the house and cradled him in my arms.

Zippee was not a lap cat and he didn't like being picked up and cuddled. Usually, holding Zippee was like trying to hold water. This was one of the few times Zippee did not resist being held. He was happy to be in my arms. Safely back inside and with the window closed, Zippee was not seen for the remainder of the day.

By the next morning, he was back to his old self, ripping and romping through the house. He engaged Badger in a game of chase and sneak attack. His adventure, like his handicap, had not slowed him down. With all of Zippee's antics, the one thing this cat taught me was we must always face life filled with zest, be willing to trust that others will be there to pick us up when we fall, and never allow our limitations to deter us from being an active participant in this great adventure called life.

~Tori Bailey

Flushing His Issues Away

Fun fact: Moving to a new home is stressful for cats
because it means they're losing their territory and
must adapt to a new one.

The move into our new home had been stressful, and each of our four cats reacted in different ways. Bobby Cat needed lots of evening cuddles. DP and Cable hung out under the bed most days, and Chai, our black-and-white tuxedo cat, had taken to following us around like a puppy. No matter which room we entered, he was not content unless he was in the middle of whatever we were doing. So when the toilet in the laundry room needed to have a leak fixed, it was no surprise to us when he insisted on sitting on the seat, peering into the tank, and watching intently as my husband took the mechanicals out and replaced them.

After repairing the leak, we expected a little relief from our higher-than-expected water bills and were baffled when the next month rolled around. The cost had inched up. We replaced a seeping faucet, lectured our teenager about shortening her shower, and made sure our laundry loads were completely full before washing. We only ran the dishwasher when it was full and didn't leave the faucets running. Another month passed, and the bill crept up even higher. We began to worry that perhaps there was a leak somewhere in the system that was going to turn into a very large problem.

My husband promised to consult with a plumber and get ideas on what steps we could take to fix our excessive water consumption.

I had come down with a summer cold and was home sick, but there were a few design jobs that simply couldn't wait. As I walked to the studio, I waved to Chai, who was soaking up some sun on a windowsill. Bobby Cat hopped into my lap. DP and Cable were curled up under my work desk. I sighed and opened my computer, ready to get to work. Our daughter was at school, my husband at work, and with any luck, I would be able to crawl back into bed in a couple of hours.

I was finishing up the first print ad when an odd sound caught my attention. I paused to listen. It sounded faintly like flushing and running water. Was someone in the house? The garage door had not opened, so it wasn't kids or my husband. I shook my head. Probably just noise from my stopped-up ears.

It happened again!

Bobby Cat, DP, and Cable didn't seem bothered or nervous, but I was! I grabbed my cell phone and began to creep back toward the laundry room. I dialed "9-1-1," but didn't press Send. Bracing myself, I slowly peeked around the doorframe into the laundry room. No one was there. Then it happened again. That was definitely a toilet flush.

I inched toward the open bathroom door, thumb on the Send button, and cautiously peered around the doorframe... just in time to see Chai place both paws on the lever and pull. He quickly shifted to the right so he could watch the water swirl and bubble as it exited the bowl. After all the water motion was gone and the bowl refilled, he moved back to the lever with both paws. It all clicked into place, and I began to laugh, startling him. He ran from the bathroom, looking as embarrassed as a cat can look.

We immediately implemented a "closed lid" policy. To this day, we don't know if it was the closed lid or sheer embarrassment that stopped his compulsive flushing. But our water bills were at a manageable level the very next month.

~Lois Bradley

A Cat Named No

*Fun fact: Kittens learn to purr when they are about
one week old.*

The scraping sound of the laundry basket against the cement floor catches my attention. I turn from the dryer just in time to see my black cat use his head to push the basket to my feet. Satisfied, he sits tall with his broad chest out and watches me with striking yellow eyes and two gleaming white fangs in his trademark "smile." Bat fangs, we call them.

"Thanks, Wookie," I say, patting his head. At my touch, he rises to all fours and drapes his tail over my hand.

Wookie is a helper cat. He thinks he must help with every task. He also thinks his name is "No."

In this next instant, he is inside the dryer standing on the warm clothes I'm trying to remove.

"No!" I say, as I reach in and pull him out.

When I run the vacuum cleaner, he is the only cat that doesn't run away in terror. Instead, I have to vacuum around him as he refuses to move. Then he follows me to the next room to sit in the way again.

"No!" I say, as I try to keep him away, but he hops over my leg and sits in the middle of the floor, forcing me to vacuum around him once more.

As soon as the broom comes out, so does Wookie. He insists on checking the dirt pile to make sure no stray treats or "toys" such as Q-tips or twisty ties have been taken prisoner.

"Wookie, no!"

I try to block him with the broom, but he heaves his twenty pounds against it, defeating my attempts, and steps in the dirt, spreading it around. Satisfied, he walks away, trailing dirt behind him.

As I prepare the sink to wash dishes, I'm relieved he's gone, although the worst he ever does at the sink is sit in the open window above it and meow at the birds outside.

From the basement, I hear a loud, "Wookie, no!" from my husband.

He is trying to scoop the litter boxes, which has to be Wookie's number one favorite chore to help with. From the time he was about two months old, he either sits in the litter box while it is being scooped or grabs onto the discard bag as if my husband is stealing the contents the cat so carefully buried.

Despite all this, he is a keeper.

We rescued his mother and her litter when the kittens were a day old, moving them out of the cold April air into a warm basement and clean blankets. Every other day, we would change the blankets, and during one of those times, when the kittens were barely two weeks old, I was lifting Wookie when he purred. I paused and looked at my husband in disbelief. This was the third litter we had cared for and the first time we had ever heard a kitten purr so young.

In my heart he was mine, even though we had decided not to keep any of them. He purred every time I touched him. When his eyes opened and his wobbly legs allowed him to explore, he would seek me out to snuggle against me while his littermates played.

At night, he sleeps sprawled out lengthwise between my husband and me. At any time of night, all one of us has to do is gently brush him with our hand and the deep purrs lull us back to sleep.

For the first year of his life, I learned to prepare dinner with him under one arm. I learned that he really shouldn't help with pumpkin carving after I found gooey seeds stuck to his fur. I learned how to decorate a Christmas tree from a cat's point of view. I needn't worry, though. If I get it wrong, he just rearranges the ornaments, the tree skirt or the presents.

Wookie likes to help. Period. Whether it's ironing, dusting, filling a mop bucket or cleaning out the refrigerator, he's the cat for the job. Every task is exciting.

My thoughts at the kitchen sink are interrupted by a crash against the closed window and a plop as soapy water soaks the front of my shirt.

"Wookie!"

The poor cat must have assumed the window was open and leapt for it.

He is drenched and covered in soap bubbles. I grab a dishtowel and begin rubbing his fur to dry him. As I do, he looks at me with big yellow eyes, bat fangs showing as he smiles and purrs.

~Valerie D. Benko

22

Pookie's Flaming Tail

*Fun fact: A human can learn to read his cat's moods by
checking out the position of his tail.*

When my beloved cockatiel, Angel, died during a visit to my grandparents, my grandmother, June, felt so terrible about it that she took me to the animal shelter to get me a cat. Knowing nothing about cats, I based my decision on looks alone — and was instantly attracted to a cream-and-white ragamuffin with big, golden eyes and a tail that looked like it belonged on a raccoon.

On her cage was the name "Taffy" and a note that said: "Doesn't like other cats." When my grandma saw me staring longingly into the cage, she said, "This cat might not be very friendly. What about this pretty gray one?" Not a chance. I was smitten with the ragamuffin. Taffy was coming home with me — and being renamed "Pookie."

Pookie was a sweetheart, but the most outstanding thing about her was her exotic tail. She'd sway it slowly and hypnotically as if saying, "Look at me, I'm Princess Pookie!"

One Thanksgiving, Pookie got a little carried away with her beautiful tail. The family had just gotten up from eating dinner, and Pookie jumped on the table to sniff out the leftovers. The room was buzzing with conversation and music, but everyone turned to look at gorgeous Miss Pookie standing on the dining table, mesmerizingly waving her fluffy, lush tail back and forth like a magic wand. Suddenly, with all eyes on her, she brushed against a centerpiece candle, and her tail went up in flames.

"The cat's on fire!" my nephew Timmy yelled. The whole tail was blazing like something in a circus act, yet Pookie didn't realize it — and just stood there looking proud while everyone gasped, screamed and pointed.

Instinctively, I grabbed a nearby glass of water and threw it — incredibly landing right on Pookie's flaming tail and completely extinguishing the fire. She hadn't been burned, but her tail fur was completely singed. From her perspective, Mommy just threw water at her for eating turkey, and she scrambled out of there for dear life. This was absolutely hysterical to witness, and we all laughed until we cried.

Pookie lived more than twenty years and was usually seen lying on my husband Mike's lap, with her front legs crossed in front of her, happily swishing her tail. The very feature that drew me to her at the shelter is also the thing that has made her a special cat in the hearts of the family forever. At Pookie's "fire show," my nephew Timmy was just a little boy. Now at age sixteen, whenever he asks how my cats are doing, he always says, "Hey, remember Pookie's tail catching on fire?" Then everyone laughs and fondly remembers our beautiful princess.

~Deborah Sturgill

23

Chicken Soup for the Soul

Home Improvement: Kitty Edition

Fun fact: Many cats have been immortalized by famous poets, such as John Keats and William Wordsworth.

'Twas four weeks before Christmas and all through our house
Not a creature was stirring, except for my spouse.
The wall had been hung, standing sturdy as steel;
It was time to rejoice with a good hearty meal.

With Dad in his flannels, feeling rightly complete,
We all settled in for something to eat.
Only twelve hours earlier, there arose such a clamor
When Tony decided to pull out the hammer.

"The shower needs fix'n," he said, lacking denial,
Then he tore down the wall, tile by tile.
A trip to Home Depot, two hundred bucks spent,
He had what he needed for this first-time event.

We all stood back just waiting to see,
Three girls, two cats, the dog and me.
Usually clad in a shirt and a tie,
Our man tightened his tool belt and gave it a try.

He measured and hammered each nail with direction
Then plastered and tiled with the greatest perfection.
He examined his labor then placed the last tile.
"This wall is complete," he said with a smile.

We all gathered 'round to share in his glee,
Three kids, one cat, the dog and me...
As we sat at the table enjoying our spread,
A noise from somewhere got stuck in my head.

"What is it?" I asked, but got no reply.
Whatever it was, it was starting to cry.
We followed the sound to the top of the stairs,
Where one cat was pacing, befuddled to tears.

He paced beside the new wall with much fright,
Like someone who knows there is something not right.
"Oh, no," said Tony, pacing along.
"I think I did something, something so wrong."

He surveyed the closets in each and every room,
Then called the cat's name, forestalling his doom.
When no one came running, he knew what was to be,
We looked on in horror, the girls and me.

He tore at the wall, ripping tile by tile;
There was no time to waste. Spike had been in there a while.
A hole in the wall would appear such a pity,
But not when it's structured to rescue a kitty.

He reached in his arm, felt around still unsure,
'Til he hit something soft, something covered in fur.
The cat came out quiet, still shocked, in a fog.
We celebrated his rescue; all but Buster, the dog.

A quick tip from a salesman who learned from his plight,
Remove cats from the wall before sealing it tight.

~Kassie Rubico

Brady

My Very Good, Very Bad Cat

My Healer Cat

Fun fact: Scientific studies have shown time and time again that cats are more than just good pets. They are extremely therapeutic, and may actually be a good form of medicine for people suffering from heart conditions.

Dancing with Joe

Fun fact: All of a cat's claws point the same way, so they can't climb down a tree headfirst; they have to back down.

s we danced to the haunting strains of Louis Armstrong's "What a Wonderful World," Joe held my shoulder with a tenderness I'd never felt before, and when he caressed my cheek with his, I didn't even mind his long whiskers tickling my skin. "This is the man I wish I could marry," I thought.

Two years before, my marriage of eighteen years had ended abruptly. Everything I had envisioned for my future vanished in a matter of months; I felt adrift. While my three young children and my job kept me going, my social life felt empty — almost like a nightmare that would not end. Joe changed all of that.

There was only one problem: Joe was my orange Tabby. Handsome, devoted, brave, patient, playful, trustworthy… he possessed all those qualities and more.

A rescue cat, Joe entered my life when he was six months old. At first, he cared more about playing with strings than anything, but by the time he turned one, he became the perfect companion. He slept by my side at night, comforted me when the kids left to visit their dad, and prompted me to continue living life in their absence — even when I didn't feel like it — with his incessant requests for food.

When I began the practice of dancing with Joe, he never resisted. He seemed to enjoy snuggling upright next to my chest, his front legs dangling over my right shoulder. As time progressed, and he knew what to expect, he would gladly grab my shoulder with both paws, purr, and snuggle his cheek to mine. He helped me pass the time, and the music and his deep purring began to heal my soul.

Of course, I let Joe have his space. He wandered my two-acre woods, enjoying nature as cats do, eyeing birds with a glint in his eye and challenging any feline interloper. But one blustery winter morning, he did not return when I called him in for breakfast. "This is odd," I thought. "Joe never misses a meal!"

The kids and I panicked. We called his name over and over again from our front door. My son decided to venture outside. The temperature was well below zero, and we were worried about Joe surviving. I could hear my son calling for Joe as he walked the perimeter of our property. Abruptly, my son screamed for me. He had found Joe, but I could tell it wasn't good news.

I tossed on my heavy coat and pulled on my boots. Stumbling through snowdrifts and fallen tree limbs, I worked my way toward my son's voice. Then I heard him. "MEOW!" Joe urgently called. My beloved cat needed me.

My son looked straight up, his head flung back, his mouth open in shock. I followed his gaze, and there was Joe clinging to a branch, high up in an old oak tree. He shook violently, and his greenish-gold eyes expressed terror. Something, maybe the coyote I had seen recently, had chased Joe up the tree.

No amount of coaxing could convince Joe to budge. We tried enticing him with food, but that didn't work. Given that he was in the middle of a small forest in the dead of winter, the idea of placing a long ladder against the tree seemed impossible.

Joe's ordeal continued for hours. The kids cried. I wanted to, but I had to remain strong. I had to figure out how to coax Joe down from that tree. With the wind picking up and nightfall approaching, I felt sick to my stomach. How would Joe survive the night? Would he freeze to death? Would he fall asleep and plunge to his death?

I called my elderly father for help. He loved Joe, too, so he came right over. He did the best he could. He pleaded with Joe to move, but nothing worked for him either. When he came back to the tree with a long aluminum ladder, I had to stop him. I couldn't let a seventy-eight-year-old man try to climb a ladder stuck in a snow bank on a hill. There had to be a better way.

Just then, a friend from work pulled in the driveway. I had forgotten he was scheduled to drop off something. Vince, a forty-eight-year-old police officer, knew something was wrong right away. He heard our shouting, and he sprinted through the snow to get to us, his six-foot, six-inch frame looking heroic.

I had never thought of Vince as anything more than a friend. We worked on projects aimed at reducing drug use among local teens, and we had volunteered at many events together. I had heard from co-workers that he was going through a painful divorce, but if you know anything about police officers, you know they don't talk much about their personal lives. Yet here was Vince, at my house, coming to my rescue.

After assessing the situation, Vince took the ladder from my dad, and he positioned it against the tree. My dad held the base as Vince climbed carefully up each rung. I watched for Joe's reaction, as he didn't really know Vince, but the cat's eyes didn't look any more fearful than before. He actually seemed to sense that help was on the way.

In one swift motion, Vince reached out his arm just as Joe inched toward his hand. In a flash, Vince whisked Joe down from the tree. Once again, my beloved cat was in my arms. I ran into the house and wrapped the shocked cat in blankets. Finally, I could cry.

I cried because Joe was safe. I cried because someone had helped me when I really needed it. I cried because I finally understood that there is an end to grief. My divorce may have crushed me, but not permanently. Through it all, I had kept my kids happy, I had excelled at my job, I had made friends, and I had learned that love can and will endure, as proven by an orange Tabby.

Joe and I still dance, and he holds a very special place in my heart. Without him, I wouldn't have seen my friend, Vince, in a new light.

Joe helped me find an excellent husband, one who possesses all the positive qualities that Joe has, plus countless more.

~Lori A. Sciame

A Miraculous Connection

Fun fact: A cat and her three kittens became known as symbols of hope after they were found in a carton of napkins in the ruins of the World Trade Center in 2001.

Four days before the World Trade Center fell, my thirteen-year-old tortoiseshell Tabby, Rascal, underwent a bilateral thyroidectomy. Afterwards, with her neck shaved, exposed, and scarred, my usually feisty old gal was subdued, still reeling from surgery and the pain of recovery. I empathized with Rascal because my world, too, had seismically shifted in recent weeks. In addition to my cat's medical needs, my dad was battling pancreatic cancer, I was in constant pain from a lower-back injury, and the unthinkable had just happened: the 9/11 attacks with their subsequent loss of thousands of lives and the spiraling devastation of countless families, friends, and heartsick citizens.

A little before noon on Friday, September 14, 2001, I sat down on the sofa with my Episcopal hymnal and prayer book in hand, ready to honor lives lost and changed forever. The televised National Day of Prayer and Remembrance service provided a much-needed collective opportunity for folks to mourn all the victims. The second I settled on the sofa, Rascal claimed a spot beside me. We'd spent a lot of time together on that couch in recent days as I watched endless news feeds and Rascal quietly recuperated. My heart was heavy as pre-service TV footage rolled. My eyes burned with tears. Hearing me sniffle, Rascal snuggled close, nudging and consoling me.

"I'm still here, and I'm here for you," she seemed to say.

As government officials streamed solemnly into Washington National Cathedral, the broadcasters became quiet. Welcoming the temporary reprieve from talk and tears, Rascal hunkered down for a nap. And then the service began. Inspiring music filled the church.

When the opening hymn began, I sang with abandon, relieved, at last, to be able to participate in some small way. The second I started singing, Rascal's head popped up and she swiveled around to gaze at me. Strangely fascinated by the sound, her green eyes glowed intently. As my emotion-charged voice continued, Rascal stood up, marched onto my lap, positioned her face inches from mine — and started to sing!

Although cat-erwauling might be a more apt description, at that moment there was no doubt in my mind that my spunky cat was singing along with the rest of us. Rascal's commiserating meows continued unabated, her head inching steadily closer to my mouth as if she were actually trying to locate the source of those baffling sounds. At once touched and tickled by my kitty's delightfully odd behavior, my singing became riddled with giggles. As each subsequent verse began, I expected Rascal to lose interest and back off, but her curiosity never waned. Even after the final note of that hymn trailed away, she hovered expectantly, eagerly awaiting one more verse.

As lessons were read and homilies spoken, Rascal curled up beside me and fell asleep. Even the voice of an eloquent soloist failed to wake her. But as soon as another congregational hymn began — and I broke into my amateur squawking — Rascal scrambled into my lap, craning her head across my hymnal, sniffing my warm breath as it fanned her face and looking deep into my mouth, searching for the source of that strange racket.

As she persistently head-butted my hymnal, chiming in with her kindred cries, Rascal and I sang a heartfelt duet. At one point, when my father briefly visited, we both got up to greet him in the kitchen. Returning to the living room after Dad left, I realized Rascal was nowhere in sight. And then another hymn began….

"This will be the test," I laughed aloud. "Was it a fluke, or will Rascal sing with me again?"

To my amazement, it wasn't a fluke. Hearing me belt out the next hymn, my elderly companion whipped around a corner from the kitchen and climbed into my lap again.

Laughing, choking back tears, I savored the miraculous connection of song that on the saddest day imaginable filled a feline with incredible compassion and support for her grieving mistress. Rascal meowed continuously that day, verse after verse, her ancient eyes riveted to mine, her silky head nudging my hymnal until, finally, I balanced the book in one hand and gently stroked her fur with the other, soothing and being soothed in return.

Prior to that poignant service, Rascal had never before joined me in song, and from that day until her death in January 2005, it never happened again. On some inexplicably awesome level, my furry friend sensed the gut-wrenching grief of that long-ago time. On September 14, 2001, an elderly cat wearing the battle scars of her own valiant fight against disease joined our nation in a profound outpouring of sorrow and support. Alone in my home, I sang with millions of people worldwide… and one compassionate Tabby.

~Wendy Hobday Haugh

26

A Different Life

Fun fact: There are more than forty varieties of
Tabbies, making them the most common breed of cat.

fter thirty-six years of marriage, I was alone, living in a nice rental townhouse near my work. My three wonderful kids, now grown, had families of their own. Thankfully, I had a job that took up my days, but the nights were long and lonely. My life fell into a dreary routine: wake, work, home, eat, sleep, repeat.

A few months after my move, a co-worker found a stray cat living under her porch. She could not take him in because she already had three cats. I was reluctant, even though I was allowed to have a cat in my unit. I had always been one to nurture and care for helpless critters. I had even raised two orphaned robins to adulthood. But right then, to agree to adopt a homeless cat, sight unseen, seemed a little crazy. But perhaps I was feeling a little crazy that day because I suddenly blurted out, "Okay! I'll take him!"

At first, he huddled in a tight ball inside the carrier and refused to come out. I could see that he was a tan-and-black Tabby, fairly nondescript. Well, that was exactly how I felt. I went about some quiet chores, and eventually he ventured out to hide under a chair and watch me suspiciously with his big yellow eyes as I moved about. I spoke to him in a soft, soothing voice, and slowly he loosened up. Crouching low to the floor, he began to work his way around the perimeter of the first floor, slowly investigating every corner and piece of furniture. At any little noise or unexpected movement, he would jump and tense, then continue on his timorous exploration.

As I watched him, I could see that he had an impression in the fur around his neck where a collar had been. I looked at my hand where there was still an indentation left by my absent wedding rings. We had similar losses. Neither of us belonged to anyone.

The Tabby looked directly at me now. I looked back, with my eyes half-closed so as not to seem threatening, and wondered: What happened to you? What have you gone through out on your own? I thought it must have been very frightening for him, suddenly out fending for himself, because that's how I felt. The world was so big, and I felt so small. He was pretty thin, too, so he obviously had not been doing very well. I could also relate to that. I had lost twenty pounds.

Watching him creep along the baseboards, the boundaries of his new world, I saw exactly how I had been living for months, creeping around the boundaries of my own newly single life, peeking around corners, afraid to venture too far out into the open, keeping to the routine. I no longer knew where or how I fit into the world, just like that poor, homeless cat.

Later on, I lay stiffly in my bed, straining to hear any sound from my feline guest. Where was he? What was he doing? Did he use the litter box? I did not even know if he had come upstairs yet. Cats are so quiet! Time dragged on. I got up once and looked for him to no avail, so I went back to bed, straining to hear any sound. At some point, though, tense as I was, I must have dozed off because I was suddenly wakened by a solid thump at my feet. I lifted my head ever so slightly and peered toward the foot of the bed. The cat stood facing me, statue still. Neither of us even twitched. My sleepy brain wondered: Was he going to attack me? Had he ever been vaccinated? I dared not move. The small nightlight in the room gave off a soft glow that reflected eerily from his big, round eyes. Was he glaring, staring, or just looking? My imagination had to choose which before I could decide what to do next, like defensively burying myself under the covers. I chose "looking," and slowly put my head back on the pillow, took a deep breath and resolved to be calm.

Then an extraordinary thing happened! The cat uttered an audible sigh, sucking in a deep breath that I could hear as he expelled it in a soft *whoosh*. I felt movement, then warm pressure on my feet as he curled up against me with his head resting on my ankle. Relaxed. Another sigh, and he closed his eyes. He had made the choice to trust me and began to purr, that gentle, contented rumbling that seems to say "all is well." My heart melted. We chose each other that night and spent the next day bonding before I had to go back to work on Monday. I named him Bailey. I no longer had to come home to an empty house because he was there, always sitting on the back of the chair by the window, looking for me or curled up beside me on the sofa, warm and comforting.

My three-year-old granddaughter was sleeping over one night and asked me to tell her the story of how Bailey came to live with me. I told her a brief version, and since I was scrapbooking at the time, I thought it would be fun to gather pictures of him and create a storybook for her. I bought a spiral notebook to begin writing what I imagined his life had been like while he was lost. I took the notebook to work every day and wrote longhand on my lunch breaks and more during the evenings. The words and situations poured out from my heart onto the pages, and I realized that I wasn't just writing a fiction story of a lost cat; I was writing my own story. It became a way to release my feelings in a safe way through creative writing. My anger and anxiety flowed onto the pages as I eagerly wrote, to see what would happen to my reluctant hero. I had to purchase a laptop in order to write more and faster!

I told my friends about my new "hobby," and they urged me to self-publish. The result was an actual book I could hold in my hands, with a cover and 247 pages filled with my words! Those who read it loved it, but I wondered how that could be. Me? An author? I couldn't write a book! I had not set out to write a book, after all. But I've always believed that God works in mysterious ways, opens windows when doors seem closed, and works all things for good. In my case, God opened a window and let in a cat I named Bailey… and a new and different life began.

~Beth DiCola

27

All My Children Wear Fur Coats

*Fun fact: All kittens are born with blue eyes, which
will change by the time they're eight weeks old. Kittens'
eyes remain closed until they're ten to fourteen
days old.*

My fiancé knew all about my love of cats up front and I began my "kitten campaign" in earnest less than a week after the wedding. Whenever I broached the subject, Mark shot me "the look," indicating further cat conversation was futile.

One glorious fall day, in our sixth month of marriage, everything changed. Mark walked into the living room and announced, "Okay, we can get a cat." Before I could respond, he moved close, pointed his coffee cup at me, narrowed his eyes and pronounced, "But you have to clean the litter box."

I jumped into his arms. I would have agreed to the daily cleaning of the elephant cage at the zoo if it meant bringing a kitten into our home.

Before he changed his mind or added any more stipulations, I grabbed his hand and dragged him out the door to begin our kitten quest.

The day we met our kitten is still one of my best memories. The shelter worker opened the cage and handed me a sweet ball of vibrating fur. I called Mark over to meet the enchanting Tabby-Siamese mix. As he approached, I rehearsed my case for bringing her home, but she took matters into her own paws. Settling into his hands, she leaned forward, put a tiny paw on his arm, blinked deep blue eyes and licked his face. The deal was sealed. He fell in love.

That sassy kitten filled our house with love, laughter and copious amounts of fur. She charmed us, entertained us, slept with us, and demanded our full attention and devotion.

I confess, without shame or apology, that we were putty in the paws of our furry diva. There were no beds soft enough, no toys interesting enough, no food healthy enough for our princess. Laser-focused on everything and anything that made her happy, we began to wonder if she might benefit from some companionship during the lonely hours we were away at work. I must confess there was another reason for considering companionship for her. It had to do with the discovery of an antique glass plate (an heirloom given to me by my mother-in-law), reduced to a pile of glittery dust on the tiles of the fireplace hearth.

We chose a long-haired, coal-black, green-eyed boy with the perfect, easygoing temperament needed to deal with the feisty Miss P and then we crossed our fingers and held our breath when they first met. Miss P sashayed toward the kitten, sniffed his coat, stared for a second, turned her back, and waltzed away, flicking her tail and shooting him a disdainful look. I swear I could hear her saying, "Get out of my way, Buster. You'd better behave yourself, Buster. Just remember who's in charge here, Buster!" We named him Buster.

Miss P and Buster settled into a harmonious existence. Their relationship was drama-free; she let him know she was the queen, and he acknowledged her superiority and sovereignty.

When Miss P reached her eighth birthday, we began another kitten search. We filled out two pages of forms for the rescue organization and had our home checked out by the kitten foster mother. Finally, deemed "kitten-worthy," we went to pick up our delightful female Lilac Point. As we moved toward the cat carrier to secure our new kitten, the "foster cat lady" picked up a little male, shoved him toward us and exclaimed, "These two are brother and sister and best friends. I simply couldn't separate them." This information might have been helpful earlier, but we fell for his crossed eyes and sweet face and drove home with two new companions for Miss P and Buster to meet.

The two "best friends," Tucker and Jasmine, proved to be anything but best friends. To this day, they tolerate each other, but exhibit no desire to spend quality time together. Note to self: Don't always believe everything the foster cat lady tells you.

Over the years, our feline family has become an important part of our lives. When I'm sick, a cat is always ready to cuddle the "patient" to sleep. When I cry, a furry, purry body presses in close, sometimes extending a paw (claws pulled in) to gently tap my face, letting me know everything will be okay (or to remind me to get up and feed them dinner). They even do us the honor of "singing the song of their people" in the wee hours of the morning.

I am childless by circumstance, not by choice. I used to avoid Mother's Day celebrations and felt empty and awkward at baby showers. In the course of emptying litter boxes, searching for delightful and delicious treats, and educating myself on the benefits of organic catnip, the empty "mother's hole" in my heart has healed in a way I'd never expected.

My feline family has taught me three valuable life lessons. First, happiness comes when I focus on what I have, rather than what is missing in my life. Second, I must never diminish the love in my life because it doesn't look exactly like the love in the lives of others. The third lesson was this: Family isn't always comprised of blood relations, nor is it necessarily comprised of humans.

People can be judgmental: "Four cats? No kids?" "Really, you seem to expend too much energy, love and money on those cats." "I understand you love your pets, but they are animals, not children!"

I let them prattle on. They don't know my story; they haven't walked beside me through my painful, childless journey. They see cats; I see healers of my heart.

"Crazy Cat Lady" is a title I wear proudly. The mockers don't understand that it's precisely because of my cats that I have not gone crazy. I am the recipient of the unconditional love of fantastic little beings who look to me to care for them, protect them and return their love in abundance.

The felines I share my life with today continue the journey of healing that began twenty years ago, the day I looked into the blue eyes of a special kitten. If that makes me a "crazy cat lady," then call me crazy.

~Anita Aurit

28

Knee Cat

Fun fact: There's an old saying among veterinarians:
"If you put a cat and a bunch of broken bones in the
same room, the bones will heal."

When I came home from the hospital after my knee-replacement surgery a few years ago, a black cat was lounging in the spring sunshine in my front yard. As my sister pulled her car into the driveway, she jokingly asked, "Oh, you have a new cat?"

"No," I grumbled. "I have a new knee. The last thing I need is a new cat."

My previous cat, which had lived with me for twelve years, had passed away a little over a year earlier. Now that I would be creeping around slowly with a walker while recovering for the next few weeks, I had decided it was not a good time to adopt a new pet.

However, this cat was not aware of my decision.

I had visits from the nursing service, my sister, my mother and my neighbor, who snuck me doughnuts and frozen pizzas to offset the fresh fruit from my sister and the vegetable casseroles from my mother. Meanwhile, that cat continued to hang around.

"Your black cat is beautiful," said the visiting nurse.

"I see your new cat is still here," mentioned my sister.

"Is that your cat out by the garage?" asked my neighbor.

"That is not my cat," I informed all of them.

But, just like them, I did see the cat every day, either wandering around the garden or napping on the sidewalk in the sunshine. It didn't seem to have a home, so in the mornings, I put out a bowl of tuna on the front porch. I couldn't let the cat go hungry.

My knee recovery continued, painfully and slowly. My mood didn't perk up either. I was bored and cranky.

"The problem is you're not walking enough," said the visiting nurse. "The weather is good. You should get outside in the yard every day."

"What for?" I grumbled. "I can't garden. I can't mow. All I can do is shuffle around with this walker."

"That's okay," replied the nurse. "The exercise will do you good."

I was totally unmotivated to get outside. I continued to sit in my chair, watch TV and complain that my knee hurt.

A couple of days later, I found the tuna in the cat's bowl had not been eaten. And it remained untouched for the next three days.

"I don't see that beautiful cat around anymore," said the visiting nurse.

"Hey, what happened to your new cat?" asked my sister.

"What did you do to get rid of that black cat?" said my neighbor.

I couldn't believe that cat had just disappeared, so hesitantly, I wrangled my feet into my sneakers, gripped my walker and struggled out the door. My steps were small and shaky at first, but I made it out to the patio where I found the cat reclining under the picnic table.

"Aren't you hungry?" I asked.

The cat meowed loudly and followed me back to the porch where it quickly gobbled up the tuna.

But the next day, the cat didn't show up again, so once more I got myself together and headed outside. This time I wandered a bit farther and found the cat sitting under the hydrangea bush.

"What's the matter?" I asked. "Your food is on the porch."

The cat followed me back and ate his meal again.

This routine continued for the next week. I would find the cat by the garden shed, sitting in the wheelbarrow or napping under the crabapple tree, but he wouldn't come to eat until I discovered where he was concealed.

It was crazy, but the cat seemed intent on making me follow the nurse's instruction to do more walking. Finally, I told others about the situation.

"Hey," replied the visiting nurse. "Anything that gets you up and moving works for me."

"There is nothing like a rousing game of 'find the kitty' to make you feel better," my sister assured me.

"Well," commented my neighbor. "I guess he must be a knee cat."

So, for the next month, Knee Cat, as he came to be known, continued assisting me with my rehabilitation by waiting for me to find him somewhere in the yard and then coming over to eat his food. Every day, I got better, stronger and less cranky.

Finally, I recovered fully and was able to go back to work. Knee Cat and I no longer had time for our game of hide-and-seek, so the cat started coming to the porch every morning to eat like he had in the beginning.

Summer passed, autumn blustered in, and before the first frost, I convinced Knee Cat to move into the house with me.

Sometimes, I still have to hunt to find him, but now Knee Cat sleeps in the closet, curls up on the bed or sits on the back porch; regardless, he never misses a meal.

And thanks to my unusual encouragement from Knee Cat, my knee is working fine, too.

~David Hull

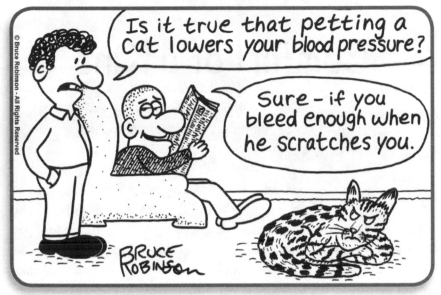

Reprinted by permission of Bruce Robinson

Comfort of a King

*Fun fact: A tuxedo cat named Simon was given a
medal for protecting the soldiers' food from mice on
board a ship in the South Pacific during World War II.*

One of our cats, KC, was the undisputed king of the
neighborhood. He would make the rounds of the
neighborhood and people would invite him in and pay
tribute in the form of treats and lots of petting.

Our next-door neighbors, the Benders, didn't know what to make
of our animal-loving household. Mr. and Mrs. B and their two children
lived a pet-free existence in their tidy ranch home. Although Mrs. B
and the kids loved our menagerie, Mr. Bender didn't like cats.

This didn't deter KC, who always started his travels outside the
Benders' kitchen door. Even though they seldom gave him a treat, he
remained hopeful. He would sit on their stoop, emitting the occasional
plaintive "Meow." If the Benders were around, they would pet him, but
KC couldn't understand why they wouldn't let him inside.

Then Mr. Bender was diagnosed with an aggressive cancer, and
KC didn't even get his petting from the Benders. Caring for Mr. B was
all they could handle. Undeterred, KC continued to stop outside their
kitchen door, tilting his head and waiting patiently before he moved
on to more receptive neighbors.

A few months later, KC disappeared one night. I was worried.
The old fellow wandered, but he was usually home by dark. I stepped
into the yard calling, "KC, KC!"

The light over the Benders' kitchen door came on, and Mrs. B, finger to her lips, gestured for me to come in. She took me to her husband's sick room. The tall strong man I'd known had wasted away. He was sleeping, and it took me a moment to realize what I was seeing. Mr. B's withered hand was resting on KC, who was tucked close to his side. The old tom was purring like a motorboat.

"I don't know how he got in the house," Mrs. Bender whispered, "but he seems to be a comfort. This is the best Mr. B has slept in weeks." She reached down and ruffled KC's ears. "Do you mind if he stays the night?"

KC quit doing his neighborhood rounds. He stayed with Mr. Bender whenever he could. He would lie by the man's side, purring to make his presence known. He seemed to be sure, in the way cats have, that Mr. Bender needed the comfort only a feline could give.

A few months later, Mr. B passed away. Thereafter, whenever KC stopped by the Bender household, he was always invited in to continue the important job of comforting the family.

~Leslie Gulvas

Missionary Cat

*Fun fact: Cats rub against people they like to mark
them as part of their "gang."*

Stripes was a silver Tabby with no remarkable features
except one: the tip of his nose was half-white and half-
brown. Despite his rather ordinary appearance, we very
quickly discovered that Stripes had a unique talent: He
was able to win the affection of practically every person he encountered. We often had meetings, home-school get-togethers and Bible
studies in our house, and Stripes greeted and saw to the comfort of
every guest. Even cat-haters would succumb to his gentle purr and
docile temperament.

Stripes patiently endured being dressed up in various outfits, carried in numerous objects, and being the accomplice in many prankish
activities, while seeming to love every minute of it. He was a people
cat. In the seventeen years we had him, I never heard him hiss or
strike at anything other than another male cat that dared to step on
our property. He would chase squirrels and birds, but would never
actually catch them.

Another talent Stripes had was exploring. This is not unusual for
a cat, but Stripes excelled in the art. He explored the interior of our
cars and took many unwitting trips. He would follow us on walks,
and people would say, "Is that your cat?" Then we would hear stories
about his visits. Our neighborhood became affectionately known as
"Stripesdom" to his regulars.

Stripes made his rounds twice a day — in the morning and in the evening. But after about five years, he suddenly had to be let out by 7:15 every morning, and he would meow and be uncharacteristically obnoxious until we did. Once the door was open, he would bolt from the house. Other times of the day, he was more flexible, but not in the morning. We chalked it up to his advancing years and becoming "set" in his ways. After about two years of this, he suddenly stopped. Finally, we could sleep in on Saturdays.

About six months later, I was working in the yard when a passerby saw Stripes sunning himself and asked, "Is that your cat?" I said yes, and she went on to tell me an amazing story about our beloved Stripes.

The lady lived about a block-and-a-half away from us. An elderly couple lived across the street from her. They had had a long and full life together traveling the globe and pursuing shared interests. One unfortunate evening, the man died. After a few weeks, the lady went to check on the widow. She said that she was doing all right, but the hardest part of the adjustment for her had been breakfast. Throughout their married life, no matter what their schedule, they always had coffee and read the paper together first thing in the morning. This was when she missed her husband the most. Yet, a couple of days after her husband died, this cat showed up in her breakfast nook window wanting to come in. She let him in and gave him some milk. He drank it, rubbed against her, began purring, and then curled up on her husband's chair next to her. She stroked his fur while she read the paper. As soon as she put down the paper and stood up, he got down and went to the door to be let out.

Stripes visited the widow practically every day at 7:30 in the morning. The widow had come to love him and wait expectantly for him, giving him treats and milk with each visit. She was sure God had sent an angel in the form of a cat to comfort her in her darkest moments.

When I asked how the widow was, the lady told me that she had died about six months earlier. She had seen Stripes visit for a day or two afterwards, then he didn't come anymore.

Another time, a woman on a playground told me how Stripes had come up to her daughter, who was sitting forlornly on a swing the day they lost a family pet. He had rubbed against her and then stood up, putting his paws on her legs and rubbing his head against her arm. Her daughter held and hugged him for quite a while. That little visit of his calmed the girl and gave her hope that maybe she could love another pet one day.

After we had Stripes almost fifteen years, we moved to another state. An elderly woman lived across the street from us. Stripes visited her daily, this time in the afternoon. She said she enjoyed how he would jump up in her lap and lie there for a while. Stripes was getting older himself at this point. About a year later, the arthritis in his hips meant he could no longer jump up, but he would still visit and lie near her feet so she could pet him.

Stripes was always affectionate with our family. But whenever anyone in the family was sick or sad, Stripes would lie by that person's side for extended periods of time, lick a hand or head, and offer his fur for petting, frequently giving up some of his outside patrols. It seemed that Stripes felt it was his mission in life to seek out and comfort people who were hurting. He definitely had a sense for detecting people who needed emotional encouragement. Perhaps the widow had been right. Maybe there really was an angel living inside Stripes.

~Ann Joseph

31

Lion's Gift

*Fun fact: The Quakers first began to use animal
therapy in treating the mentally ill in the 1790s.*

She appeared in our back yard on an otherwise ordinary day. Sitting in the grass, which complemented her autumn coloring, she stared at us with the utter surety that very few creatures possess as cats do — a kind of dignified defiance.

She was beautiful, with chocolate-brown stripes, green eyes, and a fluffy white ascot at her throat. My sister, who knows cats, decided that she was a Tabby mix, possibly with some Persian thrown in, which explained her white boots and tail-tip. She named her Lion for the way she stalked through the grass.

Why she had chosen us can only be explained by that lovely, mysterious force that is known by many names: fate, kismet, destiny, serendipity, providence, luck. My pragmatic mother said that Lion came because the family that had lived in our house previously had fed her, so she thought of our back yard as her watering hole. Personally, I think she came to us because she knew we needed each other.

Lion usually camped out in our yard, but on bitterly cold or rainy nights she came inside. She hated getting wet. She always looked disgruntled on those nights: soaking wet, ears flattened, whiskers dripping. She would purr while I dried her off with a towel.

Although she loved a cozy bed or chair, she could never bear to stay inside for more than a day. She possessed a restlessness, an innate fear of being hemmed in. Being a stray, and semi-feral to boot, she never became a docile housecat. She always possessed a bit of an edge.

One day, while I was vacationing in Florida, my aunt, who was pet-sitting Lion, called me in a panic. Lion was making awful noises, having some kind of a fit. She was sure that Lion was going to die.

I felt guilty for being so far away, helpless to stop it and unable to say goodbye. Lion was my closest friend; she needed me, and I wasn't there.

I told my aunt to put on some music for Lion. I thought it would calm her down to hear her favorite song one last time: Fred Astaire's rendition of "One For My Baby." Lion always came into my room as soon as the song came on. (She also liked the theme song to *Jeopardy!* and would emerge at exactly two minutes to seven and settle on the bed to watch.)

She thought my request was crazy, but biologists have proven that animals not only respond to music, but have listening preferences, so my aunt humored me and played the song for Lion. She called back when the song ended and said that, incredibly, Lion seemed to have recovered. I was elated.

Then one night, Lion returned the favor. I was suffering from a strange illness of my own. I had been having hallucinations, seeing things that weren't there, hearing voices that instructed me to hurt myself. It was dark and quiet, about 3:00 a.m. The household was silent; I was the only one awake. Outside, snow was falling. I sat in the den, summoning up the strength to get a knife and slit my wrists. Lion jumped into my lap and settled there. She was heavy; she felt like a furry cinderblock. She refused to get down, digging her claws into the fabric of my pants so that she clung to me like Velcro.

With the psychic ability that cats are known for, Lion sensed my desperation and kept me from acting on it by anchoring me to the chair.

Resting my hand on her back, I felt her heartbeat through my palm. The warmth of Lion's body and the rhythm of her purring began to lull me into something like sleep. Every so often, she would glance up at me, keeping tabs. She sat with me the entire night; I never did go for the knife.

The next day, I told my mother that I wanted to commit myself to a psychiatric hospital. While there, I was diagnosed with Depressive Disorder with psychotic features. Unlike situational depression, which occurs in response to unfortunate life events, a depressive disorder is biological and permanent.

I was given medication, which stopped the hallucinations and regulated my brain chemistry. I will probably be on anti-psychotic drugs for the rest of my life, but I am still alive.

I believe that Lion saved my life. If she hadn't stood sentry that night, I would almost certainly have found the strength to kill myself.

Lion passed away at the age of fifteen. The night before she died, she jumped onto my bed, climbed up my chest, and stared at me. She gazed at me, nose to nose, for a long moment, as though she were memorizing me. I didn't recognize this odd gesture for what it was until the next day: Lion had been saying, "Goodbye. I love you."

I recently saw a greeting card that said, "When I measure my life in the cats I have loved, I count myself blessed indeed." How true. I consider Lion a sort of guardian angel. In my favorite photograph of her, she is lying on her back out on the patio, with one paw stretched over her head. It looks like she is waving at me. And I think she still is.

~Jessica Goody

32

Daily Walk

*Not-so-fun fact: It's estimated that cognitive
decline — referred to as feline cognitive
dysfunction — affects more than 55% of cats over age
eleven and more than 80% of cats over age sixteen.*

The old yellow Tomcat limped along behind me on our daily walk to the second raised flowerbed. It wasn't far but our pace was slow. Upon reaching our destination, Bam Bam attempted to jump up on the old red bricks where I now sat. Sometimes the effort was too much and I would carefully lift him up and settle him beside me, scratching his ears before letting him go. This time he was able make the jump on his third attempt.

Bam Bam — sometimes called Bambi — stretched out and rolled back and forth on each side before settling down for a quick nap. After a few minutes passed, the cat roused himself, jumped down off the flowerbed and started the slow journey home. I, too, left my seat and walked alongside him.

We had just started this ritual about three months before. It took a few months after my husband's death to understand what the cat wanted. He would follow me to the community mailbox positioned just outside my gate and cry repeatedly as he walked down the sidewalk beyond my gate. When I turned in the yard, he would sit outside the gate and continue to wail.

Sixteen years earlier, I had convinced my husband, Ralph, that he needed companionship for the long days while I was at work. I made a trip to the local SPCA and spotted a small yellow kitten about six months old in a cage. As I passed, he reached out his front paw and let out a pitiful howl. When I returned home, he came with me.

Ralph liked dogs. Cats were animals that lived in a barn and rid it of mice. And while he tried to ignore the little cat, he did allow it to sit in his chair with him and watch game shows and cooking shows on television — all the while voicing his dislike for cats.

When Ralph's health began to fail, he would take two walks a day almost the length of our gated community's common area, using his cane for stability. There were three round raised flowerbeds along the way, one by our house, one in the middle of the area and the third at the opposite end from our house. The yellow cat would trot along with him, sometimes running ahead to hide and pouncing out when Ralph got close.

As time went by and Ralph's health continued to decline, he traded the cane for a walker, and the walks stopped at the second raised flowerbed. There he would sit and visit with the mailman or the gardeners or a passing neighbor. Although Bam Bam had become very thin with age and his pace had slowed, too, he continued to accompany Ralph.

The walks dwindled to once a day and cat and human both came back ready for a long nap.

When Ralph lapsed into a coma one winter day, the cat was allowed in the house to sit on his bed. The faithful cat stayed all day, leaving only for a quick trip to the sand box. He refused to eat. When my husband took his last breath, the old cat howled and had to be put outside where he continued to howl.

Now we walk every day. Down to the second flowerbed and back. The cat limps behind me, and I reach our gate long before he does, but I hold it open for him even though he could easily step between the rails. I go in the house and he shuffles to his favorite napping place. Bam Bam is seventeen years old now and deserves a good rest.

~Ruth Acers-Smith

33

Welcoming a Stranger

Fun fact: The smallest breed of cat is the Singapura.
Females may weigh as little as four pounds.

When we bought our ten-acre "mini-farm" back in 1991, our family inherited Snagglepuss, a flame-orange barn cat that the sellers had adopted. She was joined the following year by a cat of similar appearance, but very different temperament, that someone dumped by the side of the road near our house late one autumn night.

My sister had been visiting, and in the wee hours she heard a car slow down, then one of its doors slam before it drove away. She didn't think any more about it until our daughter found the cat in the morning when she was starting to walk to school. After listening to some teary-eyed gushing from her about how adorable he was and how Snagglepuss needed a friend, we told her we would keep him if no one came to claim him. Of course, no one did.

Our daughter may have honestly thought Snagglepuss would like having a friend, but the older cat quickly made it clear she had other ideas. She disliked the new cat at first sight, hissing at him whenever he got too close or tried to play with her always-twitching tail. Even worse, she seemed to hold him in contempt because he was lazy and a terrible "mouser." Those qualities, along with his golden-orange coloring, gave us the idea for his name: Goldbrick.

One of the few things those two barn cats agreed on was that no other cats belonged in the territory they shared begrudgingly with each other. There was a small tiger-gray feral cat living under a fallen tree along the creek bank, and both our cats chased the poor little stray away at every opportunity. Though our fields surely had enough mice to feed an army of cats, they weren't willing to share a single one of them with the interloper if they could prevent it.

With that as the backstory, I couldn't have been more surprised at what I found when I went out to the barn on Christmas morning to give the kitties a treat. Our barn cats were a bit spoiled, with a long table set up with a comfortable arrangement of crates and blankets to keep them warm. They also had a heat lamp designed for poultry overhead. Since it was bitter cold that was where I found them — under the heat lamp. But as they stood up and stretched, I saw that I was going to need to split their plate of sausage and eggs three ways instead of two. The little gray stray was nestled between them, out of the cold and snow. I had never before seen or heard of cats — especially barn cats — with so much "Christmas spirit"!

After that week's cold snap was over, our cats also snapped out of their holiday mood and began chasing the stray away as before. But when the stray had been in danger of freezing to death, they seemed to sense that it was no time for being territorial and selfish, and were moved to something as close to pity as cats are capable of feeling.

Animal behavior has been studied a great deal, but the animals themselves still have a lot to teach us.

~Mary L. Hickey

Tweetie

My Very Good, Very Bad Cat

My Surprising Cat

Fun fact: The first cat to appear in cartoons was Felix the Cat in 1919.

34

The Feline Follies

Fun fact: Many cats don't like to have their bellies rubbed. It's a natural protective reflex to protect their vital organs.

When I went out of town unexpectedly, I asked my friend Susie to take care of my cats. She was a bit wacky but a pet lover, and it was just for the weekend, so what could go wrong, right?

I brought her over briefly to show her the lay of the land.

Mimko, my gray one, welcomed her with a swish against her legs. The other two, Fuzik and Little B., did their normal disappearing act — under the bed, behind the sofa, who knows where? Amazing how many places they could find to hide in my tiny one-bedroom apartment. When Susie came to meet them, they were MIA.

I described them to her. "Fuzik, the black one, is a scaredy-cat at first, but lovable once he gets to know you. The orange kitten, Little B., is a feral."

"Oh, that's so sad. Maybe he'll outgrow it."

"I hope so," I sighed. "He's still young. Don't try to pet him, or he'll bite or scratch you. He's not at all approachable. He'll most likely be hiding anyway when you come."

"Maybe he lost his mama cat at an early age," she reasoned. "What does the B stand for?"

I told her that he'd been so wild and unresponsive to humans that I had named him Little Brat.

"But my mom thought it wasn't nice to call him a brat because he can't help the way he is, so I call him Little B.," I added.

Susie agreed with my mom.

"Maybe if you had named him something compassionate, he'd be more socialized," Susie reasoned. "I'll work on him."

"Do it at your own risk," I warned, laughing. "The first-aid kit is in the bathroom."

The first night, Susie called. "Your critters are fine. Mimko is a true swisher."

She went on: "The little orange one vanished into the closet when I entered. I call him Little O. for 'Orange.' Get it? Then he stuck his head out. So that's an improvement, anyway. I think he likes this new name better."

"And Floozy was all over me," she added.

"Floozy?" I laughed. "His name is Fuzik — it's Czechoslovakian for Whiskers."

She quipped, "He's Floozy to me. He does that throw-down to the floor. You know, the one that says, 'Rub my belly NOW.'"

Susie's message the next day concerned me.

"Hello! It's the Animal Farm here. I don't know how it happened, but the orange cat got out. I found him outside your sliding glass door. But don't worry. I let him in, and he went straight for his food. Everyone's fine."

It really bothered me that Little B. had been left out, perhaps overnight. My cats were indoor cats.

I called her back and left a message: "Are you sure you didn't accidentally leave the door open, even for a second? Please check the windows. Those cats are tricky."

The next morning, I received her response: "It's Susie from the Feline Follies calling. The windows and doors are shut. The cats are accounted for. Mimko is in the fridge, and Floozy's on the chandelier. Don't worry. I'm kidding."

She went on, "But seriously, you were so wrong about Little Orange. He sits on my lap and purrs. Maybe he likes me better than you. Ha ha."

I was beginning to wonder if Susie was in the right apartment.

In the two months I'd had him, he had NEVER let me pet him, much less sit in my lap. Could he be coming around? I had been hoping he'd become more domesticated when he was neutered.

Could Susie have tamed my crazy kitty so quickly? So far, he hadn't taken to anyone except Mimko. He'd nurse on her when she was in a deep sleep. When she woke up, she'd smack him. I guess she was telling him, "I'm not your mama!"

No, he was definitely not friendly with people or any cats except Mimko.

I conveyed all this to Susie. Then she said something that puzzled me even more.

"Oh, I don't know about that, Eva. Last night, the two little oranges were snuggled on the couch together. They appeared to be very friendly indeed!"

"Susie!" I exclaimed. "What are you talking about? I only have one orange cat!"

She insisted there were two orange ones. And the gray and black cats were there also.

"How many cats are in my apartment?" I demanded.

"Four! How many do you have?"

Thoroughly confused and a little upset, I replied impatiently, "Susie, I only have three!"

"But you have four plates out," she maintained.

"Yes, three for wet food and one for dry."

My trip was over the following day, and I couldn't wait to get home. As I parked my car at the complex, I noticed a sign on the gate with a picture of an orange cat. "Missing cat. Answers to Butternut Squash." It had a phone number. The same sign was on the elevator.

It became increasingly clear what had happened. It had been Butternut outside my sliding glass door that night, not Little B. And it was Butternut and Little B. huddled on my couch last night.

As I opened my door, four little critters encircled me: Mimko, Fuzik, Little B. and their new buddy, Butternut Squash. I hugged and kissed three of them and sneaked a quick pat to Little B., backing away before he had a chance to bite. Predictably, he hissed.

Then I quickly ran to the elevator to get the number of Butternut's anxious mom. She lived across the complex and had no idea how Butternut had escaped, but was ever so appreciative that he was safe. She rushed right over and happily embraced her little orange munchkin and took her home. Little B. seemed sad to see Butternut leave. However, we promised we'd get them together on play dates, and we did.

It warmed my heart that Little B. had found a friend.

Two months later, Butternut's mom left a note on my sliding glass door, "Congratulations, Grandma. Butternut had kittens. Come take your pick."

I guess Little B. had been even friendlier than I had thought.

We never did a paternity test, but one look at the four orange kittens left no doubt who was the daddy.

I took one kitty and named it Little S. for "Surprise." Butternut's mom kept two, and we thought it was only fitting that Susie should get one, since she had been the matchmaker, so to speak. She named it Little O. for "Orange."

Butternut was soon spayed, and Little B. was neutered. It helped soften his disposition. He actually let me pet him once in a while and even purred for me, a mere human, once in a blue moon. Being around other cats he loved helped with his socialization. Or maybe it was fatherhood that had turned him into a slightly gentler, more domesticated kitty.

~Eva Carter

35

The Baptism

Fun fact: The Cat Fanciers' Association has a "breed personality chart," which helps potential owners understand what to expect from each breed.

Miss Snuggles loves to steal things. Normally, she is content to play with bottle caps, bread twist ties and the occasional shoelace, but every now and again, she gets an evil notion in her head and follows through with it.

Last Christmas, I set out my nativity set with lots of special care. Each piece had its own spot, which I had set up on our oversized windowsill. Days went by, and Miss Snuggles managed to avoid the set, so I thought all was well. Then came the morning I walked in to find the Holy Family scattered about the floor with the barn animals not far away. The cradle was underneath the couch… but without its occupant. Baby Jesus was nowhere to be found.

Miss Snuggles had stolen the baby.

I looked high and low. Nothing! My desperation, as well as frustration, grew with each passing day. Where could she have hidden him? Just as with the Wise Men of old, I, too, longed to find the infant before Christmas!

Days went by, but still nothing. I began to consider that the baby was gone forever and I'd have to find a replacement, which would be no easy task as I had bought this set from a thrift store. How could my nativity set be complete without its star attraction? I even prayed,

"Lord, if you help me find Baby Jesus, I promise I will keep the cat locked up from now on!"

Or... something like that. Lock up Miss Snuggles? I couldn't do that! When she wasn't getting into trouble, she was just the sweetest cat imaginable.

Now it was just two days before Christmas Eve. I woke up very early and went to use the bathroom, which was lit only by a four-watt nightlight. There, floating in the toilet, was a brown "something." Half asleep, I peered into the bowl, wondering just what I was looking at. Was it some leftover effect from my husband's late-night snack?

Curiosity got the best of me, and I flipped on the light. After my eyes had adjusted to the sudden brightness, I peered into the toilet bowl again. There, floating face up, was Baby Jesus, all smiles and none the worse for wear from his almost two-week absence. Obviously, Miss Snuggles had decided to bring him out from her hiding place and baptize Him in the process!

I gave the baby a thorough cleaning and put him back into his rightful place in the crèche, rearranging Joseph and Mary to make room for him once again. As Miss Snuggles watched from her perch atop the couch, I'm almost certain I saw a mischievous gleam in her eye.

~Diane Ganzer Baum

Reprinted by permission of www.offthemark.com

36

The Great Fish-Tank War

Not-so-fun fact: Many cats are sensitive or even
allergic to fish; it is one of the top three most
common feline food allergens.

T he war between man and cat began the day my daughter
Emily brought home two goldfish and a ten-gallon tank
complete with gravel, filter, and one of those ancient
Greek temples the fish are supposed to swim through and
relax in but actually avoid like death. While the rest of the household regarded the fish with mild interest, Draco the cat ignored
them almost completely. It wasn't the fish that started the war; it
was the call of the water.

Draco the cat was not named for the Harry Potter character,
but he could have been. He was a sly and devilish creature whose
inner vocabulary never included the concept of "no." We got him
from a pet rescue. He was a tiny black kitten with large golden eyes
as round as a lemur's, a soft purr, and the strangest "meow" I'd ever
heard; it sounded more like the burble of some strange bird.

Like every kitten we'd ever brought home, we put Draco in the
bathroom with his food and cat box until he became acclimated.
All the other kittens had accepted this situation, even though they
would sometimes yowl to get out and explore, and they waited more
or less patiently until the day they were given free run of the house.

Draco had other plans. I was reading on the couch when, less than fifteen minutes after we'd put him in the bathroom upon his arrival, he jumped on my shoulder, nuzzled my ear, and began purring. I could not understand how he'd gotten out of the bathroom. I'd closed the door myself, and I knew it had latched. How could a tiny kitten open a bathroom door? I sat with him a while and read him some poetry. I then had to work on some writing and placed him in his little comfy box back in the bathroom and shut the door. It was maybe twenty minutes later when he startled me by hopping up on my lap where I sat at the computer. I inspected the bathroom door, and the latch worked as well as ever. I had to conclude Draco had magical powers, otherworldly assistance, or Super Cat strength in opening doors. This feat of his, though, was only the beginning.

In the years we had him, I found him perched on the tops of doors, curled up high on kitchen cabinet tops no cat should have been able to reach, and once found him asleep in the corner of a closet shelf he could not have gotten to without leaping ten feet straight up from the floor. There was no place you could keep Draco in or out of. He was the Houdini of cats.

There were three other cats living with us, all female: Little Kitty (a Sydney Greenstreet type of calculating villain), Eggnog (the perpetual damsel in distress) and Luna (the spacey hippie). Draco, as the male, considered himself a noble prince and Lord of the Realm, but it was pretty clear that Little Kitty actually ran the show, using Nog and Luna as her puppets. Maybe this was why Draco felt he had to show his superiority in scaling heights and performing grand feats. And maybe this was also how the war of the fish tank began.

As the fish swam happily around in their tank, studiously avoiding the Greek temple they were supposed to play in, the cats were watching. Once I passed by and, noticing the tank looked odd, paused for a closer look. I found Luna sitting in back of the tank, watching the fish. Another time, Eggnog hopped up and tried to get her paw in the top to scoop one out. Little Kitty even hoisted her enormous bulk up onto the bureau where the tank sat to study the fish and contemplate their untimely demise. These were all singular incidents, however; it was only Draco who never gave up.

Draco didn't care about the fish. In his world, the fish were no more than wallpaper to his actual object of desire: the water. The fish-tank pump continuously sent a cascade of water arcing down into the tank, making a soft, sibilant sound even when the tank was filled to the top. And Draco loved water. He loved the dog's water. He loved the water in the kitchen sink. He loved the water left in glasses on the kitchen counters or living room tables. He loved all water everywhere in the house except the bathtub. All of these, though, were *still* waters; the fish tank was *sparkling*, moving water — and its soft sound beckoned.

The first time I found Draco drinking from the fish tank, I told him "no" and put him on the floor. The second time I found him up there I yelled at him and tossed him onto the floor. The third time I discovered him, I squirted him with a spritzer and shouted "No!" The fourth time, I did the same. The seventy-fifth time, I repeated the above with variations. Nothing made any difference. My wife Betsy covered the opening of the tank with foil; Draco gently peeled it back and drank his fill. She covered it in plastic; he did the same. I covered it in plastic wrap, foil wrapped around with duct tape, and placed a large Styrofoam skull from Halloween on it to scare him off; he knocked the skull to the floor, broke through the plastic, and unwrapped the tank for a drink.

At first, I just hadn't wanted him bothering the fish; then I'd not wanted him drinking fish water. I also didn't want him disturbing the pump's operation — which he'd done twice. Finally, though, it became a simple battle of wills. Who was this cat to continuously defy me? I was the man, he was the cat, and he was going to learn to behave as it pleased me. Draco's view of the situation differed; in his world, he was the cat, and I was the thing he slept on. Who was I to constantly annoy him at his water banquet?

The war of the fish tank dragged on for almost two years until its dramatic conclusion. My last attempt to keep him off the bureau was to set up a number of pictures of the family in frames around the tank. I had also placed some figurines, a desk calendar, and a lamp there. None of these deterred him. Lithe as a spirit, he would hop up and manage to land perfectly between my obstacles, raise himself up, and drink from the tank. I knew this first because I heard him jump down when I was reading in the next room, and he came in to sit on my lap fresh with the scent of fish tank upon him. Then I saw him in action one time as I was coming down the stairs.

His skill at landing between the pictures and the figurines, not moving one of them an inch, was very impressive. Still, I could not let this cat defy me day after day and month after month. And so the day came when I walked into the room and there he was, draped over the top of the fish tank, absorbed in his drink. I grabbed the spritzer bottle and let him have it. He reeled away from the tank, scattering everything around him. A picture frame flew to the floor with a loud crack; another disappeared in back of the bureau; the figurines spiraled skyward and all across the floor; the desk calendar danced a pirouette and then joined them. Draco launched himself into the air and vanished into the other room.

I looked at the mess all over the floor and the cracked picture frame, thought of how I was going to have to now move the bureau out to retrieve the one fallen behind it, and realized that Draco had won. He had never been doing anything all that bad in the first place. Once I'd moved the pump farther away from the side, he hadn't bothered its operation anymore. He never disturbed the fish themselves and, since I always kept the tank clean, it wasn't like he was drinking water that could harm him. The whole war, I realized, had been one-sided, with me as the aggressor. All Draco had wanted to do was enjoy his special water dispenser.

So he won. After that day, I would sit writing at the computer, the fish tank trickling and bubbling beside me, and Draco would hop up, get his drink, and go on his way. The first time he did this after my surrender, he watched me carefully with his large, round eyes, suspecting a trap. The second time, he was also wary for any sudden moves on my part. The third time, he was a bit more casual, but still kept raising his head to make sure I hadn't moved and that the spritzer wasn't in sight. By the seventy-fifth time, he just ignored me and, after drinking, would sit by the tank while deciding his next move. He would then seem to shrug, gaze about a moment, and then hop down to go nap in his favorite corner of the living room couch.

I could have continued the war. I could have moved the fish tank, boxed the top, anchored the plastic or foil with hoops of steel, but what was the point? If you have a cat, you must at some point recognize who is master and who is not; and the sooner you do that, the happier you both will be.

~Joshua J. Mark

37

The Amazing Cat Trick

Fun fact: When giving treats to your cat, make sure
they're not chocolate, which can be toxic to cats,
causing high blood pressure, heart problems or seizures.

hen I was twelve years old, we had a cat that wandered in and out of our house. When Topsy, a gray striped Tabby, chose to stay inside, he had food, safety, and companionship. Outside, he explored, hunted and roamed the countryside, sometimes mysteriously disappearing for days. Coming and going as he desired, he had the best of both worlds.

One day, I said to him, "Topsy, you are going to learn tricks." I made this announcement after spotting a mail-order offer on the back of my cereal box featuring a booklet explaining how to teach your cat tricks. I ordered it.

During the time I waited to receive the booklet in the mail, I imagined the fantastic stunts Topsy would soon perform. I had big plans for him. I pictured my cat jumping through a ring of fire like a tiger in the circus. I went and found my old hula hoop so I'd be ready.

When the booklet arrived, it advised me to start with a simple trick: shaking hands. Following the directions, I said, "Shake hands," lifting Topsy's paw and feeding him a snack simultaneously. I repeated this procedure many times, sometimes waiting for Topsy to return from one of his jaunts before continuing. Topsy finally mastered the trick. Whenever I said, "Shake hands," he lifted his paw. I was proud of him.

Topsy had learned his trick so well that he no longer waited for me to say, "Shake hands." Instead, he constantly raised his paw and touched me, staring hopefully, as if to say, "Come on, where's my snack?" Petting him as a reward didn't work. Neither did ignoring him. He continued shaking hands. He must have believed I always carried around bits of yummy food and had suddenly decided not to share.

Then one day, when I was wearing stockings, Topsy shook hands with my ankles. His claws snagged my stockings, damaging them. I had created a "stocking ripper" cat.

Not long after, something far worse happened.

When I saw the expression on my mother's face, I knew she had terrible news. "Topsy's dead," she said. "He's been run over."

"No," I cried, rushing outside to see for myself.

In front of our house, Topsy's crushed body lay on the road. Nothing much was left of his remains. Perhaps he'd been hit by a truck or run over more than once. My insides felt like they'd been dragged along with him.

My mother scooped up fur scraps and bloody bones. She placed them in a shoebox and buried it. We sobbed and hugged each other. Topsy was gone forever. He'd never shake hands with us again. We had lost a beloved member of our family. I cried myself to sleep.

A few days after Topsy's death, I was standing outside when something touched my leg. At first, I thought I'd imagined it. Again, I felt the same sensation. It sent chills through my body. Had Topsy's ghost returned to haunt me?

I looked down. A paw rested on my ankle.

"Oh, my God!" There was good old Topsy, alive and well, and expecting a reward for shaking hands. Well, he certainly deserved one. After all, he'd performed the most amazing trick of all. He'd come back from the dead!

Clearly, my mother had buried someone else's cat. Whose gray striped Tabby was it? I never found out. I wish I could have told the owner what had happened to his pet, but that wasn't possible.

Meanwhile, I focused my attention on Topsy. He received compliments, cuddles, caresses and extra treats. He purred contentedly, probably thinking it was about time he was appreciated. I began teaching him to jump through my hula hoop. I didn't know how much more time he and I would have together, but I was going to make the most of it.

~Laura Boldin-Fournier

Fat Cat

Fun fact: To determine if a cat is overweight, vets use Body Conditioning Scoring (BCS). If they can feel the cat's ribs, but there is a light layer of fat, they're probably of normal weight.

Last month, my cat, Thor, got an e-mail from the vet notifying him that he was due for a checkup. I found the note in my spam filter.

Very clever, Thor.

But the vet was smarter and mailed him a postcard, too. It read: "Attention, Thor! It's time for a visit!"

I found the card near the litter box and scheduled an appointment.

Now, Thor is an extremely easy-going feline. Nothing rattles him except perhaps an empty food bowl, but more about that later. "You're going to go on a road trip!" I told him.

He yawned and covered his eyes.

Since our older cat, Milo, had shredded the cardboard carrier during his last vet visit, I borrowed a sturdy plastic crate from my mother-in-law.

I set it in the middle of the living room floor. Thor crawled in immediately and made himself comfortable.

Our drive to the vet's office was punctuated by Thor's pitiful mews, or "meeps" as we call them. While Milo yowls, growls, meows, hisses, and generally makes a ruckus, Thor is the strong, silent type. However, he didn't appreciate not being able to see out the windows, and he let us know.

He was much happier when we arrived at our destination. He tolerated the poking, prodding and related indignities of his exam with good cheer, and didn't even flinch when he received his shots.

Then it was time to weigh him. I knew he'd grown a lot since his previous visit, but when the vet put him on the scale, well, a lot of Thor spilled over.

"Wow, that's a pretty small scale," I ventured.

The vet just looked at me. "Thor is overweight," she pronounced.

Immediately, I plunged into denial. "Are you sure?" I asked. "I mean, he is a Tabby, and horizontal stripes aren't very slimming."

She pointed to the scale. My one-year-old cat weighed seventeen pounds. "He should weigh between twelve and fourteen pounds."

"Gosh, Mom. Thor is a FAT cat," my son, Sam, said. He scooped Thor off the scale and rubbed him between his ears.

I was mortified. "He's still wearing his winter fur," I mumbled. "He has a thick coat."

Sam agreed. "He *is* fluffy."

The vet remained unconvinced.

"Our other cat is slim," I said. "Positively svelte, and he eats the same food as Thor."

Sam shifted Thor in his arms. "Mom, we call Milo Chubsy-Wubsy."

"Do you give Thor treats?" asked the vet.

Sam raised his eyebrows and looked at me. "Oh, yes, she does," he said.

On our next vet visit, I'm leaving Sam at home.

I fidgeted with the cat carrier. "Well, uh, just once a day," I said. "But he sits up and begs for them. That's good exercise, right?"

The vet just shook her head.

We coaxed Thor back into his carrier, which somehow felt even heavier than when we arrived.

The bottom line? The cats were only to be fed one-third of a cup of dry cat food a day. No more self-feeding. Their bowls were to be set out in the morning, put away, and then put back in the evening. And no treats.

Thor seemed discouraged by the news. He didn't make a peep on the drive home. Well, until he threw up.

His humiliating day ended in the tub.

The next morning, I carefully measured out one-third cup of food into each cat's bowl. As usual, Milo pushed Thor out of the way and began eating out of Thor's dish. Thor just switched over to Milo's bowl.

A few minutes later, Milo left. Thor kept right on eating. When he finally walked away from the bowls, they were both nearly empty. I put them out of reach.

Soon, Milo returned. He looked at where his bowl should have been. He paced. He walked in circles around the water dishes. "Yeeeooooww!" he said.

I ignored him. "Meeeeooow!" he whined.

Milo was not a happy camper. He's a grazer, not a gorger. But he was paying the penance for Thor's gluttony.

I'm afraid I drove my family crazy over the next few days. "Do you think Thor looks thinner?" I asked repeatedly. "I think he looks thinner."

After two weeks of the new regimen, we weighed him. "Sixteen pounds!" Sam announced.

Whew! My kitty was losing weight! I gave him a treat to celebrate.

Our celebration was cut short when my husband brought in the mail. "Something here for Milo," he said. "It's from the vet."

I've scheduled Milo's checkup for next week. But if the vet tells me Milo is overweight, I'm going to find a new veterinarian.

~Cindy Hval

A Tail of Loyalty

Fun fact: A female cat is called a queen or a molly.

My husband and I often joke that Molly is a dog trapped in a cat's body, so it did not surprise me when she came running across the lawn to meet me when I got home from work. It had been a busy Saturday morning shift, and I was looking forward to sitting down with a cup of tea and the newspaper. I glanced half-heartedly in Molly's direction, and then did a double take. Her welcome was not a surprise, but the neat white bandage that was bobbing merrily on the end of her upturned tail was.

I had left her that morning lazily sunbathing on the kitchen windowsill alongside her sister Maisie, who doesn't have even a hint of "dog" in her personality. Maisie is the kind of cat who gives cats a bad reputation. She is independent, aloof and often downright rude, barely glancing my way as I walk by. It is rare for her to seek me out for an affectionate pat on the head or a scratch behind the ear. She is a fickle friend, sociable when I am cooking, indifferent when I am not. She would never suffer the indignity of bounding across the grass to meet me.

Molly, on the other hand, is gregarious and affectionate. She is an adventurer, and in her relatively short life, her adventurous spirit has gotten her into trouble several times. To the uninitiated, Molly and Maisie look exactly alike, both sleek and black with just the tiniest smudge of white on their chests. However, those in the know can quickly tell them apart since Molly has what I can only describe as a "flat head" as the result of a previous accident.

As I watched her bound across the grass, I wondered what mischief she had gotten herself into this time. I didn't have to wonder for long. A few minutes later, my father-in-law rounded the corner looking rather sheepish. He lives next door, and Molly adores him. She follows him around incessantly, like a faithful puppy. I may provide Molly with food and shelter, but in her heart she is Harold's cat.

I watched as Harold shuffled uncomfortably from one foot to the other, making small talk about the weather and my morning at work. My husband noticed I was home and abandoned his yard work to join us as we stood on the front path with our eyes fixed on Molly. We all looked at her as we talked about everything but the matter at hand. Neither man offered an explanation.

Eventually, Harold blurted out that he had cut off part of Molly's tail. I thought he was joking, but then I looked at his serious expression and realised he was not. Molly was now rubbing affectionately against his ankles, and I wondered if he was somehow covering for her, but my husband assured me that it was true. He had heard Harold's first confession an hour before.

Slowly, the story unfolded. It was a beautiful spring day, and Harold had decided to spend it working in his garden. As soon as he stepped through his door, Molly, his faithful shadow, was at his side. She walked beside him as he puttered about, and when he decided to prune the shrubs in his patio flowerbed, she followed, rubbing affectionately against his legs much as she was doing now. Unfortunately, Molly had embraced her inner dog at an inopportune moment and "wagged" her tail right into the path of Harold's secateurs. The result had greeted me when I arrived home.

I looked at Harold as he finished the sorry tale. He held his breath and waited anxiously for my reaction. I looked at my husband, no doubt prepared to be the peacemaker. I looked at Molly, the white bandage dancing as she continued to heap love on an oblivious Harold.

And I laughed.

It all seemed so ridiculous. Molly wasn't upset, so I wasn't either!

Relief replaced the discomfort on Harold's face, and he gave an uneasy laugh of his own before telling me how Molly sat contentedly on his knee and purred, even as her tail was being bandaged. I wondered what had happened to the bit of tail that got cut off, but decided not to ask.

If Maisie, the prima donna, had lost part of her tail, she would have tried to exploit it for every possible perk. It would have taken her years to get over the offense. Molly, however, remained unwavering in her devotion to Harold. It just goes to show that for all the negative publicity cats get, they can be every bit as loyal as dogs.

~Deborah Kerr

When the Gussycat Flew

Fun fact: Domesticated housecats can run at a
thirty-mile-per-hour pace.

t was late. Very late. Four in the morning late — that deep, dark hour when all is calm and peaceful, and nothing crazy ever happens.

Except this time something crazy did happen — and, of course, Gus was right in the middle of it all.

I was working a late shift back then, not long out of college, still living at home with Mom and my sister Paula, and our cats, WT and Gus. I had gotten home around 2:30 a.m., made myself a bite to eat, and watched a little TV. The hour had just passed 3:30 when I finally plopped down onto my bed, all set to enjoy a long morning of well-earned sleep.

Alas! The household's junior cat had other ideas.

Our Gus — formally, Augustus H.T. Cat; informally, The Gussycat — had come to us from a litter of feral kittens. After a rough start, Gus had fit in well with the family. Even WT, the senior cat, tolerated his presence fairly well. But Gus always retained that little bit of wildness, that touch of strange and crazy that sometimes led him to do unexpected things — even if the clock said, "No, sorry — no crazy right now. Go to sleep!"

Not long after I hit the sack, pandemonium broke out in the

hallway outside my bedroom door. If you've ever worked a late shift, you know how important it is to get your sleep. Any loss of that precious dreamtime is not appreciated. I dragged myself out of bed, as grumpy as you can imagine, and threw open the bedroom door, demanding an explanation: "What the (censored) is going on out here?"

My angry question generated no comprehensible response — just a stream of unintelligible, panicked cries from my mother and sister, both of whom were already tumbling down the stairs to the first floor. My fuzzy, sleepy brain could only pick out a few random nuggets of information: Gus, window, glass. Nothing that made much sense.

"What?" I asked, hoping for some clarity.

"Get WT away from the glass in my bedroom!" commanded Mom from the bottom of the stairs before she disappeared into the living room.

I made my groggy way into my mother's bedroom, where the pieces started to come together. At least, the pieces of the mystery came together; the pieces of the windowpane — which lay scattered on and beneath the windowsill — were most definitely not coming together, and never would again.

The sight of the shattered glass finally helped me do the math. Somehow, Gus had jumped through the window and plunged to the patio below.

Gus hadn't jumped *out* the window; he had jumped *through* the window, shattering the glass in the process. There wasn't a cat-shaped hole in the window, like you'd see in cartoons, but there was an impressively jagged empty space where once a pane of solid glass had stood. No wonder everyone was going crazy.

Everyone, that is, except WT, who had stationed herself by the broken window and was surveying the scene with what can only be described as detached bemusement. Given my assumptions — that we already had one mangled cat on our hands — I made sure to perform my assigned task.

"Shoo!" I said to WT, whisking her away from the carnage before she did any damage to herself. "Go on. Get out of here." WT complied, jumping down from the windowsill and slinking out of the room with a cat's typical studied indifference.

Once I had seen the sane cat off to a safe distance, I returned to the window to learn the fate of the crazy one. I peered through the jagged remains of the pane and looked down to the back patio, where the search-and-rescue operation was in full effect. Fortunately, our back yard was small and fenced off, so Gus was effectively corralled as soon as he landed. In just a few minutes, the tag team of Paula and Mom recovered our wayward cat and brought him back to the safety of the great indoors.

Later, I was able to reconstruct what had happened: Not long after I had gone to bed, Gus was seized by a fit of "the crazies." This condition, common in young cats, had sent Gus zipping around the house at top speed, running from room to room like his fur was on fire. When his frenetic path took him into Mom's bedroom, Gus decided that a flying leap onto the hope chest beneath the window would be just the thing to make his night complete.

Unfortunately, Gus did not realize that upon this hope chest's slick, ultra-smooth top surface sat a folded blanket. As soon as Gus's paws hit the blanket, the whole bundle of cat and fabric shot across the chest's lid, propelled forward by the leaping cat's full-bore momentum. The blanket acted like a magic carpet ride, launching the leaping Gus forward and upward into a low orbit that sent our feline daredevil right through the window and out into the night, until at last he landed in the yard below.

What damage resulted from this unscheduled liftoff? The window was totaled, of course; it would take several days to get a replacement pane of glass installed.

But the Gussycat, despite bursting through glass and plunging to the ground from a second-story window, survived with just a cut on his right front paw. He seemed completely unfazed by his airborne adventure.

Long after that crazy night, the legend of Gus the Flying Cat lived on. For years thereafter, Gus seemed like a Super Cat: indestructible, amazing, and capable of anything at any time.

Gus survived his night flight and lived on for another decade, until he finally made his last leap away from this world and into the next. I miss him to this day, but I will always remember the night when the Gussycat flew — the night when I learned that cats really are capable of just about anything... and sometimes "anything" happens at four in the morning!

~Stephen Taylor

41

A Sunny Welcome Home

*Fun fact: A cat's ability to find its way home is known
as "psi-traveling." One theory is that they can do this
because they have magnetized cells in their brains,
like compasses.*

Sunshine came into our lives when I was five years old. My
three-year-old sister, Candace, and I had nagged our parents for months about wanting a kitten. Our mom finally
relented when someone she knew told her of an available
litter at a nearby farm. She had one condition, though — the kitten
had to be a ginger-coloured one.

Well, as fate would have it, when we arrived to see the cats, it
turned out that there was an orange Tabby kitten. Candace and I
were jumping for joy. We were both certain that this kitten was ours.
Unfortunately, Sunshine was the only kitten that the owners planned
to keep. My sister and I were devastated. We knew we weren't going
to get a cat unless it was this orange one. Our mom had said so. When
the owner saw how upset we were, she called a family meeting. They
decided we could keep him, but only if we kept his name — Sunshine.
We happily agreed.

Sunshine came home with us, and we lavished attention on him.
He slept in the old, dilapidated barn on our property. We lived near
Belleville, Ontario, in a little house on top of a hill. Candace and I
loved to play in the gardens around the house with my mom and dad.
Sunny, as we often called him for short, ran on his own schedule. He

would wander all around the property and beyond. His visits weren't regular. Sunshine showed up whenever he was ready for some of our attention — or for some food. Our family learned to love him just the way he was.

My job was to feed Sunshine. We could almost always count on a visit from him in the morning. I would open our front door and bring out his breakfast. Once it was all set up nicely on the front step, I would sit and wait, calling, "Sunshine! Sunny! Here boy, Sunny boy!" Sure enough, he would emerge from his sleeping quarters — the barn. Happily weaving between my legs and purring, he would have some of his food. He loved to stand on my lap while getting his ears rubbed.

Work circumstances changed for my dad, though, and we had to move to Toronto. It was a two-and-a-half-hour drive from Belleville. My parents found an apartment and we moved in. They decided to keep our house in Belleville — my dad hoped the Toronto move was only temporary. On most weekends, we drove to Belleville and stayed at our house. We would then spend the workweek in Toronto. Apartment living, we soon found out, proved to be a difficult one for our wandering cat. This cat was used to roaming around outside. I wanted Sunshine to snuggle with me at night. My mom just wanted him toilet trained! Sunshine thought otherwise. He sprayed the bathroom walls with urine, claiming his territory, oblivious to the litter box.

The inevitable happened. My parents sat down with Candace and me and told us that Sunshine couldn't be with us anymore. We were crushed. We had fought so hard for a pet, found one with the specific qualifications that Mom had called for, and we couldn't keep him. My mom called some farms in the area to see if any of them were in need of a barn cat. Sure enough, a kind farmer in Aurora, Ontario, said that we could drop him off.

I remember that car ride with Sunny. I was so sad, and Sunshine hated being in the car. He meowed incessantly. We drove a good half-hour north of our apartment in Toronto to Aurora. My mom dropped off Sunny near the farmer's door, and we drove away. I cried the whole way back to our apartment.

On weekends, we continued visiting our Belleville house but it just wasn't the same without Sunshine there. Luckily for us, things soon changed. A year later, Dad got work in Belleville. We could move back home — for good! We packed up our things and drove home.

I remember asking my parents during that final drive back home if we could get a new pet because we would be settling into our house again. They just chuckled, as they usually did when I asked them, and said "maybe." It was a lot to ask for, I guess, with the move.

Well, what a shock we got that morning. As Dad drove up the driveway, we saw an orange Tabby cat emerge from the barn. I felt a smile forming on my face just as he exclaimed to Mom, "That's not Sunny, is it?"

Dad quickly parked, and we all ran out to greet him. We couldn't believe our eyes. Was it really him? This cat came up to us purring and weaving between our legs. Mom checked and there was his trademark: an extra toe on each of his front paws. My mom exclaimed gleefully, "It's him alright!"

I quickly ran inside to get some leftover cat food and milk, which I put on the front steps. Sunny came up to me, waiting for me to rub his ears. It was a wonderful, amazing thing. Somehow, our cat made the long journey from that farm in Aurora — a three-hour drive away — to our home in Belleville. Some thirty years later, it still seems unreal. I'll never forget that joyful day when our Sunshine came back.

~Rachel Lajunen Harnett

42

Game Over

*Not-so-fun fact: More than ten percent of cats will
develop an "elimination problem."*

I was reading a story in a magazine when I turned the page and found myself face-to-face with the answer to my prayers. "Toilet Train Your Cat in Less than a Month!" the ad screamed. The story forgotten, I placed an order.

When the package came, I was disappointed. Basically, it was a flimsy plastic tray shaped like a bedpan that fit over the rim and under the seat of the toilet. Somehow, I was expecting more. But they said it would work, so I got started.

The instructions said to put a bit of litter in the tray so the cat would know where he was supposed to do his business. The concept was that he would recognize how flimsy it was and perch on the edge of the seat instead of putting his weight on the tray, thus training him to use the toilet instead of a box. Sounded reasonable…

When I showed him the new facilities, my Siamese cat, Phaze, was less than impressed. He gave me a "You've got to be kidding!" look and swished his tail, but I was firm as I told him, "No, you go HERE now." To make it perfectly clear, I moved his litter box onto the balcony where he wouldn't see it.

Phaze wasn't thrilled, but he tried it. I cringed as I watched him put his full ten-pound weight on the tray. I could hear the thin plastic crinkling, but somehow it held.

About a week into the endeavor, I came home to find potting soil on the floor and a surprise in my potted plant. Phaze had found an alternative. I cleaned up the mess and moved the plant to the balcony. Phaze followed me out, and when he did, he spied his litter box.

I have never seen a cat so excited! He danced; he pranced; he leaped with joy! If he could talk, he would have been saying, "Mom, we found it! We found my litter box! Look! There it is!" He was not a happy kitty when I made him go back into the apartment and the litter box stayed outside.

The instructions said to gradually decrease the amount of litter in the tray. I did, although Phaze looked more confused each time. He was also still sitting directly in the tray. No matter what I did, I couldn't get him to understand that he was supposed to perch on the edge.

A week later, the inevitable happened. I heard a splash in the bathroom, and when I rushed in, Phaze was climbing out of the toilet. His back half was wet, and his front half was furious. He shook himself off, glared at me with disgust, and squatted on the floor.

That concluded our experiment. Game over.

~Linda Sabourin

Reprinted by permission of www.CartoonStock.com

A Toast to Thomas

Fun fact: Cats can't taste sweetness in food.

For years, Thomas was content with his own breakfast kibble. Then, one morning, I left part of the crust from a piece of toast unattended on a plate, and he discovered a whole new world of breakfast food. From that moment on, the ding on the toaster was his clarion call.

Before Thomas discovered toast, my breakfast routine was simple. I'd take my plate with my sunny-side-up eggs on toast to the couch where I'd nibble as I read a book. After Thomas discovered toast, breakfast became more complicated. As far as I was concerned, the proper protocol would have been for me to eat breakfast and then give him leftover bite-sized pieces of crust.

Thomas had a different plan. For a week or two, he yowled and tried to look imperious, hoping to shame me into feeding him first. Next he went for the sympathy vote and sat on my lap, staring up at me with huge golden eyes that said, "Feed me. I haven't eaten in hours, days or possibly weeks. I'm wasting away to almost nothing. Another pound or two and you'll be able to feel my ribs." Then he'd suck in his stomach and sigh, one of the most plaintive sounds in the world.

However, Thomas forgot two things. One, unlike him, I could tell the time. "Forget it, boy," I'd say, checking my wristwatch. "It's been exactly thirty-seven minutes since you got your real breakfast. You scarfed down every kibble and licked the dish three times to make sure not a single crumb got away. You even inhaled every molecule of the aroma." And two, like me, he was in no danger of wasting away any time soon.

I refused to succumb. Instead, I hugged the plate closer to my chest, twisting from side to side to avoid a wet nose inching toward the dish.

Unfortunately, my galley kitchen forced me to eat on the couch, making me an easy target for a determined cat. I could have cleaned the piles of papers, folders and magazines off the dining room table and sat there, but Thomas and I both knew that was never going to happen. Instead, we turned our breakfast routines into ritualized combat, with my toast as the prize.

For months, the ding of the toaster brought Thomas into the kitchen, eyes shining with love and a droplet of drool decorating his lower lip. For months, I'd plate my food and sit on the couch where I'd push him off me, only to have him jump back on my lap seconds later. Since Thomas generally doesn't like to expend energy, a trait that has increasingly shown up on the vet's scale, I was delighted I had come up with a wonderful new way of getting him to exercise.

I actually thought of calling the vet to inform him of the new fitness program, but I wasn't sure he'd approve of feeding Thomas toast. In fact, his words, "Overweight. Unhealthy. Atkins kind of cat," came to mind. Rather than stop giving him toast, I kept the good news to myself because of the added payoff. All the twisting to hold the dish away from him had added a smidgen of definition to my arms and waist. A win-win situation in my mind.

Thomas, of course, disagreed.

While he kept jumping and I kept hugging — the plate, not the cat — at least one of us was happy. Then one day, in an extravagant exhibition of energy, he sailed through the air and landed feet first in my eggs. For a moment, we stared at each other in amazement until he shook the still-runny yolk off his feet and all over the couch and me.

"Bad cat," I said. Actually, I yelled it loud enough for the entire neighborhood to hear. I loved that couch. It was my birthday present to myself. I had chosen it specifically because Thomas's hair blended in so well with the weave and color that I didn't have to vacuum it every fifteen seconds. I hadn't counted on adding bright yellow to the mix.

With a final shake of his paw, Thomas jumped off my lap and slumped down on my feet, keeping one eye trained on my plate.

I studied the eggs for a moment, noting the perfect indentations of two little cat feet. Absently removing a couple of cat hairs from my breakfast, I had the eggs halfway to my mouth before I realized what I was doing. I paused, then told myself not even a confirmed cat lover would eat that breakfast. A couple of cat hairs? Sure. Footprints? Definitely not. With a deep sigh, I returned the food to my plate.

Feeling none too generous toward my feline acrobat, I nudged him off my foot where he left partially dry, egg-colored prints on my slipper. He padded after me into the kitchen, leaving more faint footprints behind him.

"Sorry, Thomas," I said, scraping the sorry mess into the garbage. "No toast for either of us this morning." Then I pulled out an old box of cereal from the back of the cupboard. Thomas eyed me but prudently decided to let me eat in peace.

As I chomped away on stale cereal, I considered my options. I could stop eating eggs and toast for breakfast, but that would penalize both of us. I could bite the bullet and clean off the dining room table, but it would be covered with papers again within days, if not hours.

I gave in.

The next morning when the toaster dinged Thomas watched me remove one-and-a-half pieces of toast. I carefully cut up his half-slice and put the pieces into a bright blue plastic ball with holes that allow the food to come out if the cat bats it around. Now, if Thomas wanted his toast, he was going to have to run for it. I showed him the ball, let him get a good whiff of the toast, and tossed it down the hall.

As he took off after it, I got my own breakfast ready. Then I sat on the couch — alone — to the soothing sound of plastic bouncing down the hallway, with a large orange cat bounding after it. My eggs and toast had never tasted so good.

~Harriet Cooper

The Cat Who Adopted Me

Fun fact: Domestic housecats use many vocalizations, including purring, hissing, growling/snarling, grunting, meowing, and trilling. Feral cats are generally silent.

I was carrying a carton into our new home when I noticed a huge cat with luxurious white fur watching us from the picture window in the house across the street. When my husband, Joe, and I went back for another armload of boxes from the rental van, I noticed that the cat was watching us intently.

As we grabbed the last boxes I looked across the street and saw that the cat was still watching us. For the next few days it seemed like every time I went outside the cat was in the window watching me. Joe just shrugged his shoulders. "Evidently that is its favorite spot to sit and watch everything that's going on. You just happen to be in its line of vision, that's all." I accepted Joe's theory and tried to ignore the cat.

The following Saturday morning Joe went to golf with some of his buddies. I was unpacking boxes in the kitchen when I heard someone knocking. I opened the door and met my neighbor, an elderly woman with hair as white and luxuriant as the cat across the street. She carried a pie, still warm from the oven, and from the heavenly aroma I knew it was apple. She thrust the pie toward me, her huge smile making lovely dimples pop out in her cheeks. She said, "My name is Mary Shumaker. I live across the street."

As I invited her in, I realized the big white cat was with her. "Can Chloe come in?" she asked. "She has been watching your house ever since you moved in so I figured she wanted to meet you, too."

As we shared coffee and pie, Chloe checked out the house. When her curiosity was finally satisfied, she settled down on the floor at my feet and looked up at me with lovely, huge green eyes. I laughed at the look of satisfaction on her face. "I guess everything meets her approval."

Mary laughed, too. "Chloe is a strange but wonderful creature. She has a strong will and a determined mind."

When Mary stood to go, she looked a little flustered as Chloe remained on the floor by my chair. "She always gets up to go when she sees me stand." Mary said. She looked down at Chloe. "Come on Chloe, it's time to go." She took a few steps toward the door and looked back at Chloe, who had not even looked in her direction.

Mary snorted. "So now you're deaf, are you?" She looked at me. "I told you she was different, but she's never done this before." Mary finally had to pick up Chloe and carry her home.

Chloe had a cat door, and whenever she saw me out in my yard she would appear at my feet, looking up at me with eyes full of adoration. After playing with Chloe for a few minutes I would call Mary and let her know that her cat was visiting me again. This went on for a few months. One morning, Mary said, "I have a cake in the oven that will be done any minute. If you don't mind having Chloe hang around I'll just let her come home when she is ready."

I had some chores to do so I took Chloe inside with me. When I opened the door to let her go home, she gave a yawn, stretched mightily, and lay down on the rug in front of the fireplace for a nap. I had to pick her up and take her to Mary.

After that, Chloe never wanted to go back home. I was embarrassed for Mary, who obviously loved Chloe and cared for her very well. Over time it became obvious that Chloe was spending more time with Joe and me than she was at home.

One evening I went into the basement and found Joe in his workshop building a cat tower for Chloe. I laughed. "You've fallen in love with her too, I see."

Joe grinned sheepishly. "We didn't adopt her, she adopted us."

The next time Mary came to visit I saw her looking at the cat tower with an odd expression on her face. I patted her hand. "Joe just wanted her to have something to entertain herself with when she is over here. We know she isn't our cat."

Mary dropped her head. "But she is," she said softly.

"Oh, Mary…" I began, but she cut me off.

"It's okay. I don't know why Chloe prefers you over me but she obviously does. Maybe she likes being around young people or maybe…" She shook her head. "It doesn't matter why. This is where she wants to be and I know that you and Joe love her too."

Mary took a deep breath and took my hand. "I'm going to give Chloe to you. I feel mean making her come home when she makes it plain that she wants to be here." Her lips were trembling but she had a determined look on her face. When I started to protest, she held up a hand and shook her head. "My mind is made up. I love Chloe and I know she loves me, too. But that doesn't mean she can't be happier somewhere else. I told you she has a mind of her own and she is determined to have her way. That is one of the things I love about her. She can always come back home whenever she wants to. But if you want her she can stay with you as long as she wants to."

That is how I came to have a special cat named Chloe reside with me. I won't say that I own her because she is a cat that can't be owned. She might decide at some point that she wants to live with Mary again, or perhaps even with someone else. If that day ever comes I hope I will be as big hearted, kind, and understanding as Mary was when she let Chloe stay with me.

Mary still visits, and when she stands up to leave, Chloe will walk her to the door but that is as far as she will go. She looks up at Mary with wise, gentle eyes as if to say, "I love you still but this is where I belong."

And she does… for now.

~Elizabeth Atwater

Oliver

My Very Good, Very Bad Cat

My Endearing Cat

Fun fact: According to WebMD, there are about ninety-six million household cats in the United States compared to eighty-three million pet dogs.

45

Trapped

*Fun fact: Tough guy Marlon Brando loved cats and
was sometimes photographed with them.*

ast year, we lost our cat, Toby. He was a great friend, but
cats are also a responsibility and an expense. While not
pleased about his death, I was happy to be free of the extra
work.

My wife, Marie, had another opinion. She had had many cats
over the years and longed for feline companionship. It didn't matter
that we have two dogs. Having a cat is different.

However, it takes two to make a marriage. Summoning all of my
masculine authority, I made it very clear that under no circumstances
was she even to think of getting another cat.

She tried anyway. I was invited into McPhail's, the local pet store,
to view various kittens on numerous occasions. But I was rock solid.
I didn't flinch. We left the store catless.

Next came the vet clinic. I got updates on stray cats that needed
new homes. My little Mother Teresa of the cat world visited them and
told me how we would be a positive influence in their lives. I would
assure her that her saintly intentions were mixed with my fiendish,
selfish desire not to add any more pets to our household.

Marie was determined. There was the social pressure. Ann at
church asked me why I didn't want a cat. Marie expressed her desire
to many friends, who sometimes glared at me for not giving in. I had

no trouble being portrayed as the cruel husband, as long as we didn't take in a stray. I was in charge and I was sticking to my guns.

Then it happened! Marie found the perfect excuse. She went to the Mitchell Golf Club with Bonnie to play a practice round for a tournament she had entered. People often drop off unwanted cats, I'm told, at golf courses. This kitten wandered up to Marie and rubbed against her. As she would eventually explain, "He chose me. There were eight other women, and he walked right up to me. I would never have chosen a cat like him." Right! I didn't fall for that line.

He chose her enough for her to call the course the next day, pick him up and hide him in our basement, leaving a can of Pounce on the table to break the news to me gently.

She's crafty, though. We went golfing with friends after work. I had planned to go directly to the course, but had forgotten my clubs. Marie didn't complain when I asked her to bring them in her car. She seemed happy about the idea. Strange.

After an enjoyable golf game and dinner with our friends, we came home. I saw the Pounce. My first words were, "Where is he?" I announced in a firm voice that he would be out of the house at the earliest possible opportunity. I was angry. How dare she go against my wishes! How important was my opinion in this relationship? I even considered sleeping on the couch. I was upset.

Then I made the fatal mistake. I crept into the basement to see what the fuss was all about. The huge, friendly eyes of a scrawny cat greeted me. It was obvious that he needed care. I picked him up to see how light he was. He had me at the first purr.

The next day, I mentioned something about the cat going back, but as I was saying it I knew I didn't mean it. By evening, I announced that we were keeping the cat, as if it had been my idea all along.

The final seal of approval was giving him a name. Marie purposely came up with some terrible ones. She's sly. By giving me naming rights, the cat was sure to stay.

I struggled to find a name. Then it dawned on me that he was found on the Mitchell Golf Course. His name would be Caddie.

My only victory in all this? Marie is on poop patrol. Since he is her Caddie, I'm not going to clean the sand traps.

~John Stevens

46

Magic's Trick

Fun fact: A cat pregnancy lasts about sixty-three days.
Most mother cats have three to five kittens per litter,
but may have up to ten.

My husband Jim had stepped out onto the front porch to enjoy the cool September morning. And there she was: a beautiful, young black cat — sleek, shiny… and clearly hungry.

Jim came inside to tell me we needed to figure out what to do with her, since we weren't going to let her stay with us. Jim had never been a fan of cats.

I hurried out to the porch. It had been more than forty years since I had a cat to call my own. As a girl, I'd almost always had kittens around, but after marrying I gave them up to please my husband. Seeing this little black beauty begging for food, my heart was instantly won over. I began thinking of names immediately.

The first name that came to mind was Magic. After all, she was black as a midnight sky, and came to us out of thin air, appearing on top of our little mountain in the middle of nowhere. Thus, it was settled, Magic Cat she was.

Several months went by, and she settled in just fine, spending many lovely hours on the front porch enjoying the beautiful Ozark fall weather. Winter came, and with it piles of snow. Magic tiptoed through the drifts like a pro, although I was sure it was her first experience with the magical white stuff.

In the cold winter months, she took up residence in my husband's new shop building, close to the warm woodstove that he kept burning round the clock. Some days, she could be seen climbing over his fishing boat, sniffing out the corners and sleeping on the deck.

About February, I began to suspect that we might have kittens on the way. Magic's little tummy was round and tight, and she was eating enough for two or three cats. I was excited beyond words. To have baby kittens to play with was a miracle to me. Jim, not so much. He grumbled and complained that we would be overrun with cats before we knew it. I just laughed and enjoyed the experience.

Spring came, and the weeks went by. Magic and I did a lot of porch sitting, and I'd rub her belly, feeling the kittens rolling around inside. We both were waiting for that magical moment when they would be born.

One warm spring morning, I went out to check on her. She'd been acting strange for a few days, hardly eating and acting anxious. I figured the babies were coming soon. Seeing me, she meowed plaintively. I watched her closely for an hour or so; she soon began looking rather frantic. The next thing I knew she made a beeline for our shop building on the hill. I followed her, hoping to witness the miracle of new birth. I'd read that mother cats picked out their birthing spot several days or even weeks prior to the birth.

With no hesitation, Magic leaped up onto the bass boat and went straight to the small dark cavern under the steering column. Calling Jim, I alerted him that it appeared we might have a situation. Jim's bass boat is his pride and joy. I was quite certain he was not going to be happy about having a batch of kittens born there. By the time he made his way to the shop, the first baby was out. Soon, three more babies were born.

Jim was stunned that she had picked his boat as the nursery. It was fishing season, after all. The kittens would have to be relocated. He picked up a kitten and moved it to a box lined with soft towels. But Magic wouldn't allow it. Magic immediately ran to the box, grabbed the kitten in her mouth and took it back to the boat cavity. Jim knew then that it was a lost cause.

Our Magic Cat was the proud — and very protective mother — of four beautiful, black kittens.

The bass would have to wait.

~Lynette Chambers

Groundhog Double Trouble

Fun fact: About one in three thousand calicos is a male,
and he carries an extra X chromosome, making
him sterile.

"I don't want to see that cat in our yard again," my husband said as he shooed the beautiful calico across the creek and back into the neighbor's yard.

"Good luck with that! Cats aren't like dogs, honey. They are very independent and tend to roam wherever they please, especially if they are mousing."

"Well, text our neighbor and let her know I don't appreciate her cat in our yard."

Sighing, I sent off a quick text to our sweet neighbor, Cheryl, informing her of my husband's dislike of cats.

"I'll do my best," she replied sometime later, "but it's kind of hard controlling where she goes when I let her outside."

The following morning, John stood at the picture window in our bedroom. He'd installed it so that I could watch the birds visiting our feeders.

So far, it had been the best gift I'd ever received.

"You aren't going to believe this," he murmured. "Come look!"

Slowly, I approached the window, praying Cheryl's cat wasn't on our deck.

"Good grief," I gasped. Seated side by side, right in the center of our deck, were two enormous groundhogs. We'd observed groundhogs before, especially since our back yard backs up to a wooded area, but never had they been as bold as these two.

John raised the window, and the two raced across the yard and into the woods.

That evening, I happened to glance out the picture window. A hummingbird sipped nectar, twirling around the feeder we'd hung under the eaves. Then something caught my eye in the flowerbed beyond.

"John, come quick!" Hurriedly, he entered the bedroom just in time to see one of the groundhogs munching on the red dianthus flowers we'd planted around the water fountain. "Why, it's eaten every single blossom!"

Again, John lifted the window, and the groundhog made a beeline for the woods.

"Hmmm, I better look up groundhogs on the computer and see just how destructive they can be."

Before he left the room, however, he heard me gasp.

"Look!"

Across the yard, we'd planted a vegetable garden. We'd taken great pains to enclose the rows and rows of plants in chicken wire. Nevertheless a groundhog sat in the center of the garden, munching on a stalk of celery.

"How did he get in there?" I squeaked.

"He burrowed a hole right underneath," John replied angrily. "That does it... something's got to be done!"

I watched my six-foot-four Marine stalk off toward the computer, silently praying he wouldn't return to see the groundhog now devouring the lettuce.

"Hmmm, that's interesting..." John stared intently at the computer screen in the other room.

"What is it?"

"Says here that groundhogs do not like cats... in fact, they detest the scent of soiled kitty litter."

I thought about the absence of our neighbor's cat lately.

"You know, I haven't seen Cheryl's cat mousing in our yard for some time. I wonder if that's the reason these critters have gotten so brave."

John sheepishly glanced in my direction. "You might have something there. Why don't you text Cheryl and let her know the cat ban has been removed."

I couldn't help chuckling as I wandered into the bedroom in search of my cell phone.

That evening, we spotted the sweet yellow calico roaming the border of our woods in search of mice.

The groundhogs were nowhere in sight.

"It's a beautiful evening, isn't it?" My husband smiled as we sat on the back porch. The sunset painted the sky pink, purple and gold.

I couldn't help sighing contentedly. Cheryl's cat meowed in the distance. "You might say it's absolutely purrfect!"

~Mary Z. Whitney

Miracle in the Cornfield

*Fun fact: According to the American Veterinary
Medical Association, forty-four percent of pet owners
in the United States have more than one kind of pet,
most commonly cats and dogs.*

The last thing I needed was a cat. I was a twenty-eight-year-old single parent, with an eight-year-old son and a dog. But my son, Ryan, had been pleading with me for years to get a cat to go along with our dog Red. Ryan even had a name picked out for the cat — Zipper.

Every time Ryan brought up the topic of getting a cat, I would tell him that it wouldn't be fair to Red to get a cat. Red wouldn't like having a cat in the house. I wasn't being very strategic, because I never had any other excuses!

Then one rainy night we were visiting friends who lived in the country in the middle of a cornfield. They had three dogs of their own, and I had brought Red with us. When I heard a strange noise at our friends' front door I opened it to find a wet kitten looking up at me. Before I could stoop to pick it up, it scooted past me into the warmth of the house and right into the path of our friends' three large, menacing dogs.

I was totally unprepared for what happened in the next few seconds. Without any hesitation, Red came to the kitten's defence with an unprecedented display of aggression. He stood over the kitten and kept growling and baring his teeth until our friends managed to gather their dogs and lock them in a bedroom. Once Red was confident that the other dogs were no longer a threat, he calmly proceeded to lick the kitten and mother it like it was his own offspring.

Ryan was elated. "Look, Mum! It's Zipper, and Red likes him!" he squealed as he jumped up and down with excitement. I watched my single excuse for not having a cat evaporate into thin air.

While part of me wanted to think of Red as a traitor, it was hard not to be touched by his tender display of affection for this lost kitten. It was also not possible to ignore the look of sheer bliss on the kitten's face as Red licked the rain off its fur with his warm tongue.

I'll always remember the drive home the next day. Normally, Ryan would be seatbelted in the back, and Red would ride shotgun beside me on the passenger seat. We were barely out of the driveway when Red jumped into the backseat to take up his position beside Ryan, who was cradling his newly beloved Zipper. So that's how Zipper became part of our family for the next seventeen years.

We never did find out how Zipper ended up at a house in the middle of a cornfield on the only night we ever stayed there, but it was clear from the start that Ryan, Red and Zipper were meant to be together.

The dog and cat were instant best friends, and Zipper learned as much about how to be a dog as he was able to from Red. He learned to beg, never jumped up on the kitchen counters or table, and even tagged along on Red's evening walks. I was important to Zipper only because I had the ability to open cat-food tins and change the litter box.

Ryan was Zipper's special person. He trusted that Ryan would never drop him no matter how awkwardly he was being toted around the house. He slept on Ryan's bed while he was at school and again during the night. And while he would never lie on his back for anyone else, he was at his most contented when he was in that position on Ryan's lap having his tummy rubbed.

In 1994, Ryan, Red, Zipper and I all moved into a new house that my future husband, Dave, and I had bought in Richmond Hill, Ontario. Although Dave was allergic to cats, he assured Ryan that Zipper was welcome in our new home. However, watching Dave live in a constant state of allergic reaction was not easy, and by the end of our second week of living together, Ryan admitted that he was ready to find Zipper a new home. Considering how much he loved his cat, I was touched that he'd come to this decision on his own.

I thought Dave would have been hugely relieved when Ryan told him about his plans for Zipper, but Dave, with red eyes and a drippy nose, said that Zipper was part of our family, and he would eventually get used to him. While he never became totally immune to the cat, Dave did become less reactive to Zipper over time, and they developed their own special relationship. And when Ryan moved out of the house four years later, Dave became Zipper's new special person.

As Red aged, Zipper took to sleeping beside him during the day and often acted as his hearing aid. When Red died in 1999, Zipper was beyond distraught. He would sit on our stairs and yowl inconsolably as if his wanting Red so badly would bring him back to life. After a few weeks, Zipper got on with his life by simply attaching himself more closely to Dave, who would patiently pat him with his foot and share his food with him.

Oddly enough, sometimes the best things that come into our lives are the ones we think we want the least. I hadn't wanted a cat, but I wouldn't trade my seventeen years with Zipper for anything. I am eternally grateful that he found his way to us at our friends' house in the middle of a cornfield on that rainy night.

~Laura Snell

Another Baby Boy

*Fun fact: Baby rabbits are also called "kittens" or
"kits"—not bunnies!*

'm crazy about him. I think about him all the time. When we're
apart, I check my watch frequently, counting down the hours till
he's in my arms again. I'm constantly buying little gifts just to
surprise him. Friends say he's all I talk about.

His name is Milo. We adopted him two weeks ago, and I'm amazed
at how wonderful it feels to have a baby in the house again. You'd think
with four sons, ages nineteen to nine, the last thing I'd want is another
boy. But when I picked up Milo, he sighed deeply and snuggled into
my arms, and I was smitten.

"Uh-oh," said my husband, Derek. This newest addition, just
like our other boys, is all his fault. Our two-month-old fluffy ball of
black-and-white fur might still be languishing in a cage if Derek hadn't
gone to PetSmart on an errand for his mother. The Humane Society
was sponsoring a pet adoption weekend at the store. I'd talked about
wanting a cat for quite a while—a female. "It'd be nice to have another
girl around the house," I'd said.

With that in mind, Derek had spotted a one-year-old, elegant,
blue-eyed, white cat. Like all pets at the event, she'd already been
spayed, and her immunizations were up-to-date. So, later that evening,
we loaded the family in the van to take a look at her. She was indeed a
lovely lady, but as I wandered down the double row of metal cages, a
hyperactive kitty caught my eye. He was literally bouncing off the walls.

"My goodness!" I said. "This little guy needs Ritalin." He jumped. He hopped. He spun in circles. In short, he was just like the rest of the boys in my house.

"No," Derek said. "Not that one."

Even nine-year-old Sam seemed leery. "Too wild," he pronounced.

I dutifully looked at the other cats, but I couldn't help wondering if all Milo's frantic activity was just a desperate plea for attention. "I want to hold him," I said.

"Not a good idea," Derek replied. But a store employee unlocked Milo's cage. I picked him up, fully expecting him to squirm or scratch or climb up my hair, but instead he laid his head on my shoulder and sighed.

The boys each took a turn holding Milo, who seemed to relish the loving pats and soft murmurs. "Okay, let's put him back and cuddle some of these calmer cats," Derek urged. But when I placed Milo back in his cage, he gave a piteous meow and reached his paw through the door.

"That's it," said fourteen-year-old Zack. "I'm bonded to this kitty. He's the one for us."

I stood in front of Milo's cage, and he stretched both paws out to me and cried. I looked at Derek. The boys looked at Derek. He sighed. "Who wants to help me pick out a bed for Milo?"

While they shopped for kitty supplies, I filled out the adoption paperwork. I signed more release forms for this cat than I did when my children were born.

At last, we were able to take Milo (and $200 worth of accessories) home. Already, it seems like he's always been part of our family. And while everyone loves him, Milo and I share a special bond — a bond that has some family members concerned. Everyone except Sam found it worrisome when I gave Milo a middle name. "How else will he know he's in trouble?" Sam asked. "When Mom says, 'Milo James, come here!' he'll know he'd better hurry."

One evening as I rocked him to sleep (Milo loves lullabies), his brothers sat on the couch across from us. "I get it," Zack said. "You really just wanted another baby."

"No, I didn't," I replied. Just then Milo woke and stretched and patted my cheek with his tiny paw. "Oh, there's Mama's biggity, biggity boy," I crooned.

"She used to say that to me," Sam observed.

"Yeah, well, you're not the baby anymore," seventeen-year-old Alex replied.

"I'm a big brother, though. I've never been a big brother before!"

"We are not his brothers. We're his owners," Zack clarified.

Derek walked into the room as Milo buried his face in my hair and began purring loudly. "I'm worried," he announced. "I think you wanted a cat because Ethan moved out. When the next boy moves out, you'll want another kitten. Soon, it'll be just me and the lady with four cats."

"And your point is?" I asked.

"Just tell me: Are you going to replace me with a cat?"

My sister-in-law reassured my husband. "Don't be too concerned unless she starts dressing him up."

Listen, Milo likes his itty-bitty Mariners cap.

~Cindy Hval

Meatball and the Chipmunks

*Fun fact: Some cats don't recognize certain animals
as food because they haven't been taught to eat them.
They just like to play with their prey because it moves.*

"Mom, there's a black cat on the front porch," my kids said when they came in from school one afternoon.

"I know. He was sitting there when I went out to get the mail," I said. "He started purring and rubbing against my legs."

"We need to feed him, Mom," my daughter said.

"I already did."

She frowned. "Did you have any cat food?"

"No, but I had some meatballs left from last night's dinner," I said. "He sure liked them."

"You fed him meatballs?" my daughter said, and at the same moment, my son said, "We should name him Meatball!"

"Guys, let's not get too attached to this cat," I cautioned. "He just appeared on the porch this morning, and he may be gone tomorrow. We don't know if he's a stray or if he already has a home. So let's not get attached to him."

But they didn't listen. My kids spent hours on the porch that evening playing with their new pet. They came in and asked me for old towels and a cardboard box so they could build him a bed.

I was worried that they'd be heartbroken when the cat was gone in the morning, but Meatball was waiting on the porch, ready to rub his head on whoever would stand still long enough to allow it. That morning, the kids nearly missed the bus because they were so busy playing with the cat.

And when twelve-year-old Julia got off the school bus that afternoon, she couldn't wait to tell me what her friend had said about Meatball's name. "I told Chloe that we named the cat Meatball because that was the first thing we fed him, and she said, 'Well, it's a good thing your mom didn't do that with you.' When I asked why, she said, 'Think about it, Jules. What was the first thing your mom fed you?'" Julia laughed and said, "Oh my goodness, Mom, my name would be Breast Milk!"

I shook my head and laughed. Silly girls.

The days went on, and Meatball stayed. And despite my warnings to the kids not to get attached, I found myself falling in love with this stray cat.

We invited Meatball into the house, but he was only content to stay inside for short periods of time. When he wanted out, he'd sit by the front door and meow until someone opened the door for him.

One day, I went to the door to see if Meatball was ready to come back inside when I saw him darting through our yard, zigzagging back and forth.

"What is Meatball doing?" one of the kids asked. "He looks like he's chasing something."

"He probably found a mouse," I said. But when I went outside, I discovered that it wasn't a mouse he was chasing, but a chipmunk.

I was concerned that Meatball would kill the chipmunk, so I attempted to chase it into the woods behind our house where I doubted Meatball would follow. But the more I chased the chipmunk, the more Meatball chased me. The three of us darted around the yard until I was sure my children were cracking up if they were watching from the window.

I ran out of energy before Meatball did, and he eventually caught the chipmunk. He smacked his paw on the chipmunk's back, and the animal flipped over onto its back. It squealed and I cringed, waiting for the cat to eat it. Instead, Meatball licked it once and then lifted his paw, setting it free. The chipmunk jumped up, and the chase began all over again.

He caught the chipmunk for a second time, and the same thing happened. Meatball wasn't hunting the chipmunk. They were playing. And it was hilarious to witness.

A few days later, I saw Meatball zigzagging through the yard again. I called for my children to come and watch. "He's playing with that chipmunk again," I called.

We all went out into the yard and watched their game. The kids and I were laughing and chasing them until, quite abruptly, the game stopped.

The chipmunk had run toward our wall of landscaping bricks and squeezed into a hole between the bricks. And Meatball had followed.

The chipmunk fit into the hole; Meatball did not.

By the time I caught up to them, Meatball had wedged his head into the hole. "His head is stuck," my kids reported.

I tugged on his body and realized that he was indeed stuck. I could hear the chipmunk squealing from inside the hole, and Meatball howling and squirming in response.

"Quick, guys, help me pull down these bricks," I said. "We can make the hole bigger and free Meatball."

We pulled down several of the landscaping bricks until Meatball wriggled free. He had a few scratches on his head and face. I tried to grab him to clean his wounds, but at that same moment, the chipmunk popped out of the hole and ran away. Meatball darted after him, and their game began again.

Meatball and the neighborhood chipmunks have formed an unlikely friendship. He allows them to eat out of his food dish, and I've even caught glimpses of them snuggling on our front porch.

My children have even named Meatball's chipmunk friends. They call them Cat Food, since that's the first thing we fed them.

~Diane Stark

The Calico Puppy

Fun fact: Kittens enter their primary socialization period at two–three weeks of age. This is when the brain is primed for attachment to other beings.

We have no idea when Poppy, our Golden Retriever, had her rendezvous but by mid-summer it was quite evident that she had been naughty. When our vet confirmed that Poppy would soon present us with a litter of grand-puppies we were at first stunned but that soon gave way to excitement. Since we had no idea whom our naughty girl had seduced we were eager to see what her pups would look like.

On the Fourth of July the local fireworks were forgotten when Poppy went into labor. Leave it to Poppy to upstage the annual celebration. The sound of distant fireworks heralded in the birth of her three pups. Their parental lineage still escaped us. One short-haired male was brown and white, his brother had a long silky coat like Poppy but was black, and their sister looked a lot like Poppy, right down to her golden fur. Tired but exhausted, Poppy beamed first at her babies at then at us, clearly delighted in the fuss we were making over her and her pups.

My husband, Joe, came in from feeding the horses one morning, scowling as he cradled something against his chest. "Some people," he muttered, as he showed me a tiny, frightened calico kitten that was small enough to nestle in one of his big hands. We live in the country and it isn't unusual to find abandoned pets, but we never get used to the callousness it takes to leave an animal on its own to slowly starve or become wild. The most heartbreaking of all is to find babies who either were tossed out to die or whose mother was killed.

"I couldn't find any more," Joe said. "The mother and any other kittens that there may have been are most likely dead. This one wouldn't have made it much longer." He put the kitten in my hands. "I'll go into town and get a dropper and some formula. She might make it if we can get some food into her soon."

While Joe was gone I found a shoebox and an old soft receiving blanket and made a bed for the kitten. In a few days she was putting on weight and mewling happily when I took her out of her bed to be fed and cuddled for a while.

Poppy's puppies were getting fat and beginning to frolic, though never venturing far from her watchful eye. One morning, out of curiosity, I placed the kitten next to the pups to see how they would react to each other. The pups looked curiously at the funny little thing that made such odd sounds. They examined her for a few moments, then lost interest and wandered back to Poppy for some milk. To my surprise the kitten followed the pups timidly, mewling all the while.

When Poppy saw her brood approaching she dutifully lay down so they could nurse. She eyed the kitten and decided the tiny thing posed no threat to her pups, so she relaxed and turned her attention to her babies as they nuzzled around for a spot to nurse. To my surprise, the kitten started pushing forward between two of the pups, instinctively knowing what her reward would be if she could snag a teat.

I jumped up, ready to snatch her away. I didn't know how Poppy would react to this intrusion. Poppy looked alarmed for few seconds as if she didn't know how to react either. She looked up at me for guidance. I patted her head and talked softly to her. "It's okay, girl. She's just another hungry baby."

I never had to feed the kitten after that. Poppy totally accepted her into her family. As time went on Poppy became very protective of her special baby. And the kitten followed the pups everywhere they went and seemed to think that she was a puppy too. We began to call her Rover because she clearly identified with the dogs.

When Poppy watched her babies play she kept a close eye on Rover, who was diminutive next to her large puppies, who turned out to be part Husky. Often, if one of the pups got too rough with Rover, Poppy would run over to inspect her smallest baby to make sure she was all right. Then she would give the offending sibling a warning look.

Initially we had planned on finding a home for Rover when she was weaned. But Poppy got so attached to her little calico "puppy" that we didn't have the heart to separate them. To this day the two of them are inseparable. And Rover still thinks she is a dog.

~Elizabeth Atwater

Three Little Kittens

*Fun fact: People who are allergic to cats are actually
allergic to their "dander," which is a mixture of cat hair,
saliva and skin particles.*

It was the first cold evening in October, and I was wearing only a cardigan. By the time we got home from Bible class, my teeth were chattering. I rushed inside with the kids, leaving my husband to tend to whatever chores needed finishing outside. A few minutes later, I heard a knock on the front door. I looked out the window, puzzled — even more so when I saw my husband standing there. He was grinning and pointing down. My eyes followed, and I gasped.

"Kids! Come look!" I said. "Kittens!"

There were three of them. Two Tabbies — one gray and one orange. The third one was the color of charcoal. He was the bold one, already weaving around my husband's long legs while the other two vocalized their support. My eyes rose to lock with his.

What would we do with them?

We were allergic. I had explained this to the kids often when they asked why we didn't have a pet. I had no doubt it was true. Whenever my son spent the night with his cousin (two cats, one dog), we had to dose him with Benadryl. I also struggled whenever I slept over at my sister's house, with my nose tickling all night as I eyed her cat suspiciously.

There was no way we could take in three cats!

That's what my mind said. Meanwhile, my mouth was betraying me. "Lead them to the back porch!" I heard myself say.

My husband complied, proving himself to be either a natural cat wrangler or the Pied Piper. They followed him without fuss.

My mind said no but my hands and feet sided with my mouth. Before I knew it, I was grabbing a Costco box, an old blanket and a towel. I pushed them into my son's hands and pointed him to the back door.

"Get out a plastic cereal bowl," I told my daughter. "Fill it with water." Meanwhile, I rummaged in the pantry, coming up with a can of tuna.

My mind was telling me to stop. My mouth said, "They must be hungry."

I opened the tuna and followed my kids outside. The kittens responded immediately, circling my legs and softly mewling their pleasure over what they could smell.

"Okay, okay." I stooped to place the dish in front of them. "You like tuna?"

Watching the kittens gobble up the tuna, I forgot it was cold. The gray boy was pushy with his two Tabby sisters, so I intervened, pulling him away so they could get their fair share. It wasn't difficult to coax them all into the blanket-lined box we set up in the corner. My kids were thrilled with all of it, exclaiming happily over every yawn or meow, cooing every time the kittens stretched or curled up in a ball to sleep.

When I checked on them the next morning, they were still there.

Now what were we going to do?

Buy cat food.

The kittens wandered over the next couple of weeks, but always came back at night to sleep on our porch. The gray Tabby was the least likely to roam far. From time to time, I would hear her on the back porch, crying toward the stream, beckoning her siblings home. She remained skittish when we tried to pet her, but was bold in other ways. Occasionally, she would dash inside the house when I opened the door.

"No," I told her. "That will never be okay."

Would it surprise you if I said that today, three years later, she's curled up in the middle of my unmade bed?

We found a home for the orange Tabby with a friend of a friend. She is now a fat and happy house cat named Mango. Her brother ran off one day and, sadly, we never saw him again. By that time, I knew I couldn't part with our little gray Tabby, despite my sniffling nose. We named her Katniss and cautiously invited her indoors from time to time while I wracked my brain trying to figure out how to handle all the cat dander. By Christmas, she was letting us hold her, sleeping under the tree, batting at the glittering balls, and begging to go outside so she could pounce through the fresh snow.

Over the years, Katniss has been the perfect pet for us. Yes, we've had to figure out how to deal with our allergy issues, but it hasn't been as bad as we feared. And we all agree that caring for a cat is easier than caring for a dog — we even have a wonderful cat-loving friend who checks in on her when we travel. Having Katniss has also been wonderful for my autistic son, who has always been nervous around dogs. Having a gentle, purring fur ball to snuggle with has been especially helpful for him.

One night, not long after we decided we would keep Katniss, she was lying in my daughter's arms, her head flung back against the crook of her elbow, her tummy exposed and enjoying a good scratch.

"God works in mysterious ways," my daughter said solemnly.

My lips twitched. "How's that?" I asked.

"Well," she said. "I prayed for a dog, and He sent us a cat."

~Jennifer Froelich

The Truth about Cats and Dogs

*Fun fact: A person who loves cats is called an
ailurophile. The Greek historian Herodotus called cats
"ailuroi," which means "tail wavers."*

All of my friends are dog people. They own Corgis and Shepherds and Puggles, shuttle their dogs between each other's apartments, and even take them away on vacation, only leaving their canines home alone when absolutely necessary. I've always liked animals, but I never understood this obsession. Why can't you just leave your dog at home when you run to the grocery store or go have coffee with a friend? Don't you want to at least take a trip without having to worry about feeding and walking and picking up your pup's poop from the sidewalk?

I guess you could say that I just wasn't a dog person, and because of this, I didn't always fit in. There were many conversations I couldn't join and Dog Dates I couldn't attend, so when I decided to adopt my cat Cleo from a local shelter, I thought it would certainly alienate me further from the group. Little did I know that the opposite was true.

Within a few days of adopting Cleo, I began noticing that she had a number of traits unusual for a cat. She wasn't quiet or disinterested, and she didn't ignore me for most of the day the way my previous cats often had, happy just to bathe in the sun and nap. She wanted attention. She wanted to steal the food off my plate and chew on my shoes. She waited at the door, meowing fervently when she heard me walking up. She followed me around from room to room, staring at me with big, sad eyes until I got out her feather toy and played with her. At night, I would often wake up with her body curled in the curve of my knees, peacefully snoozing, her belly exposed and ready to be scratched.

Because she was so dependent on me, I started to feel bad when I left her alone for long periods of time. Though I didn't need to rush home from work to make sure she didn't have an accident on my beautiful white shag rug (thank goodness for litter boxes), I knew that she missed me and would be watching the door, waiting for the sound of my key in the lock. A few times, I even turned down the offer of happy-hour drinks with my co-workers to go home and check on my cat. For a while, nothing about this seemed strange.

Then one day it struck me.

Oh my God, I thought, watching my cat chase her tail in a circle. My cat is just like a dog. I am just like a dog person.

My friends didn't understand. "What do you mean, your cat's like a dog?" they asked. But when I tried to explain, they just scoffed. All the cats they knew were prissy, aloof and, from their perspective, utterly unlikeable.

"No offense," my friend Jane said. "I'm just not a cat person."

That day, I was forced to confront the fact that Cleo would never completely fit in. She would not be able to go on a Dog Date to the park and likely wouldn't be happy on long road trips with the group. But despite these obstacles, I decided there was one thing Cleo could do: She could help change my friends' minds about cats.

I started by inviting them over one at a time, worried that if Cleo were confronted by the whole group at once she would feel outnumbered and uncomfortable and take up residence behind my bed until everyone left.

It worked like a charm. Cleo ran right up to each friend that came over, sniffing and meowing and trying to make sense of the foreign-smelling dog hairs on each stranger's pants and shirt. Once she was satisfied, she began licking the friend's hands. They always laughed at the strange feel of Cleo's rough feline tongue. "I've never met a cat who likes to lick," they all said. "It really does feel like sandpaper!"

My friends saw how charming and fun Cleo was, not at all like the stereotypical cats they had imagined, and admitted to enjoying the many quirks unique to cats: sandpaper tongues, subtle ear movements, the soft kneading of paws on your lap when a cat is blissfully happy. One by one, they converted. All of them, that is, except Jane, who went everywhere with her dog Pepper, and used that as an excuse to not meet Cleo.

"Just bring Pepper with you," I finally suggested. And though she resisted at first, we ultimately set a time for her and her long-haired Chihuahua to meet Cleo.

I was extremely nervous about the meeting, as Cleo now had to impress not one but two harsh judges. When the pair finally arrived, Cleo held her ground. Both animals hesitated, skirting each other's general vicinity with narrow, hesitant eyes until they finally got close enough to sniff each other's rumps. This sizing up went on for a few nerve-wracking minutes while Jane and I watched in silent awe. Then, Cleo and Pepper started to play.

"I can't believe it," Jane said in disbelief. "Your cat really is like a dog."

There's no denying that Cleo taught us all valuable lessons. She taught me to appreciate dog people and the energy it takes to properly care for such a loving, sweet, and — let's face it — needy companion. As for my friends? Well, they now understand that not all cats are alike. That old curmudgeonly Tabby their childhood neighbor once had is not indicative of the entire feline species. Just like dogs, each cat has an individual, disparate, and often very endearing personality.

Now, when people ask me whether I'm a dog person or a cat person, I shake my head, explaining that it's not that simple. I tell them about Cleo, how she has become an honorary member of the dog pack, and how my dog-loving friends opened themselves up to her. When confronted with non-believers, I just smile. "Come meet her," I tell them. "You'll see."

~Clara Blake

Home Invasion

*Fun fact: In general, a cat that approaches complete
strangers is most likely a stray or abandoned
domesticated cat, not a feral.*

ne might consider "Mousey" a strange name for a cat,
perhaps even an insult. I consider the name appropriate for the way our cat became a member of our family.
My son and I were watching television one night
with a friend when I noticed something moving by my friend's chair.
Upset because I thought I'd seen a mouse, I sat up straight and stared
down to see what had caught my eye. A young gray cat sat looking at
me, uncertain whether to stay or run.

"Where did that cat come from?" I asked suspiciously, looking
at my son for confirmation of his guilt. He had been asking for a cat
for years and I had been unrelenting in turning him down. We had
already been through too many pets and wildlife rescues.

"Cat?" he asked.

"What?" asked my friend.

Both males looked in the direction I pointed, with equally surprised
looks on their faces.

I stood up. The cat backed up. I walked forward. The cat turned,
ran into the laundry room, and out the pet door.

The pet door wasn't new. It, and the one in the outer garage door,
came with the house. I'd never known them to be used. Evidently,
the scent of our chicken dinner, the sound of talking, and the chilly

temperatures outside had encouraged the cat to chance entering.

I felt sure she wouldn't be back, and she wasn't… that night. The next night, however, a gray shadow once again peeked from around my friend's recliner.

"Outside, cat. You're not staying," I insisted. My statement, meant to sound emphatic and made more for the benefit of the males in the room than the cat, might have been a little louder than necessary, but I was going to win this war.

"Mom, it's cold, and the cat looks hungry. Can't we give her something to eat and let her sleep in the laundry room for the night?"

"Not a chance. It's not happening! That cat can find food elsewhere and sleep in the garage." I wasn't giving in, although I had to admit my conscience bothered me at the thought of sending a poor little creature outside in the cold without food.

"I'll take her out," my son volunteered.

I thought I saw him grab a piece of chicken as he walked through the kitchen, but I wasn't sure and, like I said, my conscience was bothering me.

The cat didn't come back that night. Score round two for me. The next evening, I found myself keeping an eye on the corner of the recliner, prepared for an ambush. No cat. I gave up and became engaged in the movie. Suddenly, as quiet as a mouse, a gray ball of fur landed on the footrest of my chair. I nearly jumped out of my skin! My friend chuckled and my son laughed out loud. The cat curled up and snuggled down by my leg, pretending to be oblivious to her surroundings.

The ball was in my court. I reached down to stroke her soft gray fur. The purring of the cat sounded loud, despite the volume of the television. The cat had adopted a family for herself, and she knew it. I never had a chance.

~Rita Durrett

55

Chicken Soup for the Soul.

Chosen

*Fun fact: Cats are very particular about people and
will often choose a special someone to bond with.*

ll my life, my family and I have adopted things — people,
wounded animals, strays (both the human and animal
variety) — so it shouldn't be any wonder that we currently have two rescue dogs and a feral cat that followed
me home two years ago.

I can remember feeding baby raccoons when I was eight. I can
remember researching everything from hermit crabs to baby rabbits
to hamsters so that we could make a proper shelter for each and
nurse them back to health. When I grew up and became a teacher, I
remember carrying a baby squirrel around my classroom when my
students brought it in to me after finding it injured.

People were no different... I can remember a Thanksgiving at
which we had twenty people, some of whom we didn't really know,
but they had no place to go so we took them in. And there was
the Thanksgiving at my sister's with a mixture of Spanish-speaking
immigrants, former inmates, and a couple of elderly people who lived
in a nursing home. Both days were full of laughter and unexpected
perspective. Then, there's work. As educators, my mother and I were
constantly adopting families and sending bags of food, clothes and
books or supplies home with children.

That was my upbringing. The family motto was to leave things,
people and places better than we found them. It makes for an unusual

life, but it also makes life a rich tapestry of color and emotion and creates a family everywhere one goes.

Last winter was no exception. When I arrived home from work, there was a message waiting for me: "April, your sister has found three stray kittens. It looks like someone has dumped them, and it's getting cold. We need to catch them and figure out what to do with them."

I was a dog person and had no idea what do to with a cat. Did I need a laundry basket? How would we attract the kittens so we could catch them? Would they come if we called them, like a dog?

A half-hour later, I drove part of the way down the mountain armed with a laundry basket, towels, a blanket, kibble, tuna, milk, and water. I figured that something had to work. I parked and listened for the faint mewling sound. Nothing. It was cold, too. Really cold. I'd parked on a patch of frozen ground about halfway down the mountain and dreaded the cold trek back up. As I began to walk toward the woods, I noticed a little flash of white. I stopped in my tracks on the empty winding road and saw a small head peer out at me. It was black and white and about the size of my palm. I said, "Come," and out popped this little ball of fur, maybe four pounds soaking wet. She walked across the street and sat down beside my feet as if to say, "I'm ready. Let's go." I tried this again to reach the others, but to no avail. I decided to put this little lady in the car so I wouldn't have to chase her around later, and when I opened the car door, she climbed in and sat primly in the front seat.

My sister managed to catch another one of the kittens that day and gave her to an elderly lady nearby who was lonely. That cat has been wearing knitted, matching dresses and bonnets ever since.

I caught the final one, the tiniest, the next day, and he went to one of my students, a little boy whose father had recently lost his fingers in an accident. The boy's mother and I had decided that a kitten would be the perfect new companion for the boy, and that evening, I managed to get the kitten out of the drainpipe where he'd been hiding with the remains of the food and the blanket I'd left after trying to coax him out for hours the previous day.

I still had to find a place for the first kitten we rescued, the prim little miss who was now residing in my home. I pulled out my cell phone and pulled up Facebook, asking for suggestions from my friends and family. I didn't know anything about cats and wasn't sure where to take her. The unanimous response was, "I'm sorry, but cats are different… it sounds like you've been chosen."

Over the weeks, my little cat flourished. I named her Jane (as in Jane Austen) for her pretty manners, and I trained her like a dog. (As humans, we stick to what we know.) She can sit, never scratches, doesn't eat treats, never snarls at the vet, and likes to have conversations. She likes boxes, loves the shower, talks to the neighborhood birds, and only chews on the dogs' tails when playing. We travel together, and she's learning to walk on a leash. Each night, as I fall asleep, she puts one paw on each side of my hand, and reminds me that I've been chosen.

~April Riser

Nilla

My Very Good, Very Bad Cat

My Clever Cat

Fun fact: The brains of cats are about ninety percent similar to the brains of humans.

56

A Very Smart Cat

Fun fact: It's called "dream chasing" when your cat's
leg muscles or face twitch while he sleeps.

J o was a very good cat. His full name was Jo Jo Precious, Tiger Kitty, a name he was barely able to tolerate, much preferring the single syllable. Unlike Jo, our dog Sir Corwin the Beautiful Dog-faced Dog, Brindled Beast of Sylmar, is very proud of his long name but is willing to tolerate our tendency to call him Corwin. Jo, though, was far too dignified and practical to be bothered with anything as ornamental as a lengthy and descriptive name.

Jo was far smarter than cats are generally presumed to be. I used to say that he did my taxes, but this was just a fanciful joke. Jo was smart, but he couldn't hold a pencil or work a calculator. No opposable thumbs. Jo's intelligence expressed itself in other ways. Jo could, for example, tell time.

I'm not saying that he knew the rhythms and patterns of our life so that he knew when it was time to eat and when it was time to go to bed, though that was all true. I'm saying that he could actually tell time.

My wife is a schoolteacher. We lived for many years in a small apartment in Studio City. Nancy's alarm would sound at 5:00 a.m. every weekday, and she would get up and open the sliding glass door so that Jo would be free to wander the courtyard and relieve himself in the flowerboxes. If she did not get up right away, Jo would stand on her and say, "Now, now, now," until my wife slid out of bed and opened the door.

The natural and common awareness of life's rhythms allowed Jo, on weekends, to know when it was 5:00 without the alarm. He would announce it on Saturday morning until one of us got up to let him outside. We didn't love that. We wanted to sleep in.

It occurred to us one Friday to tell him what was going on. He came to bed in the evening, and Nancy spoke to him about it. "Listen," she said. "Jo… Leave the fly alone for a minute and listen to me." He did. He was a very smart cat. "Tomorrow is Saturday. We don't have to get up. We'd like to sleep late. So, if nobody's up by 9:00, you can wake me up. But no earlier. Okay?" Jo slid his tail back and forth across the bedspread, looking at Nancy until he was certain she was done talking and then curled up to go to sleep.

The following morning, an odd chorus dragged me from a confusing dream about a doorway in the middle of Hollywood that led to a bright green forest. Jo was singing, "Now? Now? Now?" And Nancy was saying, "Dylan. Dylan. Seriously, Dylan, you have to see this."

I slipped back from dream body into waking body and rolled over to find out what was so urgent. Nancy was holding up her clock for me to see. It was 9:00. I said, "Wow," and then it was 9:01. We got up, and she let Jo outside while I made coffee.

Thereafter, we were able to tell Jo with confidence what time he could wake us and, indeed, he proved a reliable furry alarm clock on days when our needs were not so urgent that we required the security of an electronic backup. We experimented: 9:30. 8:05. 8:37. I'm not kidding. The cat could tell time.

Nancy said once that when she told him the appointed time, she would imagine the numbers so that he could see the symbols. She suspected that he didn't actually read a clock but rather read her mind and then waited to see the shapes she had shown him. I have no idea why, but I find that far less credible than the theory that he was able to tell time.

Nancy and I both wanted a dog, but the apartment building wouldn't allow one. For years, we imagined that some day we would have a place where we could keep a dog and that we would get a puppy so that Jo could be dominant and train it to behave respectfully toward him. We knew he was capable of using both his claws and teeth as training tools. He had very quickly trained us to keep our feet under the blankets at night and not to pet him when *Jeopardy!* was on TV unless it was the part where Alex questions the contestants about their personal lives. He didn't care about the players' anecdotal ramblings at all and frequently used the interview segment as he did the commercials, to practice his impressions of Ed Asner and other grumpy-but-kind hearted character actors.

In 2002, Nancy and I decided we were ready to own property. Jo was fourteen years old when we moved to our townhouse in Sylmar. The vet told us that moving is one of the most stressful experiences in a cat's life, right up there with falling in a swimming pool and getting divorced. We felt we should give him a month or two to adjust to life in the new place before we confronted him with a puppy.

Six weeks after we moved in, Jo started dying. He had some sort of stroke or seizure. He couldn't meow properly. Instead of doing impressions of Charles Durning and Walter Matthau, he began to do Marlo Thomas. We took him to an emergency vet, who kept him overnight and then told us that they didn't know what was wrong. They charged us several hundred dollars for the overnight visit and suggested that we have them conduct thousands of dollars worth of tests over the next few weeks to figure out what was going on with him. They implied that if we did not spend thousands of dollars on these tests, we simply didn't love our cat enough. They admitted that there were many probable causes of the illness for which they would be able to do little or nothing.

Jo had always hated the vet. We couldn't imagine that he would want a series of trips to the vet in his waning days. We took him home and swore that if he seemed to be in real pain at any point, we would have him put to sleep.

He ate less from then on and lost weight quickly. He never got his proper voice back. He stayed fairly near to us when we went from room to room and up and down the stairs in our new, beloved home. He grew steadily weaker and sadder. We made an appointment to have him put to sleep on a Saturday morning when we would both be able to go with him to the vet.

The night before he was to be put down, Jo told us he was done. Unable to stand up properly, he meowed at us in his sad, whispered voice. We called the vet to ask if we could bring him in right then rather than waiting for the morning appointment.

Leaving his travel crate in the garage, Nancy held Jo in her arms, wrapped in his favorite blanket as I drove us all, weeping, to the vet's office. At the reception desk, Nancy filled out paperwork while I held Jo in my arms. We handed him off to a veterinary assistant who said she would take him to the back room, and they would bring us in momentarily when he was set up so that we could be there when they gave him the final injection. A minute later, a vet came out to tell us that the injection wouldn't be necessary. Jo had died naturally as they set him on the table. As always, he knew when it was time. He could tell, with or without a clock.

He had held on just long enough. Nancy got to hold him lovingly and say goodbye on the car ride. I got to hold him lovingly and say goodbye at the reception desk.

Then he died without an injection, saving us fifty dollars.

Jo was a very good cat. Smart, dignified and eminently practical.

~Dylan Brody

The Switch

*Fun fact: Cats can jump up to five times their height
from a standing start thanks to their strong
hind-leg muscles.*

"Darn it! Not again!" I stomped over to the entry-hall
wall and clicked on the light switch. Although Mom
was nearly ninety, it still upset me when she mistak-
enly turned off the switch that controlled the electri-
cal outlet for the television set.

I hadn't mentioned anything to her about it because I understood
it was merely a minor inconvenience. It was my selfish lack of patience
that caused me to overreact.

Although it was only a matter of minutes, it seemed to take forever
for the TV satellite box to reboot whenever the power source was
interrupted.

Mom had recently suffered a stroke and had to deal with enough
issues without the extra burden of knowing she was causing me anxiety.

However, on this particular day, I decided I should gently remind
her about the switch. She might just need a little prompting, I reasoned,
and everyone would be happy. Well, everyone being me.

"Mom, it's no big thing, but I've been noticing that the light switch
that controls the TV is turned off when I get up in the morning. Maybe
you can be a bit more careful when you use those switches on the
entry-hall wall during the night."

I did not expect the response I received. Even though she often had problems relating thoughts because of the stroke, she came through loud and clear!

"I never touch the light switches on that wall when I get up at night. I turn on the light from the other side of the kitchen. Why would I walk all the way to the entry hall to turn on the kitchen light?"

With four light switches on the wall, I knew that it would be easy for her to get confused, and I couldn't blame her for that. But she was right. She really had no reason to be using those particular light switches. I was baffled, to say the least.

Things did not improve in the following weeks, and I began to worry more about Mom's mental state at night and less about having to reboot the TV in morning. I couldn't help mentioning it to her a few more times to see if she'd remember turning off the switch, but she always gave the same response and was justly becoming agitated with my accusations.

I finally gave up questioning her altogether and chalked it up to her declining memory. There was no need to pester her further.

Then, late one night, while we were watching a scary movie, the TV suddenly shut off. We both nearly jumped out of our chairs. Mom looked at me as if to ask, "Are you going to blame me for this, too?"

Normally, things don't scare me, but this did. I inched quietly across the carpet on my hands and knees toward where we'd heard a thud in the hallway. I poked my head ever so cautiously around the corner and stared into the large green eyes of Pumpkin, our year-old orange Tabby cat. She was sitting on the floor beneath the light switch with a smug look on her furry face.

"Pumpkin!" I giggled with relief. "You didn't!"

But she did!

Although it took another few days for me to actually witness her awesome jumping skills, it was well worth the wait.

I was sitting in the living room with a perfect view of the entry hall when Pumpkin crept around the corner. She sat on the floor and studied the light switches above her head. After a few moments of plotting her strategy, she sprang nearly four feet straight into the air and made perfect paw contact with the switch. The TV snapped off, and my mouth flew open. It was a sight to behold!

All is finally well at home. Mom is relieved that she was proven innocent. I'm relieved that she is mentally stable. Pumpkin is happy to be out in the open with her antics and has yet to meet a light switch she can't turn off.

~Connie Kaseweter Pullen

What in the Sam Hill...?

Fun fact: Some cat species, such as cheetahs and cougars, can purr like domesticated cats, but lions and tigers can't purr. They roar instead.

"**N**o more cats!" That's what my husband Fred told the kids and me. "Three cats are more than enough." My daughter Summer and I just looked at each other and grinned. Yeah… like you can ever have too many cats! Then again, we weren't planning on adding any new cats just then, so the issue didn't seem worth debating. But that was before Sam came on the scene.

My friend Denise and I had stopped for dinner at a country-western pub on the outskirts of Portland, and on our way in a black-and-white cat came flying past to perch on the hood of a nearby car.

What can I say? I'm a sucker for cats, and this one was oozing with charm. I walked right over and scratched him behind the ears. His purr kicked into high gear and he leaned against my fingers.

I wondered where he came from; there were no houses nearby, just an empty field on one side and a tree farm on the other. I picked him up and gave him a warm snuggle. The cat burrowed his face into my neck in obvious ecstasy. "It's a shame he's so unfriendly," I laughed. I put him down on the sidewalk, and Denise and I went inside.

During dinner, I found myself thinking about the little guy outside in the cold, obviously hungry for attention. I asked the waitress if she knew anything about the young cat in the parking lot. She told us that someone had abandoned a mother cat and her four kittens in the field next door. The restaurant staff had fed and looked after them until the kittens were weaned, and then, one by one, the mother cat and the kittens had been adopted, except for the one outside.

He was still there when we went outside, sitting on the hood of another car. If cats could smile, he was smiling his face off, and we could hear him purring from six feet away. I scooped him up, said goodnight to Denise and headed for my van. Putting him on the passenger seat, I belted myself in and prepared for him to freak out when I started the car. He didn't. He stretched languidly across the seat with his front paws curled beneath him and looked expectantly at me. His expression was clear. "Home, James!"

When we got to the house, I picked him up from his comfy position and wrapped him in my coat. As I walked into the family room where the gang was watching TV, our son Aaron looked up and, seeing a tail dangling from beneath my jacket, said, "What in the Sam Hill is under your coat?" giving my hitchhiker the perfect name.

"It's our new kitty — Sam Hill!" I announced, opening my coat with a flourish and hoping Sam's cuteness would win Fred over.

It did. Sam grinned his irresistible cat grin, Fred groaned and muttered, but before the evening was over, he, along with the kids, became a Sam fan. The other cats hissed at him once or twice, but then, like the rest of us, fell under his spell. The kitty without a home had found a family.

The first item on Sam's agenda was to establish his number-one rule: No closed doors! He promptly set about teaching himself to open said doors, which, fortunately for him, were equipped with latch-type handles. Within a few weeks, he had set off the burglar alarm in the house three times and shocked unsuspecting guests who were using the bathroom.

The laundry room, off the TV room, was where we kept the litter box, but when the dryer was running, it was hard to hear the television, so we always closed the door. Sam didn't approve — he'd open it. We'd close it, he'd open it, and so on. It was through this little idiosyncrasy that we discovered another aspect of our endlessly entertaining boy:

He was apparently psychic. When the other cats found the door to the laundry room closed, they would sit, staring patiently at the portal until, only minutes later, Sam, from wherever he had been sleeping in the house, would come and open the door for them. Eventually, Fred changed the handles to regular doorknobs.

All creatures, two-legged or four, were friends in Sammy's book. People were great, cats were cool, and dogs were dandy. He didn't even bat a whisker when I brought home a dwarf rabbit named Bunny Jean. Before a week was out, they were best buddies, chasing each other around the family room. We had a sheepskin rug in front of the fireplace. Sam would dive under it, every part of him covered except his nose, and then wait patiently until Bunny Jean came hopping by. When he pounced, the two would roll around on the carpet, wrestle and play hide-and-seek until one or the other finally collapsed into a nap. They were infinitely more captivating than most of the television shows.

Every day, it seemed, we would discover a new component to our Sam's repertoire of personality quirks. One afternoon when I was working around the house, I heard Sam meowing loudly. He rarely did this, so when it continued for quite some time, I got a little concerned and went to see what was going on. Following his voice, I found him in the kitchen, sitting on the floor, looking up intently at and having a heartfelt conversation with… the oven. He glanced over at me, then went on chatting. When he was finished with his tête-à-tête, he smoothed a whisker and headed to the sofa for a nap. Off and on after that, I would find him in the living room having the same dialogue with the drapes. He was a nut, but never boring.

Samuel William Hill was cherished by our family for nine wonderful years. These days, he's hanging out in heaven, keeping the angels amused, opening doors for them, I'm sure, and waiting for his family to come home.

~Tina Wagner Mattern

Trained in a Flash

Fun fact: The scientific term for a hairball is a "bezoar."

"Y ou can't teach that cat to do tricks," a friend of mine declared, as he watched me throw wadded-up paper across the room in Flash's direction.

"Fetch!" I commanded, ignoring my friend's negativity. Flash, short for Flash Dance Gordon, was lying where the sun came into the room and warmed the carpet. He yawned and stretched, then rose to his feet and nonchalantly walked over to sniff the paper.

"Told you so," said my friend.

"Fetch!" I repeated, throwing another paper ball his way.

Now more awake, Flash pounced upon it, batted it around, threw it in the air and then flopped back down on the carpet, totally disinterested.

"Ha, ha, ha!" said my friend. "Is that all he's got?"

"Roll over, play dead!" I instructed, and Flash closed his eyes.

"At least he got that one right!" crowed my friend.

But over the course of the next few months, I worked with Flash on a daily basis, sure that he could, and would, follow direct commands — especially if I found the right reward to motivate him.

The motivation came unexpectedly during a trip to the vet to find the root of his persistent cough.

"Since he's a long-hair," said the vet, "he's predisposed to getting hairballs." She handed me a tube about the size of a large tube of toothpaste. "Squirt a little of this down his throat as often as directed. You'll only need to give him about half an inch of this medicine at a time. You can start right now."

Tentatively, I removed the cap. I'd had to wrestle Flash to the ground and hold him between my knees to give him his worm pills, and I wasn't all that keen on showing the vet how inept I was.

I wondered if I should put it on my finger or maybe try to hide it in his food. Instead, I gave Flash a pat on the head, then held the tube in front of him and squeezed a little out. Flash got one whiff of the medicine and went ballistic — in a good way! He licked the medicine right off the tube, and then pawed at it, trying to get me to give him more.

"It's got a cod-liver-oil base," said the vet, smiling and nodding. "Most cats love it."

Happily, I took Flash home and let him out of his travel crate. I set the tube of medicine on the dining table and went into the kitchen.

When I returned, Flash had the tube on the floor and was trying to get it open. He'd obviously gotten on the table, which he'd been trained (with a squirt gun) not to do. And there he was, rolling on the floor, pawing at the tube as obsessed as a junkie after drugs.

I started to yell at him, but then I realized that I might be able to use his desire to get more medicine to my advantage.

A few weeks later, when my friend came over for coffee, he asked if I'd had any success "training" my cat.

"Of course," I replied. "Would you like a demonstration?"

He laughed. "Flash already knows how to play dead," he answered, observing my cat snoozing away the afternoon in the sunshine.

I nonchalantly went to the cupboard where I kept the hairball medicine and let the cupboard door bang as I slipped the tube into my pocket, unobserved by my friend.

Flash was instantly on high alert and came running to me.

"Sit!" I commanded. And Flash sat. "Beg!" And he sat up straight with his front paws in the air in front of him.

Then I threw a wad of paper across the room, and Flash retrieved it. My friend's eyes got big, and his mouth gaped open.

"How in the world…?"

But Flash knew the routine, so as soon as he dropped the wadded paper in front of me, and without any commands, he instantly rolled over — twice — and then began head-butting me and meowing.

"Roll over, knuckle-bump, and speak," I said in a rush, laughing. "You've got to wait till I tell you which trick to do, Flash Dancer!"

"But how? Why? I don't believe it!" said my shocked friend.

"Cats are smart," I replied, retrieving the tube from my pocket and squeezing a little of the gel directly into Flash's mouth. "It hardly took him any time at all to train me."

~Jan Bono

King Murphy

Fun fact: In the Italian version of Cinderella, *the fairy godmother was a cat!*

Murphy was regal from the start. Even at the shelter his aloof attitude set him apart from his cage-mates. He was long-legged and long-haired. He confidently cruised up to the cage door and looked directly into my five-year-old daughter Bridget's eyes. He was unperturbed as the attendant pulled him from the cage and deposited him into the arms of his new valet. No scared kitten mewling from him — he purred contentedly on Bridget's lap as we motored to his suburban palace.

As the weeks and months passed, Murphy grew bigger and fluffier, and he fell in love with us despite his haughty manner. A visit to the vet confirmed what we had already surmised: He was a Maine Coon cat. He followed us everywhere, learned how to retrieve, and gave kisses on command. We were amazed at how intelligent he was. He was as big as a small dog, and his antics were quite dog-like as well. His size astonished us. His full weight held steady at twenty pounds.

Particularly unnerving was Murphy's more feline penchant for perching. He would resourcefully find his way to the tops of open doors and lie lengthwise on the narrow frame, his bulk evenly distributed and perfectly balanced. He would survey his kingdom, patiently wait for visitors to enter, and then surprise them as they passed with gentle smacks on their heads with his large paw. Even more disturbing was his nightly trapeze act on the exposed beams of the cathedral ceiling in our bedroom. He would begin the show with a jump to a tall dresser, a quick hop to the top of the door and then a perfect mount onto the beam. We would watch his progress along the bar. He would pause above the bed and, after a few seconds of staring down at us, he would perform a perfect dismount, solidifying his place as the king of the bedroom. Instead of applause, his reward was our reaction as we scattered when he dropped from the ten-foot-high girder onto our bed!

His most loyal subject in the family was Bridget. She swaddled him and walked him in her doll carriage. He would lie beside her as she read or watched television. He slept on her bed and sat beneath her chair at meals as she dropped morsels of her dinner for him.

His favorite activity was playing Barbie with her. He would crawl among her dolls' extensive wardrobe and nose out outfits that Bridget would promptly put on Barbie. One day, I heard her giggling uncontrollably. She was in the kitchen standing by Murphy's water bowl, watching him play with something in the water. When I looked in, I saw a tiny pair of Barbie panties being swirled around in the water. Through her giggles, Bridget exclaimed, "Mom, he's washing Barbie's clothes!" Murphy laundered Barbie's unmentionables from then on. Each time Bridget opened up her doll cases, Murphy was right there, pawing around in search of Barbie's underwear.

Murphy's quirkiness reached new heights one rainy afternoon. I was preparing dinner, and Bridget was playing upstairs in her bedroom. I overheard Bridget stating firmly, "Okay, it's my turn," then "Okay, you go." Knowing she was alone in her room, I ran upstairs, wondering who was playing with her. Sitting opposite each other on the floor were Bridget and Murphy. The *Pretty Pretty Princess* board game was spread out between them. The game requires a player to spin a basic flat spinner, move a playing piece the appropriate number of moves, and put on or lose jewelry pieces as directed.

The winner earns the most jewelry and wears a tiara as his or her prize. This certainly seemed like an appropriate game for our kingly cat. As I watched from the doorway, I noticed a necklace hung around Murphy's neck. Bridget spun the spinner, moved her piece and put on a ring. She then told Murphy it was his turn. To my surprise, he reached out his paw and hit the side of the spinner. Bridget moved his piece and put his earned bracelet on his paw. She then spun again as Murphy calmly sat across from her watching her move. She again said, "Murphy, your turn," and I was astounded as he delicately pushed the spinner and Bridget moved his piece. I watched in awe as this game played out until the end when Bridget eventually won. She was ever the gracious princess and thanked her King Murphy for playing the game with her.

Murphy has been gone a while now, but the joy and love he brought into our lives will never be forgotten. We now have a Golden Retriever, Charlie, who seems to have inherited Murphy's quirkiness and love for our family. I am, as ever, prepared to be amazed.

~Ann C. Kenna

Bell Ringer

*Fun fact: Many cats don't like closed doors and will
meow or paw at the door to get you to open it.*

TB was a gorgeous black cat with soft fur and huge golden eyes. He was such a deep black color, that at night, when he would stand up on his hind legs at the screen door quietly mewing to be let in, all you could see were those huge golden eyes floating in the dark looking exotic and rather magical.

When we found him as a kitten, he was really tiny, alone and hungry. And though warm and affectionate, he was still fiercely independent in that very cat-like way.

My husband and I loved TB, but we were a little worried when I became pregnant with our first child. I'd heard many scary tales about how cats could be a danger around infants, so when our daughter was born, we did our best to keep them apart. But tired new moms cannot be everywhere at all times. One night, exhausted, I fell asleep in the chair in the baby's room. When I awoke I found TB curled up in the crib near the baby's feet. Both of them seemed perfectly content, and I realized that maybe I'd been overthinking the cat-danger thing.

Another time, I was in the kitchen cooking and heard the baby cry, then stop crying and start laughing. I went to check on her and found TB licking the bottom of one of her bare feet, soothing and calming her the way a mother cat would lick a kitten to comfort and clean it.

The two of them grew very fond of each other. I couldn't believe the rough handling TB would allow eighteen-month-old Becki to put him through. She would sit on his belly, tightly hugging his neck with one arm, while pulling his tail up on the opposite side to wrap around her and, to my utter dismay and bewilderment, she would often chew on the tip of his tail. Becki pretty much used old TB like her own live rug, shawl, and teething toy!

But TB took it all in stride without flinching, a master of quiet suffering and calm endurance. We'd tell Becki she had to be nice to the kitty and be careful not to hurt him, but TB never seemed to mind or complain.

Then, as our family grew in numbers of children and other pets we found that TB also got along beautifully with our parakeet, dogs, and gerbils. In fact, when the gerbils would escape their habitat, TB would help us round them up, herding them in our direction so we could catch them and return them to their home. TB never bit them or so much as ruffled a lick of fur on their little bodies. He really was an amazing creature.

He did these things and many others with the greatest finesse, but one of the best tricks he ever did was learning how to ring the doorbell.

From time to time, I would hear the doorbell ring and go to answer it, but there would be no one there. I'd open the door to see who it was and TB would run in!

I didn't make the connection at first, but one day I happened to look out the window when the doorbell rang and, to my total amazement, there was TB hanging onto the screen door and leaning way over to push the doorbell button!

Later, we figured out how TB must have learned this little trick. He would see someone come to the door and touch that spot — to ring the doorbell — and the door would open. At first, when the bell rang and the door opened, he'd just run inside with whoever rang the bell. But, over time, he figured out that if he touched the same spot that people touched to get in, the door would open, and he could come in all on his own.

Sadly, he is no longer with us on this earth, having lived a long and happy life. As for us, although we've loved and lost many cats over the years, all of them wonderful creatures, TB's spirit and cleverness made him an extra-special cat.

~PJ

62

Phantom's Thanksgiving

*Fun fact: Most cats like their food at room temperature
and won't eat it if it's too hot or too cold.*

T he first cat I ever had, a gift from my girlfriend, was a black kitten that came into my life because his previous owner (my girlfriend's co-worker) was looking for a new home for him. They had to give him up when they had a baby and the cat thought she was a plaything.

Phantom would lie asleep at the other end of the couch as I watched television, but would be waiting for me in the kitchen when I got up to get a snack. I never saw him run past me; he simply appeared in the kitchen before I did. He also developed the habit of finding ways to get to the human food he wanted so much. I swore he could walk through walls (or at least pantry doors).

Several years later, my now-wife and I moved to the other side of the country, to Los Angeles, to start a new job for me at a new school. The two of us and Phantom moved into our new home in August. My wife and I both came from big families and were used to large gatherings for Thanksgiving, so we were a little sad that we could not afford to fly back home for the holiday. Determined to make the best of the situation, we invited several friends in the same predicament over to celebrate "Friendsgiving" on that Thursday.

As the cook in our family, I spent the early morning hours preparing the turkey and a dozen side dishes, constantly shooing Phantom out of the kitchen. When our guests arrived, we asked them to help us keep Phantom away from the food. Eventually, he made such a pest of himself during dinner that I put him in the bedroom and closed the door.

After dinner, we left everything on the dining room table and the kitchen counter in order to go to the living room, watch some football, and relax after eating. A few minutes into the game, I heard a noise from the kitchen. With my wife and all of our guests sitting there, no one was in the kitchen, so I got up and looked down the hall. The bedroom door was open a crack.

Moving quickly to the kitchen, I could not believe what I saw. I had carved the turkey and left the uncarved part sitting on the counter. Phantom was sitting inside the remains of the turkey, very contentedly eating around himself. He was in the act of pulling some meat off the thigh I had not served.

"Phantom!" I yelled, startling some of the guests, who jumped up to see what was the matter. The cat simply gave me a look and kept eating. The guests, on the other hand, found it quite funny, although we now had a lot fewer leftovers.

I finally went over and removed him from his seat in paradise, cleaned him off (threatening him with a bath later) and set to work cleaning up. By the time I left the kitchen, he was contentedly licking himself clean on the couch in the spot I had vacated, no doubt enjoying the turkey flavor.

Phantom is gone now, but our friends still laugh about the year that we did not have a "turducken" but rather a "turkitten" for Thanksgiving dinner.

~Kevin Wetmore

63

Bait and Switch

Fun fact: "Community cats" are made up of feral cats, which have never been socialized around people, and stray cats, which are lost or runaway pets.

'll never be smarter than a cat. I'm okay with that. Really. Every cat lover knows and accepts one simple truth: Cats are smarter than people. What's upsetting is the extent to which cats can outsmart me.

It all began after my beloved cat, Toonsie, passed away. Not only did I miss her daily antics, but my yard was becoming overrun with chipmunks, squirrels, and other little critters. The cat was away, and the local wildlife wasn't merely playing; they were having an all-out free-for-all party on my property. The only things missing were itty-bitty beer kegs and mini ping pong balls.

Getting another cat was out of the question. "We're not having another pet in this house," declared Prospero. "I miss Toonsie, too, but we finally got our lives back." By this he meant that we hadn't had a proper vacation in the thirteen years since we took her in. She got mad when we left the house, so we stayed home. Toonsie had us well trained.

One day, I saw a cat in the yard. I had some leftover dry food and decided to leave out a dish along with a bowl of fresh water. Word along the kitty telegraph must have gotten out because, before long, I had several regular visitors. Of course, cans of wet food soon began to supplement the dry, and I had a new job directing traffic and breaking up fights among the diners.

A rough-looking Tabby began making appearances but was a bit skittish about staying around. He was huge and scruffy, and we named him Chestnut for two very large, obvious reasons. Soon, a little black kitten showed up, also very skittish, but would circle back around if food were left out for her. It soon became apparent that whenever Midnight was eating, Chestnut would join her. The tough Tabby and little kitten happily shared whatever was in the dish. Of course, I would then go out with another plate of food so they could both enjoy a meal. I realized that whenever the cute little kitten would come begging for food, Chestnut would be hiding beneath a bush and join her when it arrived.

It was a pure bait-and-switch scam. I'd feed the little kitty, and the big cat would then move in. The two cats outsmarted me!

What was really amazing was how well the two got along. Little Midnight always finished her food first, and then shoved Chestnut aside and ate out of his plate. They were an odd couple, but also the best of friends.

Feral cats rarely come close enough to make human contact, and these two wonderful cats were no exception. The only way they would come to a plate is when I was firmly enclosed back in my habitat. That's why it was impossible for me to rescue Chestnut when I saw a large, bloody gash on his shoulder. He ran off, never to be seen again. My heart was broken, not only for the injured cat, but also for little Midnight, who lost a good friend and protector. For all we know, Chestnut may have gotten his injury defending his little buddy. What a loyal friend.

Cats are smarter than people. Not only did those two little scamps fool me with their bait-and-switch routine, but they also taught me a true lesson about selfless love and putting a friend before one's self. Rest in peace, Chestnut. I'll keep an eye on your friend for you.

~Lynn Maddalena Menna

A Purrfect Escape Artist

Fun fact: The first Siamese cat came to the United States in 1878. It was a gift to President Rutherford Hayes's wife, Lucy, from the U.S. consul in Siam (now Thailand).

Cats, while being clever animals, are sometimes too clever for their own good. One such feline was my parents' elegant Siamese named Perky (a testament to his always perfectly perpendicular tail).

Perky had lived with Mom and Dad for many years; however, due to my parents' declining health, a move to a seniors' home became necessary. As Mom and Dad remained quite independent, the appropriate choice was a property where each resident had his/her own apartment but shared a common "great room" and dining room. Many of the residents had small pets, so Perky was free to move in with Mom and Dad. Following the chaos of downsizing and moving my parents, the frightened cat hid under the bed for a few days. However, he soon reappeared, adjusted well, and continued to provide good company and comfort for Mom and Dad.

Things changed, however. My mother eventually passed away, and Dad had to be moved to more secure housing because he was becoming increasingly forgetful but wasn't ready for a full-scale Alzheimer's facility. Instead, we found him a home shared by a handful of other residents with early-stage dementia. Full-time staff monitored this home's residents and managed their care. To make this facility more home-like, each of the residents' families was encouraged to bring in personal belongings to help make the home more familiar and comfortable.

Instead of supplying yet another chair or bookshelf for this home, my two sisters and I wondered if we could donate Perky. The answer was a resounding "yes," and the cat was warmly welcomed. As cats often do, Perky made himself very much at home in his new surroundings and regally prowled the hallways. Both the residents and staff seemed to appreciate their new houseguest while Perky appreciated the increased number of laps to sit in. This may have been the perfect answer, save for one big problem.

Perky soon learned he could let himself out of the house. He would stand on his hind paws, reach up, and pull the front door handle down with his front paws. The front door would gently swing open, and Perky would casually saunter outside. A smart move, yes? One might think so; however, while Perky could now open the front door, he could not close it behind him and had absolutely no understanding of the huge safety risk this presented. Unless it was noticed immediately, the home's open front door was an open invitation for the residents inside, who were prone to wandering away.

No doubt about it, the cat had to go — and quickly! Thankfully, Perky did not have to be turned over to an animal shelter; my older sister adopted him so he remained with the family. Perky could now go outside in my sister's back yard whenever he wanted — no assistance required!

~Rick Lauber

The Kleptomaniac Kitty

*Fun fact: Cats are right-pawed or left-pawed just like
people are right-handed or left-handed.*

After responding to a Craigslist post, my mom and I made
the half-hour drive to adopt three-month-old Suki and
her sister Kimi. Their owner met me in the driveway
holding Kimi, who was purring happily. Suki, I was
informed, was in the process of "being found." I was handed Kimi
and instantly fell in love. It was a good thing the owner had her
hands free, because at that moment a little black thing zoomed out of
the open front door and headed straight for the street.

The owner, clearly well practiced in events like these, made one
graceful dive, caught Suki by the tail, and lifted the protesting kitten
into her arms. "I'll just hold her until your mom finishes parking the
car," she assured me. "This one can be a bit squirmy."

I loved Suki and her lively act of rebellion instantly, but I was
fourteen and the decision to adopt the kittens ultimately lay with my
mother. I begged the owner not to inform her of Suki's latest escape
attempt. Probably eager to be rid of the "liveliest" kitten in the litter,
the owner agreed.

It didn't take long for the whole family to realize what we'd gotten
ourselves into, but by then it was too late; each of us had fallen in love
with Suki. And as long as she would have us as her humans, we'd be
honored to have her as our cat.

True to her free-spirit nature, Suki spent most of her time outdoors roaming the neighborhood. One day, I noticed she was playing with a gray stuffed elephant, and I asked my parents about it. No one in the house had given it to her so we wrote it off as one of the many things about Suki we'd never understand.

The very next day, there was a stuffed squirrel in her bed, the same size as the elephant. Now it was clear something fishy was going on. Either the manipulative feline had cajoled an innocent cat-lover into providing her with a second set of toys and other luxuries, or an unfortunate pet had fallen victim to our little kleptomaniac. Knowing Suki's love of rebellion, we suspected the second.

Every day, Suki added a new stuffed animal to her collection, and she was accumulating quite a zoo. We were at a loss. How could we return them to their rightful owner when we had no idea where the toys were coming from? We weren't even sure if they belonged to another pet. What if Suki was swiping them from a child?

The mystery continued for over a week, until we finally made a breakthrough in the case. While sitting at the kitchen table trying desperately to focus on anything but my geometry homework, the corner of my eye caught movement outside the kitchen window. It was Suki, slick as the day she'd escaped from her first home over a year ago, jumping over our back wall and into the neighbor's yard.

With her love of adventure and her tendency to treat rules as merely suggestions, I didn't think anything of it until she reappeared a few moments later with a stuffed turtle clamped firmly in her mouth.

A-ha! I'd caught her in the act. Now it was time to get to the bottom of this. Despite Suki's protests, I retrieved the turtle and grabbed a ladder — my alternative to scaling the eight-foot wall my little kleptomaniac kitty had climbed with ease — and peeked into the unfamiliar yard.

Sure enough, a basket of stuffed animals belonging to some other pet sat at the doorway. We later returned the pilfered goods and learned that their rightful owner was a two-year-old Collie named Randy and his best friend, third-grader Noah. Apparently, Randy went with Noah's mom to pick him up from school every afternoon, and recognizing this schedule, Suki took the time to swipe beloved toys from a dog more than four times her size!

The toys were returned to their rightful owner with no hard feelings and a few good laughs, and that night I had a talk with my furry thief. "Suki," I told her as I scratched her favorite spot below her chin, "you're not a bad kitty, but sometimes you make bad choices." She kept purring as if she was exceptionally pleased with herself. Somehow, I don't think the lesson sank in. We're still vigilant — always on the lookout for Suki's next "adventure."

~Elizabeth Batman

66

The Secret Passage

Fun fact: If you can't find your cat anywhere in your
house, she could be trapped inside an HVAC duct,
drop-down ceiling, wall, or sub-basement.

The house was in a frenzy. All of our out-of-town relatives were arriving, along with my sister's closest friends. Extra tables were brought in, draped with elegant tablecloths and filled with fancy hors d'oeuvres in pretty dishes. We were hosting a bridal shower for my sister.

When we hosted parties, we usually let Snickers, our adorable, but un-trainable cat, partake in the festivities. But this time we had to exclude Snickers because Kathy, one of our guests, was afraid of cats.

It is rare that we have to confine Snickers, but when we do, we usually put her in the basement or in a bedroom. But we figured some of the cousins would want to use the ping-pong table in the main room of the basement, and the house would be so chaotic someone would forget and open the door of any bedroom we tried to put her in. So we decided to fix up a storage room off to the side of the basement with her litter box, food, water and her softest bed.

Just before Kathy arrived, Mom carried Snickers down to her room and closed the door. But not long after Kathy arrived and walked into the dining room, so did Snickers.

Fortunately, Mom noticed Snickers before Kathy did, quickly scooped her up, and took her back down to her room.

"We need to keep Snickers locked up for the party. Don't open the door to the store room," Mom called to all of us as she came back upstairs. She figured that one of us kids must have opened that door and that was how Snickers got out.

But just a few minutes later, we heard Kathy say "Eek, a cat!" Sure enough, Mom looked and saw that indeed, Snickers was back!

Now Mom was embarrassed and apologized profusely to Kathy. She had told all of us that this guest was afraid of cats. Was this someone's idea of a mean joke?

"Who keeps letting the cat out?" Mom hollered in exasperation when she saw Snickers.

When all of us kids swore we hadn't let her out, Dad decided to stand watch outside the door. He didn't have to watch long before he saw Snickers walking in the ceiling rafters which extended above the door of the storage room and led right out into the main room of the basement. When she made it out to the main room, she just jumped down to the floor and ran upstairs!

When Dad reported this, everyone, including Kathy laughed. We had lived in this house for eighteen years, ten years longer than Snickers, and we never knew about this secret passage in the ceiling rafters. When we saw it, we were also amazed that Snickers had jumped so high.

Ever since this incident, I look at Snickers with an increased sense of wonder. I always imagined that she just slept all day while we were at school and work, and I am still sure she does a lot of that. But I wonder if she also takes advantage of this time alone to explore every nook and cranny of her world. If she could talk, I would love to ask her what else she knows about this house that we don't.

As for that bridal shower, and every event thereafter when we needed to confine Snickers, we went back to locking her into the main room of the basement. She hasn't found a secret passage upstairs from this room, at least not yet.

~Allison Nastoff

Delly

Chapter 7

My Very Good, Very Bad Cat

My Therapist Cat

Fun fact: There are several organizations that certify pet therapy teams. Pet Partners' Therapy Animal Program is one of the largest in the U.S., and the organization has been training volunteers nationwide since 1990.

67

Chicken Soup for the Soul

Kitty Bites

*Not-so-fun fact: About 40,000 people in the United
States are bitten by cats each year.*

When he was younger, there was nothing my cat, Mr. Meow, enjoyed more than wrestling with me. He'd seek me out with this look in his eyes that said, "You ready to play, Mom? Because I am!"

The second I got up, he'd dash to the pop-up cube ("hut") that he liked to hide in. I'd throw one of his little toy balls on top, and he'd punch the roof to send it flying off. When I'd reach down to pick it up to throw it again, he'd lunge out and grab onto my arm, biting and kicking me. Or "wrestling," as I called it.

"How can you let him do that?" my husband would often ask, appalled.

It looked much more vicious than it felt. It didn't hurt. Not usually. Mr. Meow didn't have front claws, only back ones. He mostly used the pads of his paws, not his claws, when he kicked. And he mostly just mouthed me and didn't sink his teeth in when he bit.

Of course, he did get carried away sometimes. He'd get so swept up in the frenzy of playing, he'd forget to be gentle.

"Owie Meowie!" I'd say to let him know when he bit or scratched too hard or drew blood. He'd respond by taking it down a notch.

It was actually our wrestling matches that gave me the courage to face my biggest fear: needles.

"Fear" is perhaps too tame of a word for how I viewed needles. I had an extreme case of needle phobia. It came with lots of drama — tears, profuse sweating, nausea, diarrhea and fainting. It was usually in that order and rapid-fire, one symptom right after the other.

It was humiliating and embarrassing. I was a grown woman, for goodness sake. I should have had better control of myself!

For most of my life, I'd been able to avoid needles as much as possible. Then I was diagnosed with cancer. It quickly became clear that routine injections and blood draws were inevitable.

Most nurses were sympathetic and tried to do everything possible to assuage my needle-phobia symptoms. The nurses at my oncologist's office quickly realized that lying me down helped with the nausea, diarrhea and fainting. I still cried and sweated, but it beat them having to worry about me falling over and breaking open my head.

For a couple of months, chemo left me too sick to play with Mr. Meow, which he seemed to sense. He'd never been a particularly snuggly cat, but during my chemo days he'd perch on my chest for hours.

One of the first times I felt better enough to wrestle with him, he bit too hard. I realized his teeth hurt more than most of the needles I had to deal with.

"How come I can handle you biting me, Mr. Meow? I don't experience all the chaos I do when I get shots."

His answer? He grabbed me tighter and bit harder. It was so hard that he drew blood — and quite a lot of it.

"Yowie Meowie!" I hollered, quickly rushing to tend to my wound.

As I cleaned myself up, I thought about how much his teeth puncturing my skin still hurt afterwards. It was rare for shots to hurt me like that.

And blood draws? As Melissa, the phlebotomist at my oncologist's office, said before she'd stick me, "Get ready for the bee sting in three, two, one…"

They usually weren't much more than a bee sting, either. Just a quick little prick.

Yet, I didn't much like bees either. They conjured up images of suffering, too.

But my cat? He conjured up happy feelings of fun times.

I decided the next time I had my blood drawn, I was going to tell myself "Kitty Bites" and see if it helped.

A couple of days later, I got the chance to put my theory to the test when I went in for my three-week checkup. The familiar anxious feelings were fluttering in my stomach. Tears welled in my eyes.

Melissa took me to a room and lay me down. As she got ready to put in the needle, I closed my eyes and repeated silently over and over, "Kitty bites. Kitty bites. Kitty bites."

"All done," she said. "Wow, I'm impressed. No tears today. What gives?"

"Wait, what? You're done?" I asked, incredulous. I hadn't felt a thing! I didn't even feel sick afterward.

I couldn't wait to get home and tell Mr. Meow. Of course, he couldn't understand me. All he wanted to do was wrestle, and I happily obliged.

It wasn't long before I was able to sit in a chair and have my blood drawn — sans tears, nausea, diarrhea, or fainting.

Needles to this day are still not my favorite thing. However, as long as I repeat "Kitty bites" and think of Mr. Meow when being poked, I can handle it.

~Courtney Lynn Mroch

Angel

Fun fact: All Tabby cats have a distinct M-shaped mark on their forehead.

On the way home from the hospital, I stopped at the hardware shop and bought the rope. I discreetly camouflaged it behind a rug in the boot of the car. I was just about to slam it shut when my neighbour appeared by my side.

"Becky? How are you?" she asked.

"Feeling much better, thanks," I lied.

I'd just been discharged from St. Michael's psychiatric hospital. It had been my sixth admission, and I only ever seemed to come out marginally improved. It seemed pointless to tell her the truth, that I was worse than ever. I remember thinking that if I'd been in a general hospital and been diagnosed with heart disease or cancer, I'd probably have gotten a more sympathetic ear. All I had was plain old depression — an invisible cross that had weighed heavily on my shoulders for two decades.

"If you need anything…" she patted me on the shoulder.

"Just ask. I know…" I said in my head, getting into the car.

It wasn't her fault. It wasn't anybody's fault. My malaise was mine, and mine alone.

In my self-absorption, I forgot to thank her for looking after Angel, my five-year-old Tabby cat. Mind you, there wasn't much minding to be done when it came to Angel. While I spent long spells of time inside, she spent most of hers outside. Still, we were two of a kind. We lived together, but we weren't living. Not really.

In the kitchen, I ran my hand under the tap, but no water came out. Reality kicked in faster than a Serena Williams serve. The taps in St. Michael's had electric eyes and only released water in short bursts — a safety precaution designed to deter those considering drowning. I wasn't in there anymore. I was back home. As I turned the handle to open the tap, I heard that familiar voice in my head:

"You're as good as institutionalized, dear."

I didn't disagree.

My family hadn't visited me once during my incarceration. Judging by the disapproving glares from Angel, she'd had enough, too. I could see her nose pressed firmly against the cat-flap entrance outside. I reluctantly lifted the plastic screen, and she crawled in. I filled her bowls with fresh food and water, hoping she'd allow me to pet her. As soon as my hand went out, Angel flinched.

"What am I going to do with you, Angel?" I sighed, but my words fell into the empty space she left behind as she fled from me.

In fairness to Angel, she had good reason to be disappointed in me. When I'd adopted her from the local cat rescue home, she had undoubtedly hoped for a better life than her old one. She'd been abandoned and badly abused and didn't take kindly to physical contact from any human being. She wasn't the prettiest of kittens either. Her left ear was missing, and her belly was almost bald. She'd literally torn out her hair. The vet told me it was a nervous habit. Poor Angel was all out of trust, and nobody wanted her. Angel and I had so much in common. I'd walked in her paws many times.

I'd been thinking a lot about giving her away to a better home. It would have been the decent thing to do. I'd been away so much due to my recurring bouts of depression, it felt wrong to keep holding on to her. Despite all the years I had spent trying to heal Angel's trauma, she remained unresponsive. I could relate to that. When I looked at Angel, all I could see was my own troubled future. I didn't want to see it anymore.

I'd practised with the rope before, so I knew what I was doing.

My Therapist Cat | 237

As I wound it around the sturdy attic beam, my conviction grew. My family had suffered enough. I could never give them back the days they had spent worrying about me. My illness had robbed them of the one thing they needed the most — peace of mind. I was going to give it back to them. I had to touch death in order for them to feel alive again. I loved them that much.

I climbed up onto the old, rickety chair from the dining room. The double knot of the rope felt comfortable around my neck. I gave it a little tug just to make sure it was secure and tight. My feet were a full foot from the floor. I rocked the chair from side to side as I offered up a final prayer for forgiveness. I closed my eyes and readied myself to kick the chair away. I was scared I'd fail, and of all my options, failure was not one of them. I started to count. One. Two. Three…

Suddenly, Angel was clinging to my left leg, wailing and crying. Her claws dug into me, tearing through my clothes and slicing into my skin. I looked down at her and then back up at the rope. It was clear she needed to go to the toilet and wanted to get out through the cat flap.

I tried to shoo her away, but the more I did, the more agitated she became. I couldn't leave her like that. It wouldn't be long before she went into some corner and peed there. That would be degrading for her. I didn't like the thoughts of her watching what I was doing either. She'd had more than her fair share of suffering already. Reluctantly, I slid the rope from my neck and climbed down from the chair.

"Angel," I sighed, walking down the stairs. "You sure know how to pick your moments."

I opened the screen door of the cat flap for her to go through.

"Go on then," I encouraged her, but Angel sat down by my heel and didn't move an inch.

Suddenly, I felt very tired and walked upstairs to my bedroom. I passed the hanging rope on the landing, a grim reminder of my aborted mission. I'll try again later, I thought to myself, as I lay down on my bed. Angel crawled up on my chest and spread herself right across my body. She'd never done anything like that before.

I was so taken by surprise and overcome with joy that I lay frozen and still. I was aware that any movement from me might cause her to leap in fright. I cried as I felt her breath against my face, her paws possessively clinging to my shoulders. I was so startled by her uncharacteristic behaviour that I forgot about everything else.

Eventually, I fell into a deep sleep. When I awoke the following morning, Angel was still there, huddled close to my chest and purring gently in my ear. It was only then I remembered that the cat-litter tray was where it had always been — at the bottom of the stairs and not outside. She hadn't needed to go out. She was truly trying to save me.

As the new day dawned, so did the miracle. It was the day Angel lived up to her name. It was the day I realized we all have a purpose, and it was the day I chose to live again.

~Catherine Barry

69

The Scar

Fun fact: Cats don't actually "sharpen" their claws.
When they scratch on furniture, they are stripping
away worn layers from the claw to reveal a fresh layer.

"Since this is such a beautiful day and it's Saturday," Jerry said, reaching for the hairdryer, "why don't you fix a picnic lunch while I run a few errands, and then we can drive up into the mountains? Maybe toss our lines in the lake and catch a few fish for dinner?"

As my husband and I planned our day, our large tuxedo cat, El Gato Gordo, purred softly in my arms, gazing lazily at the lush green trees through our upstairs master bath window.

When Jerry turned on the dryer, Gato bolted in panic. In his hurry to escape, Gato's claws ripped the soft flesh on the underside of my lower left arm. The cut was deep and bled profusely. After stopping the bleeding and inspecting it closely, we decided no stitches were required. Jerry helped me treat and dress the wound while I insisted no amount of discomfort would interfere with our day's plans. He left, and I began searching for Gato.

"Gato!" I called, several times, but there was no answer. Since cats are so intelligent and sensitive to human emotions, I wondered if perhaps he felt my shock at being scratched and feared I was unhappy with him.

Finally, I found him huddling beneath the stairwell, wide-eyed and trembling. I picked him up gently, favoring my bandaged arm. As I held

Gato close, I felt the wild thumping of his heart. Kissing him on the head, I whispered, "It's okay, sweetheart. It was just an accident. I know you didn't mean to hurt me." I sat on the stairs holding and stroking him in my lap until he relaxed. Finally satisfied that he was over his trauma, I released him and started preparing for our afternoon outing.

I dashed to the store for some chips and dip, and while waiting in the checkout line I met the husband of a neighbor who lived at the end of our street.

"What happened to your arm?" he asked, noting the bandage.

After I explained, he responded with raised brow, "I tell you one thing, if that had happened to me, that would be one dead cat!"

Horrified, I said, "It was an accident! He didn't deliberately hurt me — he was just frightened."

"I don't care whether it was an accident or not, I'd get rid of that cat!"

Driving home, I thought angrily, "Well, it's obvious he's no cat lover!"

Several weeks later, the wound was completely healed, but in its place was a prominent white curved scar — almost three inches in length.

Early one morning as Jerry and I sat enjoying our freshly ground vanilla-nut coffee, he glanced at my arm and said, "I'm so sorry, honey. Maybe the scar will fade with time, and you won't even be able to see it."

I surprised him with my response. "I hope it never goes away! I want to always have this scar — as a reminder."

"Why on earth would you want to remember that Gato scratched you? Are you mad at him?" he asked, eyes wide. Gato, dozing in the corner, raised his head at hearing his name.

"Of course not!" I responded, blowing Gato a kiss.

Then I related the comments made by our neighbor's husband and how it got me to thinking.

"Seeing this scar will remind me that, yes, I suffered a minor injury, but it wasn't about me — it was about Gato and what prompted his action. Gato would never deliberately hurt me. His lashing out at me was a reaction — not a malicious intent — because he was suddenly frightened and felt threatened. People can do the same."

I refreshed my cup, inhaling its sweet aroma. After adding more half-and-half with sweetener, I took another bite of my cinnamon roll.

"How so?" Jerry asked, eyeing the last doughnut on the plate.

"Cutting remarks can sometimes be made by those closest to us — someone we trust and feel safe with — and I want to remember that. Shouldn't a friend be given the same compassionate understanding as a pet? Just as I wouldn't think of getting rid of Gato because he hurt me, neither should I immediately react by getting rid of a friend."

Jerry nodded as he gave in and took the doughnut.

"Rather than taking offense," I continued, "wouldn't it be better to learn what prompted their out-of-character action? Maybe their response was due to something totally unrelated to us, and they simply reacted out of fear, insecurity or pent-up frustration — by lashing out at whoever was the nearest."

Setting down his cup, Jerry reached for my hand and clasped it gently. "You mean like the other day when everything had gone wrong at the office, and I came home and rudely lashed out at you? Oh, I know I later apologized, but it had to have cut you deeply at the time — it was so unlike me," he said, eyes watering. Releasing my hand, he took my arm and gently caressed the scar. With a boyish grin, he said, "I noticed how you looked at your scar after my inconsiderate comment, and I wondered why — after all, it was healed. You never retaliated or lashed back at me in response, but the tears in your eyes said it all. Now I know why."

That was decades ago, and since that time both Gato and my husband have passed on. But just as I wished, my scar still remains. I thank God that although it has faded, it is still visible. It is an ever-present reminder that validates an old proverb, "A friend loves at all times."

And since I am a friend lover as well as a cat lover, it helps me to resist the temptation to kill a friendship over a self-defensive swipe or an unintentional wound.

~Kitty Chappell

70

Mother Love

Fun fact: In order to be fertile, cats require at least ten hours of light a day.

From the moment a child enters the world, the mother knows she will do whatever it takes to protect her child—even giving her life if she is called upon to do so. One of the strongest and most courageous examples of Mother Love I ever saw was demonstrated, brilliantly, by our feral cat, Miss Henrietta. It happened a number of years ago. Our family of four resided in the old McClew farmhouse in the small town of Burt, New York, three miles south of the Lake Ontario shore.

Along with purchasing the 125-year-old farmhouse and orchards, we inherited a beautiful, golden-colored German Shepherd named Sandy and two female barn cats. I became especially attached to the beautiful, black-and-white feral I came to call Miss Henrietta. Our other cat, Matilda, was much more aloof than Henrietta and not at all interested in any kind of relationship with us.

We were told Matilda and Henrietta had lived outdoors all their lives. They were used to being on their own. However, we still provided them with daily food and water, and also took them to the vet for checkups and vaccinations. They more than earned their keep by helping to control the rodent population in our barn, certainly a greener alternative than using toxic poisons.

Both cats had minds of their own. Each knew exactly what she wanted and what she did not want. For example, I was certain that friendlier Henrietta would want to live inside our cozy farmhouse, but I was wrong. She had no interest in staying in our home and let us know that. When I brought her inside to feed her, she would hightail it out the kitchen door if someone opened it, not even finishing her meal. She did, however, accept us fixing up a warm and cozy home for her on the second floor of our barn.

When my small boys, Chrissy and Timmy, were outside with me, Miss Henrietta purred when she saw the three of us coming toward her and often followed us on our excursions around the farm. I took those soft, soothing sounds as a greeting — like she was saying to us, "Hello, happy to see you again." One day, she surprised us all with a gift — a frog she had caught near our pond. I broke into a big smile, realizing this was a sure sign she was becoming fond of us. After all, you only give gifts to those dearest to you.

One day, this independent feline finally let us pet her — a real breakthrough. She actually seemed to like our affectionate behavior. However, if a relative or friend came for a visit, Miss Henrietta was nowhere in sight. She only responded favorably to our little family — no one else.

I have so many happy memories from our five years on the farm. I learned many lessons about country living, as well as life lessons from our farm animals. One of those "animal lessons" happened during a short period when we had auctions. People would drop off articles they wanted to sell, and we would keep everything in our barn until there were enough items collected to warrant an auction. We would then hire an auctioneer and make all the arrangements necessary for a successful event.

I remember one particular auction that turned out to be the largest sale we had at the farm. People came from as far away as Kansas. My husband and I, of course, wanted everything to run smoothly.

The Friday before the big Sunday afternoon event was a beautiful, sunny day. My boys and I were outdoors having a grand time exploring the farm grounds. I heard a truck pull up in our driveway and immediately recognized our neighbor, Doug Bottom, who was bringing over last-minute auction goods.

Doug had brought a friend along to assist with the unloading. My boys and I quit our exploring to watch what was happening. We noticed Doug's two German Shepherd dogs had come along. They were beautiful, lively dogs, running all over the place and exploring the new surroundings.

Miss Henrietta had just given birth to four adorable kittens. The birthing had taken place in her warm, safe living area on the second floor of the barn. Mama cat was extremely protective of these little ones, as well she should be. And though she would let our family near her new babies, she did not want anyone else hanging around them.

When I saw one of Doug's dogs begin to race up the barn steps to the second floor, I immediately thought of the kittens' safety. I started running in the direction of the stairs, but Miss Henrietta was well ahead of me. She had already sensed the possibility of danger to her little ones and was now in "protect" — or should I say "attack"— mode. To Henrietta, those two words meant the same thing.

That fierce mother cat, about one-eighth the size of one of those dogs, hurtled down the stairs, two at a time, screeching loudly and looking quite ferocious. Miss Henrietta leaped onto the back of the intruding dog, burying her claws deeply into the shocked animal. Our German Shepherd visitor, now scared to death, howled in pain. Before you could say "lickety-split," both of Doug's dogs were speeding back to the safety of his truck. Once Henrietta saw the danger had passed, she went back to tending her babies.

Henrietta in action was something I will always remember. Because her babies were in danger, no mountains were too high to cross, no oceans were too deep to swim, and no German Shepherd was too powerful to tackle.

I never really understood that kind of protective love until I became a mom. Once that happened, I knew I would put my life on the line to keep my children safe and protected. It is just what mothers do, like courageous Miss Henrietta, our beautiful black-and-white mama cat.

~Kay Johnson-Gentile

71

Healing Heartache

*Fun fact: According to the Delta Society, the presence
of an animal produces positive results in safety, self-
esteem and in dealing with loneliness and depression.*

The guy I was interested in fell for a nun instead of me. When I first heard the news, I called an old boyfriend who I could depend on. I cried, "Now I'm losing guys to nuns! These women aren't even trying!" He responded with all the compliments I needed to assuage my humiliation, but his true opinion on the matter manifested in a package he sent to me three days later containing a calendar called "Nuns Having Fun" and a note that read simply, "Hahahaha! Nuns really DO have all the fun!" The vintage photos on the calendar showed nuns on roller coasters, nuns doing tricks on bikes, and nuns having more fun than I'd had while dating in my thirties. These were single women the world didn't pressure into finding love or living a fairy tale, and they were happy.

I decided to move out of my apartment and into an actual house, one where I could set down roots and redefine my version of "happily ever after." I found a sweet, historical home previously occupied by an elderly couple. The wife had died, and the old man wanted to live near his children, but he would have to leave one thing behind. "Will you please take good care of my cat?" he asked. "She's spayed and doesn't need anything but food and some attention now and again. It would mean so much to me if you could take care of her." His eyes were so earnest, I couldn't say no. I had never owned a cat, but I understood his broken heart. I told him I would pamper her. He smiled, then said, "Well, if you're a woman living alone, you'll need a good cat. Her name is Ms. Thang, you know, like slang for 'thing.'"

My first act as the owner of this gray fluffy creature was to change her name to Edie. She responded with approval to the new name with my first pop of a cat-food can. Edie ate her food like a lady, and then spread out like an odalisque on the patio table. Then the others appeared.

The neighborhood cats apparently received a newsletter stating that a single woman had moved in and was serving posh food to all the other singles. They descended on my house and hung around as long as Edie let them. Regardless of the number of cats that came and went, it remained her territory. Even the neighborhood dogs respected the invisible boundaries. Edie regally sat on my porch railing, presiding over the yard. She never left the property — after all, she wasn't seeking a mate and had no need to do anything other than hang out and be free. I understood this and found myself adopting a similar lifestyle. I shopped for books, went to movies, and had no obligations to anyone. It was glorious.

Together, we formed a daily routine with minimal effort, even as my house became a revolving door to friends visiting for summer beach weekends, including Andrew, a friend who came into town for a few job interviews. We had agreed that he could stay and share the rent if any of them worked out. Before he arrived, several people asked if I had romantic prospects with Andrew, which I always denied. I had known him for years, but the timing was never right for us, and we remained comfortable friends. Lots of my girlfriends had crushes on him. He was handsome, freakishly smart and had the sort of wit that made you wonder why Jon Stewart hadn't yet discovered him. He was everything I should have wanted, but I can be guilty of missing the obvious at times.

Two days after Andrew arrived, a hurricane developed in the Gulf that seemed to be on a direct path to my town. Rather than leave, he climbed on my roof to check the durability of my shingles. He also checked the sewage lines, the storm shutters and our cars in case we needed to leave town. He went to the store to buy supplies. When he got back, his mother called to try and convince him to leave.

Andrew was in the kitchen, but I could hear him say, "Mom, I know you're worried, but I'm not going to leave her. If it becomes clear that we need to leave, then I'll help her with that, too, but I have to make sure she's okay through this." He loved me and had patiently waited for the right time for us. More importantly, he knew I was beyond the fantasies of dating life and spared me the discomfort of wooing me with sappy songs or deep thoughts on Dostoyevsky. Instead, he demonstrated an ability to share my life as couples really lived, completely committed to each other despite potential storms.

I walked over to help with the supplies and found that he had purchased enough provisions for Edie to survive Armageddon. I reached for a can of cat food and smiled. It was the posh kind.

"Andrew, we're getting married, aren't we?" I said.

He looked at me and smiled. "I hope so."

Fortune was on our side, and the storm never came. We married the next year, and Edie remained a fixture at our house long after the birth of our son. She was sitting on the porch with us when we got word that Andrew had a new opportunity that would move us out of town. Edie had become frail that year and she quietly disappeared before we started packing. She had seen me through the aftermath of heartache and helped me learn to embrace myself before I embraced anyone else, and I am a better wife and mother for it.

~Tanya Estes

72

Angel Kitten

*Fun fact: Some cats seem to have an uncanny ability
to know when a person is near death, and will lie with
him or her to provide comfort.*

"Yes, Darren, I agree he is adorable, but the last thing we need right now is a new kitten."

Our son and his girlfriend had come to visit my terminally ill husband, who was in his final stages of metastatic prostate cancer. On their way out to our place, they had stopped at the feed store to buy dog food and were drawn to the tiny rescue kitten. They couldn't resist his pleading eyes, but, more importantly, they believed he would be a comfort to my ailing husband.

We had moved Larry's bed to the living room so everyone could be together when the kids and other visitors stopped by. I didn't want him to miss out on a single thing during these final days.

Thus, he overhead my comment to Darren, and responded in his weak, toneless voice, "Honey, I think we should keep him."

Knowing my husband like I did, I knew exactly what he was thinking — the kitten would be a comforting companion for me after he was gone. He was not particularly fond of cats, so I wasn't about to let him make this sacrifice for me.

But Darren wasn't about to give up.

"Mom, he shouldn't be any problem. We bought everything he'll need. There's a bag of kitten food, litter and a litter box out in the car.

Why don't you give him a try? If you don't think he's a good fit for you guys, Dawn and I will keep him."

He was pretty adorable, especially when he looked up at me with those big, soulful eyes. I picked him up. He was as soft as silk, and had the most soothing purr I'd ever heard.

"Hon, are you sure he won't be a nuisance to you?" I queried my husband one more time. He was in a lot of pain, so even a pet as small as the kitten could be troublesome.

Larry held out his thin, unsteady hands, and I gently placed the kitten in them. When he clutched the furry, black-and-gray bundle to his chest, I had my answer — we owned a kitten.

The kids and grandkids loved our new pet. Although he was pleasant to everyone, he was absolutely devoted to Larry. When Jacqui, our daughter, first observed the bond between her father and the kitten, she was in awe — so much so that she bought a little red collar for the kitten with his new name engraved on the tag. From that day forward, he was called Little Larry.

Little Larry left my husband's side only to eat and use the litter box. If someone picked him up, he became restless after a few moments and jumped right back on Larry's bed. He didn't just lie at the foot of the bed; he had to be touching Larry at all times. He preferred to be snuggled up on his chest or resting his head on my husband's frail shoulder.

There was something almost mystical about the bond they shared. Everyone, including the grandchildren, learned to respect and admire their closeness and didn't attempt to separate them for even a moment. It was understood that Little Larry's mission was to be there to comfort and support Grandpa.

About six weeks after the kitten's arrival, Larry passed away peacefully, surrounded by our five children. Our faithful little kitten remained at his side until his very last breath, imparting comfort not only to Larry, but to the rest of us as well.

Strangely, we never saw the kitten again after the night Larry died. It was as if he had accompanied my husband's heaven-bound spirit on its final journey. I know Little Larry was more than just a kitten. Maybe, just maybe, angels come to us in our time of need disguised as little, furry bundles of love.

~Connie Kaseweter Pullen

73

Biofeedback Cat

*Fun fact: Studies have shown that people can reduce
their chances of a heart attack by having a cat.*

Fear-induced aggression. That is what the veterinarian and
animal behaviorist called it. Finally, we had a name to
describe what could turn my otherwise affectionate cat
into a tormented beast.

I first noticed there was a problem when Mindy was a few months
old. Arriving home from work, I dropped a bag of groceries and cans
crashed to the floor. Mindy, who had met me at the door, now cowered
behind the kitchen table. Not thinking too much of it, I reached out a
hand to pet and reassure her. The yowl that arose was unlike anything
I had ever heard before. I froze. The possibility of being attacked by
my own cat was suddenly very real.

I snatched my hand back and quickly retreated. Minutes later, I was
making supper when a long tail looking like a bottlebrush appeared in
the doorway. I backed away cautiously, but my fears were unfounded.
The little cat started purring and rubbing her silver-gray head against
my ankles.

I was puzzled but pleased at the change in her attitude. Later I sat
down at my piano, and as the music filled the house, Mindy stretched
her little body, no longer arched in defence, and closed her eyes. We
ended the evening on a happy note.

As weeks went by, I observed her more carefully and discovered that she over-reacted to sudden noises and movements. Simple things, like dropping the TV remote or someone knocking loudly on the door, would bring on a reaction of the now-familiar threatening growls. These often escalated to bloodcurdling yowls, which could make the hairs on a person's neck stand up.

Contradictory as it may sound, Mindy was affectionate and tolerant between such episodes. She'd calmly sprawl on her back while I clipped her nails. She loved baths and enjoyed the hair dryer afterward. She was fond of riding in the car, and we travelled many miles together.

As I started to piece together this tangled web of Mindy's psyche, I realized that my pet often reacted to my own stress level: my frustration and anger when I dropped the groceries, my startled reaction to an unexpected knock on the door. I realized that I had to find a way to deal with rude drivers and work stress before I got home, because Mindy would tune in to my own emotions. If I was sad or feeling discouraged, she would jump on my lap and pat my face with that big, fluffy paw as if to console me. And on the days when I did not want to be bothered, she'd lie at a distance and respect my need for space.

I turned to the Internet for information to understand my cat better and was soon participating in a study led by a group of researchers in the United States. The result? The relationship between Mindy and me was a classic example of "twinship." The research paper said, "In the study, twinship was represented in animals described as being very adept at reading body language and external cues, along with being very focused on their human companions. Therefore, it would often seem like they were capable of being able to 'read minds.'"

Other cats I had owned over the years seemed oblivious to the fact when I was working on something and did not need, or want, a cat sprawled on my papers. But Mindy always knew. Whether she read my mind or discerned my body language matters little. What mattered was that she was an extremely perceptive cat with extremely poor coping skills.

And I was to make another discovery. When I played the piano, Mindy would often wander out from her latest favorite spot to sleep and lie near me. I noticed that her tail would gently flick in time to the music — my personal metronome. I was not a good player by any stretch, and Mindy had an aversion to my incorrect notes. When I made a mistake, her tail swishing increased in a rapid, agitated manner that had no musical timing. At first, I assumed it was my imagination, but even my piano teacher reached a point where she just shook her head in disbelief and admitted that it was too predictable to be merely coincidental.

One year, I was preparing for Christmas, and in my haste to decorate my tree, I knocked over a vase while grabbing a box of ornaments, which clattered on the tiled hearth of the fireplace. The noise startled Mindy, and she took her predictable pose — arching her back and swaying on her hind legs. Growling and hissing followed as she was focused on me, the enemy. I was tired and frustrated. I had invited friends over for drinks, and I did not have time for this! Somehow, I managed to remind myself that it was Christmas, and if I should ever have tolerance, it should be now.

I sat down on the piano bench to play some Christmas carols. I fumbled through a couple of songs and then settled on "Away in a Manager." By the third verse of the song, Mindy was lying by the piano, swishing her tail gently, and a feeling of calmness descended. Then it hit me: Mindy not only liked piano music; it had a soothing effect on her. A more profound revelation was that it had a calming effect on me, as well. From that point forward, I found I could avert her aggression or rapidly bring it to a close by playing the piano. "Away in a Manger" had a particularly consoling effect on Mindy. Fortunately, the carol was easy to play, and I played it almost perfectly. Since she seemed quite conscious of the errors in my playing, the smooth flow was probably the biggest factor in her serenity. But whatever the reason, it became "our song."

My relationship with Mindy spanned more than eighteen years. They were not easy years, and there were plenty of ups and downs. But I learned so much about myself from that cat. She became my stress barometer. I could assess my own stress level by Mindy's reaction. She taught me to leave my cares outside, and that sometimes, "Away in a Manger" played in July is just what a person (and a cat) needs.

~Brenda Leppington

A Tiger-Sized Heart

Fun fact: The biggest cat in the wild is the Siberian Tiger, which may grow to more than twelve feet in length.

He was the ugliest cat I'd ever seen, a young black-and-brown Tabby, so skinny I could count his ribs. One ear was ragged and matted with dried blood, like he'd been in a fight and lost. He probably had fleas and ticks.

Why did he have to show up on my patio? Why couldn't he have gone to the neighbor's house instead?

I decided to ignore him. He would leave, off to find another home. Or so I hoped.

I should have known better.

We live in the country and people seem to think country folks are just waiting for their throwaways. Over the years, my husband, Jack, and I took in many dogs and cats. We loved them all. At the present time, however, I did not want another cat. I had my calico that also had showed up on the patio a couple years earlier. One cat was enough, one too many in Jack's opinion. He wasn't a big fan of the feline family and only tolerated Patches because I loved her.

As if sensing me watching him, the cat peered through the sliding glass door. Maybe it was his droopy ear. Maybe it was the sadness in his eyes. I'm not sure, but at that moment, in spite of my reluctance to take in another stray, the cat won my heart. How could I send him away to face coyotes, wild dogs, and whatever else roamed the countryside?

"Okay, you can stay, Tiger," I told him through the glass door. "You'll be an outside cat, though. Understand?" Wait? Had I called him "Tiger?" Yeah, I had. So Tiger became his name, and the patio became his home, briefly.

He was shy at first. When I went outside to feed him, he kept his distance. It was summertime and hot, so I put soft towels in a large box and set it in a corner of the patio where there was shade. Even though he had a huge back yard with grass and trees that provided shade, he seldom left the patio. A week or so after Tiger first showed up, something happened that changed my mind about him coming into the house.

I was sleeping soundly when horrible hisses and rumbles and meows woke me up. At first I thought I was dreaming. Then I heard growls and screams and knew Tiger was in trouble.

Jack, bless his sleepy heart, grunted and rolled over. A tornado wouldn't wake him, so I didn't even try. I stumbled out of bed, ran to the sliding glass bedroom door that also opened onto the patio, and looked out. I flicked on the light to get a better view. What I saw scared me. A big gray cat, creepy sounds rumbling from its throat, crouched over Tiger, who was lying, unmoving, in the flowerbed.

I hated bullies, and the gray certainly was a bully, or worse. With a screech that probably woke our neighbors two acres away, I ran outside, hissed at the bully cat and chased it into the back yard, where it scrabbled over the fence and disappeared into the dark. From that night on, Tiger lived in the house.

Once he became an indoor cat, I took Tiger to the veterinarian for his shots and treatment of his ear. He also treated Tiger for ear mites and vaccinated him. At first, Tiger was so starved that he ate anything and everything he could get his paws on. I had to put all food out of his reach to keep him from eating too much. Once, he even found the cake on top of the fridge and demolished it.

With love and good food, his fur turned soft and the missing patches grew back. His ear healed, even though eight years later it's still ragged, scarred, and smaller than the other ear. Tiger's physical appearance would win no contests, but he has a beautiful heart.

Tiger became Jack's buddy. He'd crawl onto Jack's lap, rest his paws on Jack's chest, and gaze into his eyes, communicating in his own special way. What amazed me the most was the fact that Jack loved Tiger. He petted Tiger, talked to him and took him on long walks. The two of them would wander down to our pond and watch the fish and ducks. They'd stroll across the pasture, Tiger exploring everything that moved, from insects and small critters to flowers and weeds. The walk was their special time.

In the evenings, they watched TV together, Tiger napping on Jack's chest.

When my husband passed away three years ago, Tiger roamed the house in search of him. He meowed at me, like I should make Jack suddenly appear.

Tiger lost his buddy and walking partner, but he now gives me the pleasure of his company. At night, he curls up in bed next to me, his paw on my shoulder as if to tell me "It's okay." He talks to me in his squeaky little voice. I suspect he's telling me of the times he walked with Jack. We go on walks together. I think he understands me.

Last year Tiger was having trouble breathing, so I took him to the veterinarian for a checkup. The news was bad. He was diagnosed as FIV positive. He either caught the virus in the fight with the gray cat or from the animal that mangled his ear. Right now, he's doing fine. He's not as playful as he once was. He doesn't roll the ball back to me when I roll it to him. He still walks with me and talks to me. Sometimes, if he gets tired, I pick him up and carry him. He's very thin, the way he was in the beginning. But his heart is still filled with love.

One day, Tiger and Jack will walk together again. Tiger will talk to Jack in his soft, squeaky voice. Jack will understand what he's saying.

Until that day, I pray God will let Tiger stay with me a little longer. We still have a lot to talk about on our daily walks: the fish, the flowers, the birds and the insects. Mostly, though, we talk about Jack.

~Beverly Stowe McClure

Therapy Appointment

*Fun fact: Only female calico cats are fertile; males are
few and they are usually sterile.*

"**Y**ou want out again, Marmalade? You were just out.
What, not the back door, you want out the front?" I
was very surprised that our beautiful, long-haired, ten-
year-old calico cat wanted out again.

Several days later, I realized that almost every day she had been
asking to be let out at 1:00 p.m. and always wanted the front door
instead of the back door she normally used to go to the yard. As a
busy housewife and mother, I hadn't been paying much attention, but
I realized this had been going on for a while, and I had no idea why.
Therefore, the next time it happened, I watched out the front room
window to see what Marmalade was doing at one o'clock every day.

"Marm" meandered down the front stairs and out to the city sidewalk — then just sat there. About three minutes later, she flopped
down and rolled over so her belly was showing.

"This is weird," I thought. "She never does that unless she wants
to be petted — but there is no one there." I looked up the street — no
one; I looked down the street — no one. Wait — on the sidewalk just
crossing a block down from our house was a group of about fifteen
young adults from the nearby group home for young adults with Down's
syndrome. They were out for a walk with their chaperone.

As they approached, I could hear, "There's the kitty; there's the
kitty," coming from multiple mouths. When they were close enough

to touch Marm, she lay quietly while each person took a turn petting her. This took quite a while, and obviously these teens were very comfortable petting her and talking to her. When everyone, including the chaperone, had given Marm a petting and a belly rub, she turned over, stood up and gave herself a shake, then meandered back up the sidewalk to the front door where I heard her scratching to be let in. As I opened the door, I watched the group continue on their walk down the street.

It had been a breathtaking experience to see.

The next day, at the same time, I watched it happen again.

After a few more days of this, I needed to find out how long this had been going on, so I went out just as the last few were giving Marm the required petting, and asked the chaperone.

What I was told was both interesting and humbling. Our wonderful cat had been doing this every weekday for months, and these young adults thought it was the highlight of the walk to be able to have a chance to pet her.

How she had come to understand that these young people would enjoy petting her and could trust them, only God knows.

Marmalade had the most loving and caring personality I have ever seen in a cat. She would cuddle any of the family when they felt sad, and she would lick away the tears and purr in their ears until she had made them feel better. To see that she extended that love to others was incredible.

~Shirley K. Stevenson

76

Finding Peace Together

*Fun fact: Cats love their owners just as much as dogs
do; they just don't show it in the same ways.*

"**M**uffins is at your house and safe," read the text from
my friend, Nikki, which came along with a picture
of an orange Tabby perched on one of my kitchen
chairs.

"Great," I thought to myself. "I can only imagine how this is going
to go."

Muffins had belonged to Nikki's horrible neighbor, who left him
outside, barely giving him food or water. The woman had recently
moved away, leaving Muffins to wander the neighborhood to completely
fend for himself. My husband had a co-worker who was looking to
adopt a cat, but couldn't take him in for a few weeks, so we agreed to
foster him in the meantime.

It's not that I didn't feel bad for the little guy. I wanted him to
find a good home. But never having owned a cat in my life, I really
didn't see this going well. I didn't dislike cats, but I couldn't imagine
ever bonding with one like I could a dog. They all just seemed so
arrogant and aloof.

To top it all off, I had still never gotten over losing Berkeley, my
beloved dog who had died almost a year earlier.

When Berkeley was diagnosed with cancer at not quite six years
old, the veterinarian told us it was too aggressive to cure. Instead of
allowing myself to be consumed with sadness, I spent the next four

months using all my energy to make Berkeley's life as wonderful as possible, taking her on countless trips to the dog park and the ice-cream stand. But once the cancer became too much for her and we had to say goodbye to our sweet girl, I suddenly had nothing to do with my grief anymore. I had spent most of the year in a deep depression, angry that she was taken so soon and convinced I had somehow failed her. I would dream of her regularly, and the feel of her downy fur under my fingers always felt so real, that waking up was always a disappointment.

By the time I got home from work the day Nikki dropped off Muffins, he had taken to hiding behind one of the living room chairs. Our dog, Rain, took somewhat of an interest in our new houseguest, but curiosity quickly turned to fear after too many claws-out swats to her nose when she would try to sniff around the chair.

Muffins eventually emerged into the living room. I can't say he was a holy terror, but this cat meowed incessantly, constantly messed up the blinds on our windows and didn't seem to understand that my laptop wasn't meant to be walked across.

Two weeks went by, and we learned that my husband's co-worker was interested in a female cat only. A couple of other leads on a home for Muffins also fell through. By this time, Rain's anxiety caused by this feisty feline was making her physically ill. She had always been a skittish dog, and the fear of constantly wondering if Muffins was waiting around the corner, ready to attack, was taking its toll.

This cat had to go.

Even though I wanted Muffins out of my house in the worst way, I wasn't heartless. I wouldn't take him to the pound or turn him out on the street like his awful first owner, but I was exhausting all efforts by contacting every animal-rescue group in the area, desperately trying to rehome him.

In the meantime, I took Rain to the veterinarian to see if there were any solutions to calm her nerves.

"We are fostering this cat right now until we can find him a home," I told the vet, trying to explain why Rain was so out of sorts.

"Sweetie, he already has a home," the kindly vet responded gently.

"Oh, no," I said. "Absolutely not."

Over the next week, the anxiety medicine prescribed by the vet did seem to help. Rain also started to assert herself, letting out a firm growl whenever Muffins would overstep his bounds.

With Rain steadily turning back into her old self, I guess I began to relax, too. Muffins really wasn't so bad. In fact, he was pretty adorable to watch while he was rolling around on his back with his paws tangling around the string attached to his furry toy mouse. And I have to admit I enjoyed it when he would fall asleep on my chest in the evening when my husband and I were watching television. I couldn't exactly say I loved him, but I had learned to like the little guy.

A few weeks later, Berkeley appeared again in my dreams. Somehow, even in this dream state, I knew it was just a temporary visit. I gathered her in my arms and buried my face in her fur.

"I'm not letting you go, baby," I cried. "Mommy is right here."

When I woke up the next morning, I found Muffins nestled in my arms, looking up at me with his big green eyes. I wiped away my tears and rubbed the top of his head as he purred with contentment.

"Hey, little guy," I whispered. "Mommy is right here."

After that morning, I found I could think of Berkeley and smile instead of cry. Her life may have been short, but it was full of love — something that Muffins' life had lacked for so long.

No one could ever replace Berkeley or change what she meant to me, but I finally realized the same goes for Muffins.

A few months later, when I took Muffins to the vet for some shots, I happily told the doctor that he was right.

This sweet little kitty has found a home.

~Emily Canning-Dean

Cooter

My Very Good, Very Bad Cat

My Hunter Cat

Fun fact: Cats are called "obligate carnivores," which means they must have meat to survive because it has nutrients their bodies need.

77

Neighborhood Cat Burglar

*Fun fact: Bengals, Munchkins, Pixiebobs and
American Bobtails are more likely to be attracted to
shiny objects and steal them.*

Who is three years old and has red hair and extra large toes on his front paws, which aid him in his kleptomania? Our neighbor's cat, fast-fingered Uther Pendragon (named in honor of King Arthur's father) alias Klepto Kitty, has everyone laughing but his owners!

His pet parent, Preston, is an artist who understands creativity, but what his cat does goes way past creativity into the art of criminology. As good parents, Preston and his wife, Barbara, raised their children to be model citizens, but they never expected their cat to become a delinquent and go "a stray," becoming the neighborhood's cat burglar. What led Uther into this life of crime is a mystery.

"This has being going on for years!" laments Barbara with a hint of a smile. "We wake up to various stolen articles — washcloths, tea towels, children's hats, dog toys, lots of socks — but Uther specializes in gloves. After breakfast, he goes back through his cat door and returns with the matching glove to the one he stole before breakfast! He has misappropriated dozens of matching pairs. His thievery is a full-time job!"

"Uther may be smarter than we give him credit for, as none of what he stalks and brings home fights back — so he is never clawed or injured. If a neighbor leaves anything outside that fits into Uther's mouth, he claims it and carries it home. The oddest thing is that when I am gardening and lay down my gloves Uther is not the least bit interested in them."

Their other cat is a shy, innocent black female. Thank goodness she is a "normal" cat and in no way Uther's accomplice. Sometimes, Uther tries to look innocent and blame Natalie for items that mysteriously show up… but we have his number! He can't fool us with those big yellow eyes.

Uther knows about cat doors, so Barbara's greatest fear is that one day her thief is going to expand his territory, house-breaking through neighbors' cat doors. Then what? What if his keen senses help him pull off a daring heist, and he carries home expensive, sparkly items? Then she and Preston might be in legal trouble. Imagine explaining "what the cat dragged in" to a judge and jury!

Uther is a Humane Society rescue. He appeared to be a gem at the time. Little did they know he would grow into a cat burglar. He was neutered as a kitten to stop him from roving after female felines, but how can they stop this kind of extracurricular criminal activity?

Preston sacrificed one of his artist easels to help alleviate the guilt of owning and feeding, i.e. enabling, the neighborhood's cat burglar. Preston attached three crossbars to the easel and glued on a dozen clothespins to display the cat's loot. The easel sits at the end of their driveway, adorned with gloves, socks, and other purr-loined items for the neighbors to retrieve.

"The oddest thing," said Barbara, "is when three understanding neighbors came by to collect items off our 'wall/easel of shame.' They mentioned that, at one time, they too had an orange cat that stole from neighbors!" Do you think the theft gene and his feline-onius behavior is in the orange cat's DNA? If so, it is a good thing Uther was neutered.

The sign above the loot-filled easel reads:

Please retrieve your things.
Our cat collects what you leave out.
He is a Cat Burglar!
Check back often.
SORRY.

Like the rest of our neighbors, we have learned that when things "disappear," we'd better take a walk over to Barbara and Preston's house and check out their easel!

~Mary Ellen Angelscribe

Jupiter, My Not-So-Vegetarian Cat

Fun fact: Even if kittens lose their mothers, who are normally their hunting teachers, they still have a natural instinct to chase and catch fast-moving small items.

I'd never wanted a pet. I worried I'd make a dog unhappy by leaving it locked inside our house alone, or that I'd lose a cat to a coyote. And then I moved to the country. Everyone in our rural neighbourhood had cats or dogs (or both). And all of them seemed to be living a happy, free-range life.

My sons were desperate for a pet of their own — preferably a cat. My excuses for turning them down were endless. How were we going to give attention to a pet when we could barely look after ourselves? What would happen when we went on holiday? Who was going to deal with the litter box?

But the biggest issue was this: How could we feed it meat when we didn't eat it ourselves?

The tipping point came a year after we moved in, the day I pulled a mouse out of my running shoe thinking it was a crumpled-up sock. We'd been overrun with rodents — and their droppings — since the moment we'd arrived in our new home. I'd tried my best to claim our space with a humane trap: a catch-and-release contraption that didn't work at all. I'd actually watched a mouse stroll into it, lap up the peanut butter bait, and then saunter back out smacking its lips.

The mice were winning the battle. We needed an animal on our side. It was either a cat or a hinge trap that would snap the invaders in half. If we were going to stay in the house (moving wasn't really an option), mice were going to have to die. And with relentless logic, my family convinced me it might as well happen as part of the circle of life.

We strapped ourselves into the car and headed for the SPCA, the wide grins on my boys' faces never wavering despite my constant reminders that "I wasn't making any promises." The scene that greeted us was overwhelming — so many creatures cramped into a tiny space that reeked of cat pee and kibble. I had no idea how to care for a pet or what to look for in a cat. But I knew we weren't leaving without one. I had to give one of these animals a home.

"That one's gotta be a good mouser." The SPCA volunteer pointed to a fat tomcat that looked like he could inhale me in one bite. All I could think about was the amount of food — all containing meat, something I hadn't eaten since I'd witnessed the slaughter of my favourite rooster at the age of twelve — he was likely to consume.

"We'll take that one." I motioned toward a petite orange Tabby that was squirming on his back, already delighted to roughhouse with my boys.

"James," the volunteer confirmed over the expressions of delight that exploded from my children's mouths. The cat purred loudly in response to their jubilant hugs.

I fed James — who was promptly renamed "Jupiter James" and then simply "Jupiter" — dry cat food containing free-range chicken. At my children's urging, I got him a few treats as well, but not the stuff Jupiter no doubt wanted most. I could not handle the wet, slimy, fishy-smelling concoctions that came in a tin. I considered vegetarian cat food, but in the end decided against it.

Cats are carnivores. And Jupiter had been welcomed into our home, in part, for his skills as a hunter. Naively, I hoped that just having a cat would keep the mice away — no death necessary.

For the first few weeks, we kept Jupiter — a former stray — inside so he could get to know his new home before he started wandering around our acreage. I referred to him as the kids' pet and encouraged him to sleep in their beds because I wanted them to bond. Plus, I didn't really want to bond with him myself. My excuses — even still — were endless. How could I possibly find time to groom and care for a cat? Why attach myself to a solitary creature that often seemed indifferent to us? Who was going to do all the extra laundry that resulted from a single petting session that left my black pants coated in beige fur?

But my real concern was this: What if something happened to Jupiter when we finally let him loose?

Because the truth was, this little fur ball had already purred his way into my heart. I looked forward to the feel of his whiskers against my bare leg in the morning. I loved the weight of his warm body curled up in my lap as I read. And when he tilted his head in response to my rambling? It was like he was really listening (unlike my human family members).

By the time he was ready to go outside, I'd also convinced myself that my cat was vegetarian. He liked cuddling, not hunting. And he didn't seem too crazy about the chicken. Maybe he really could be satisfied with quinoa and kale (like the rest of my family members). Because really, how could a cute, affectionate cat like Jupiter also be a killer?

It only took two days for him to prove me wrong. That's when the first dead mouse appeared on the doorstep.

With a shudder, I ordered my husband to remove it. And I did not praise Jupiter for the kill, even though I couldn't help feeling flattered. He'd given us a Thanksgiving present. How was he supposed to know that our turkey was made of tofu? The way I saw it (or chose to see it), he'd saved the mouse from the torture of sneaking into our house, discovering its comforts (a warm bed in my box of spare toilet paper; a yummy dinner in my cereal bin), only to be crucified by a snap trap.

After the mouse came the decapitated bird. Then the bunny. Once, Jupiter even took out a baby gopher. Every time he leaves a prize at the door, I know it's there before I even see it. I can tell by the toothy grin on my kitty's face.

By now, I've lost track of Jupiter's gifts. I continue to feed him the chicken — processed beyond recognition — and my husband continues to pick up the carcasses at the back door. I can't say that I'm used to it, but I will say this: I've accepted our differences.

He's a cat. He likes to hunt. And he keeps the mice out of the house, in the woods where they belong. (I try not to think too much about the ones that trespass on his territory — with deadly consequences.)

I'm a vegetarian. But I'm in love with a carnivore, and I can't imagine my life without him. Jupiter: my not-so-vegetarian cat.

~Yolanda Ridge

"It's your lucky day. I just went vegan!"

An Unexpected Guest

Fun fact: The party game called The Vicar's Cat
is a traditional word game played in Britain since
Elizabethan times.

Mrs. Pitt frightened me. Blue hair and stooped shoulders could not diminish the authority she wielded with just a look or word. Meekly, I followed her on a tour of the parsonage as she shared both her wisdom and expectations for the new pastor's wife.

We stopped briefly at the kitchen sink. "See how this shines?" she asked in her sweet southern accent. The gleam of the stainless steel was only slightly less than that in her eyes. "I expect to see it look just like this the next time I come. And I'd better never see any bits of food in the trap." She smiled pleasantly, but I wasn't fooled.

At that most inopportune moment, Kitty rounded the corner with a trill. Mrs. Pitt stiffened. "You know," she stated, "no pastor has ever had an animal in the parsonage before." She wrinkled her nose and sniffed.

"Yes, I know." I shot her my most engaging smile. "I'm so grateful that Kitty has been allowed that great privilege."

Kitty was sixteen, my beloved black cat since I was eight years old. I had pleaded with my husband to ask that he be allowed to come with us to North Carolina, and pity for the new preacher's wife had somehow swayed the parsonage committee to allow him to live with us.

Apparently, that decision was made over the objections of Mrs. Pitt.

Kitty obligingly gave Mrs. Pitt's legs a friendly swish with his tail, and she recoiled. "I don't like cats," she said, stating the obvious. I gave Kitty a gentle shove toward his food dish in the pantry, and he was distracted enough to leave her alone for the moment. Our tour over, Mrs. Pitt marched to her giant Oldsmobile and left, although I didn't believe for a moment that Kitty was truly welcome in the parsonage.

"A cat is always on the wrong side of a closed door." Garrison Keillor's wry observation was proven right. Endless trips to the patio to let Kitty in or out made life tedious, and we surreptitiously replaced a window in the basement with a pet door. I didn't plan to let Mrs. Pitt see it. Kitty was most pleased with his new freedom and explored the nearby woods like the predator he was.

Our first Christmas in the parsonage brought my debut as a hostess. The Women's Missionary Fellowship always had a party at the parsonage, charmingly dubbed a "carry-in dinner." I smiled at the name, unaccustomed to the differences in some terminology in the South. I slipped in the substitute term "potluck" one day, and Mrs. Pitt glowered. I would forever be a hapless Yankee.

Mrs. Pitt's words during our tour rang in my ears as I scrubbed, dusted, and polished everything in sight, especially the sink, before the party. I wanted everything to look perfect. With only minutes to spare before the ladies arrived, my last act was to banish Kitty outdoors. I felt a little twinge of guilt because it was cold, but reasoned that he was used to being outside. He stood at the patio door, meowing and glaring at me, but I shut the blinds.

I shooed my husband out a few minutes later since the party was "ladies only." Giving me a peck on the cheek, he squeezed my hand and whispered, "Good luck."

A few deep, cleansing breaths were all I had time for before the doorbell rang with the arrival of the first guests. The fireplace crackled with warmth, cranberry-scented candles shone, and my Christmas tree was a glowing masterpiece. The ladies toured the entire house, as I knew they would, and I was confident that every square inch was spotless.

Mrs. Pitt's arrival was the cue to begin, and she placed her trademark sweet-potato pie on the buffet table with a flourish. Following a brief prayer, the ladies began to fill their plates and gathered to enjoy the meal.

The parsonage had a large dining room, but there were so many women that a few had to be seated in the living room, balancing their food and drinks on tray tables. Their gentle conversation and kind compliments about the beauty of our home helped me to relax, lulling me into a false sense of security.

In the last-minute rush, I had forgotten to latch the door to the basement. I didn't realize my mistake until I heard a familiar yowl coming up the stairs. I nearly knocked the contents of my tray to the floor as I flew across the room trying to beat Kitty to the door. I was too late.

I screamed when the mouse, still writhing, was dragged across my feet. Kitty ran by me so fast that I missed him when I tried to grab any part of him, even his tail. He trotted into the living room, proud to show off his most recent catch. When he rounded the corner, pandemonium erupted.

Screams echoed from the walls, and women scrambled to climb up onto the furniture. Some women simply froze in fright, forks poised in midair as their brains tried to comprehend what they were seeing. My first instinct was to call for my husband, but then I remembered he had been banished. I was on my own.

Ignoring my fear, I scrambled to grab Kitty, latching onto his furry belly with ferocity. He was so startled that he dropped the mouse, which then wobbled off toward the couch in a last-ditch effort to survive. After a few steps, he fell over, succumbing to his injuries. Perhaps he was just scared to death.

Eerie quiet descended upon the room as every eye turned to Mrs. Pitt. Her expression was inscrutable. I wondered what it would be like to have to be packed and gone before New Year's Day.

The corners of Mrs. Pitt's mouth twitched almost imperceptibly. Instead of a glare, I saw a twinkle in her eye.

"Oh, y'all," she drawled, "just calm down. We said it was a carry-in dinner."

~Rhonda Dragomir

80

Asleep on the Job

Fun fact: Veterinarian and author James Herriot once said, "Cats are the connoisseurs of comfort."

Arriving home from work one day,
I thought I'd find my cats at play.
Instead, I found a quiet house,
A house as silent as a mouse.

Dear Pete was sleeping, safe and sound,
but brother Twink was not around.
I checked in all his usual spots,
but did I see him? I did not.

I found him, finally, asleep on a boot
in the back of a closet. Oh, what a hoot!
His wide body straddled the boot on each side
with his head in the hole as if trying to hide.

My laughter awoke him. He looked up and yawned,
then raced to the kitchen as dinner-thoughts dawned.
I started to follow but heard a strange squeak,
an odd little sound… in a strange little speak!

I picked up the boot, and deep down I spied
a poor frightened mouse cowering inside.
My Twinkie had done what a good cat would do.
He'd chased that wee mouse straight into a shoe!

Unable to reach the mouse deep in the toe,
Twink opted to catnap on top of his foe.
I carried the boot to some shrubs in my yard
and set the mouse free, scared but unscarred.

Gone in a second, it never returned,
and from my cat, Twinkie, that day I learned:
If you can't catch a mouse, then you must guard its trap.
But don't let the hunt interfere with your nap!

~Wendy Hobday Haugh

81

The Moth Hunters

Fun fact: A group of grown cats is known as a "clowder." A group of kittens is called a "kindle."

One evening, after a long day of classes, I was home relaxing and reading in our living room. I had inadvertently let a moth in with me, which flitted about aimlessly. Several of my cats had noticed, and their interest was piqued. It continued to float about, as moths do, but unaware that four hunters sat in a circle below, waiting patiently for it to come closer.

The cats worked in tandem, two calling for the hapless bug, the other two prepared to capture their quarry. Samantha, a plump orange Tabby, and Coco, a Siamese with piercing blue eyes, alternated calling for the bug. Samantha chittered like a mouse might, while Coco caterwauled. Somehow this seemed to entice the moth to glide lower and lower until it was in range of the two designated monster slayers: Sammy and Kitticus. Sammy was a loveable, black-and-white, high-maintenance fluff ball and not a very adept hunter. Kitticus was also black and white, but unlike Sammy he was a wily, patient stalker with a goatee and the attitude of a Roman gladiator.

As the moth flew lower at the beckoning of the two criers, the two hunters waited for it to fly low enough to be captured. This, of course, was where Sammy was not an asset to the team. Each time the moth flew halfway down to them, Sammy would bolt and jump into the air, flailing wildly at the moth and almost never connecting. This would cause the moth to fly high again, forcing the group to repeat the process. Each time, without fail, Sammy would repeat the same error, which engendered dirty looks from his hunting party. At one point, Kitticus, who never jumped early from his position, whacked Sammy several times on the head when an attempted assault caused him to land right on Kitticus's head.

This process went on for ten minutes with the same results every time. It was four cats versus one tiny moth and the moth was winning.

Then Murphy, the fifth cat, entered the room.

Murphy was a unique cat. If Kitticus was a Roman gladiator, then Murphy was the grand champion of the Coliseum. He was a brawler by nature; when one of the other cats did something he didn't like, he would let them know. Most of the cats, except Kitticus, seemed to fear him — keeping their distance and respecting his space. Kitticus would often scrap with Murphy, like some contest for dominance, but would lose every time. You could sense the respect Kitticus had for Murphy.

Murphy was also the most able hunter of all five, despite his long orange hair being a disadvantage. Yet, he seemed to have no interest in the moth. He took in the situation, watching all the cats for a few minutes (after their brief pause upon seeing him, of course). He then jumped up on top of the old-fashioned box television and curled up, watching the peons beneath him continue their attempts to get the moth.

By this point, the moth was about halfway from the doorway to the television, where the king himself was sitting. He yawned and stretched, rolling onto his back in the process. He slung his head over the front of the TV, watching them all upside-down, seemingly amused by their display. The debacle continued, but this time Kitticus nearly snagged the moth because Sammy had finally developed enough patience to let it fly low enough. A few more minutes passed, and the moth now floated in front of the TV, about three or four feet from the screen.

Murphy sat up and watched the moth with an intensity he hadn't exhibited before. Samantha and Coco called for the moth, their mouths watering for this delectable meal they had all spent the last half-hour trying to get. The moth descended as before, with the four waiting patiently below, but this time they would not get their chance. Murphy dove from the top of the TV and caught the moth between his front paws, dragging the poor creature down to earth and crushing it beneath him. Before the other cats could react, he ate it. The look on their faces was priceless! They all seemed so dejected. Here they had expended all this energy trying to hunt the moth, and yet Murphy accomplished it all in seconds while he lounged about almost the entire time.

Samantha walked past him, looking at the ground and dragging her feet like a two-year-old child who doesn't want to go to bed. Sammy hissed at Murphy and went upstairs. Coco complained and complained and complained until Murphy turned and swiped the air near him; that made Coco flee the room. Kitticus sat motionless, staring at Murphy with a look of hatred in his eyes. Murphy locked eyes with him, and the two remained that way for five minutes until Kitticus decided to leave. That was one of the last times they were all together.

Now, several years later, only Kitticus is still around, but that night with the moth has given me a fond memory of each of those special companions and their unique personalities.

~Sean V. Cronin

Shadows

Fun fact: Cats can become addicted to chasing shadows or lights. It's like hunting prey that they'll never catch.

At first, I wasn't sure what my cat, named Kitten, did when she hid herself away in the front hallway. I would peek around the corner and watch as she stared at the bare wall. She sat with her tiny pink nose against the beige drywall, her striped body alert and her brown eyes entranced.

Every night, at roughly the same time, she positioned herself in the hall. Patiently, she would wait. For what, my family and I did not know, until one night when the sound of scraping claws and scampering paws sent us rushing into the hallway. That was the first night we noticed the shadows.

Brilliant golden beams danced across the dark hallway. Kitten trailed them as they billowed along the wall and rolled along the floor. She tried to catch them in her little paws. As excitedly as if she had discovered a new toy, she chased the illuminated shapes until they faded away. Engulfed in darkness once more, she would gape at the spot where the shadows had at one time brightened the hall.

Kitten had come to learn the sound of my mother's car pulling into the driveway every night after work. She knew where to position herself so that the beaming headlights of the minivan would reflect through the front window and create the dazzling light show she anticipated every single night. The sound of a car venturing down the street would send her scurrying to her spot, sometimes just as the last shadow dwindled away.

She waited for the show of shadows as excitedly as a child waits for a fireworks display. Her body was still and unmoving, and not even the prospect of a crunchy treat could pull her away from her favorite spot, lest she miss the first light pass along the wall.

Even as Kitten's playful personality drastically changed, a side effect of the feline leukemia she was born with, her love and excitement for the shadows was a constant. Sometimes, a member of my family would purposely pull in and out of the driveway, just so Kitten would get her nightly light show. My dad liked to flicker the headlights' high beams on and off and on again. Kitten ran and jumped and pounced and followed the silhouettes along the wall as if she herself were dancing with them.

My mom always called home when she was minutes away from our driveway. "Get Kitten ready," she would say.

Kitten's ears would perk up when I would then exclaim: "Kitten! Let's go look at the shadows!"

Together, we raced to the hallway. Kitten took the steps two or three at a time and skated around corners, her paws sliding from beneath her on the linoleum flooring.

Kitten watched the shadows nearly every single night during the short year she was a part of our family. The night before we had to put her to sleep, when the leukemia had rendered her body weak and unmoving, my mother carried her into the hallway, and I turned out the lights all around the house. The street outside the window was dark, with not a car's headlights in sight. My younger brother stuffed a miniature flashlight in his pocket and snuck out through the side door.

Lights and shadows began to flicker and flash all around the hallway. I could see my brother's face through the window, partially hidden in the darkness. He waved the light around and waited patiently. We all did. Kitten could no longer move. She no longer had the strength to stand on her paws, let alone chase the shadows down the long length of the hallway as she once had.

But her eyes, big and bright and as excited as they had been when she first watched the shadows, followed them back and forth.

~Keri Lindenmuth

83

Chasing Butterflies

Fun fact: On average, one pounce in three results in a successful catch for a cat.

KC, our fat Tabby, loves chasing butterflies. Fortunately for them, her enthusiasm far outweighs her skill, and they are never in any real danger. But that doesn't stop KC. Throughout the summer, she crouches patiently and watches for anything that flies past. Some days, she resembles someone watching tennis, with her head bobbing from side to side. When the buddleia are in bloom, the butterflies are in profusion, and then it's hard to get her to come indoors. From her point of view, there are simply too many cat toys fluttering past.

KC is rather chubby, so there is something comical about her trying to flatten herself and move across the garden like a shadow — she generally succeeds at being a moving bump. Then comes the pounce, which shows a cheerful exuberance, as she leaps spread-eagled into the air and lands, looking around in confusion to find the butterfly. The joyful abandonment and total lack of skill in the pounce ensures the butterfly has time to escape, and KC's eyes dart around, seeking her long-escaped prey.

The fact that KC is hopeless at catching butterflies does little to dim her enthusiasm, and she keeps watching, a gleeful picture of a cat totally enthralled in her activity, persisting in spite of constant failure, but having a wonderful time in the process.

Watching her, I realize there is a lot we can learn from her: We can't all be successful at everything, but we can still enjoy trying.

~Denice Penrose

84

The Art of Hunting

Fun fact: Tasmania established a program in 1997 to eradicate feral cats from Macquarie Island because they were decimating endangered seabirds. After removing 2,500 cats, the island was declared cat-free in 2003.

As far back as I can recall, my daughter has had a special connection with animals. I remember a visit to a local zoo when I told Emily, "Look at the monkey." From her three-year-old vantage point, she observed, "That's no monkey, Dad. That's a lemur." Or the time at a farm when a bull rushed the fence and everyone stumbled backwards, except for Emily, who reached out to touch it. She has always had a love for all creatures, just like her mother.

Needless to say, we've had more than our share of pets over the years, everything from mice to turtles to mangy dogs. We had a cat named Kitty who lived with us for more than twenty years. When Kitty died of old age, our family was heartbroken.

A short time later, Emily found a black cat in the hills behind our home. It was a female, skinny and starving, that apparently belonged to no one. Emily brought the cat home, nursed her back to health, and named her Blackjack.

Our new cat got the full treatment — a visit to the vet, a pillow to sack out on, water and food bowls beside her bed, and a daily ration of affection. In return, Blackjack began to supply us with gifts of her own. Sometimes, it was gophers or moles. Other times, it was frogs, chipmunks or bats. We usually ended up chasing them around the house in order to release them back to nature.

One day, Blackjack popped in through an open window next to my computer desk and dropped a green snake onto the keyboard. It coiled, ready to strike. After I peeled myself off the ceiling, I placed the snake in a bag, took it outside and set it free.

Once, in the middle of the night, I got up to go to the bathroom and stepped on something cold, wet and slimy. It was a fish Blackjack had snatched up from a nearby creek. Another time, I came home to find a live shrew scampering around the kitchen table.

I slowly came to appreciate Blackjack's unique gifts and often chuckled to myself over the wide variety of wildlife she caught. There were cicadas and salamanders and centipedes and sparrows, and once even a live woodpecker — so many critters that I started to think she was knocking off pet stores. Happily, most of the animals she brought us were still alive. Blackjack and I became a top-notch catch-and-release team.

For a while, her favorite prey was live moths. Blackjack would step into the house, open her mouth, and out they would fly. It was a sight to behold.

One morning, on the way to school, Emily's younger brother, Tyler, was pulling on his shoes when he shouted so loudly it nearly caused me to career off the road. In the bottom of one shoe was a lizard — a skink.

We kept Blackjack's food bowl full, but that didn't stop her. Hunting was hard-wired into that cat's brain.

One Thanksgiving, her gift was more traditional. Our family was seated around the table when she came in the pet door, dragging something between her front legs. It was a dead rabbit. The scene immediately put me in mind of a cheetah on the African savannah with its fresh kill, and the loud scream coming from my wife verified that.

Blackjack dropped the rabbit beside my chair and stared at me, as if to say, "I didn't want to show up for dinner without bringing something."

A week later, she trapped one of my neighbor's geese under our house. The goose was big, but Blackjack was a strong cat. I heard all the commotion — thumping, wings flapping, hissing, quacking, yowling — coming from beneath the floorboards. Then total silence. I rushed outside just in time to see the goose waddle away, unharmed. A minute later, Blackjack appeared, shaking her head and looking baffled. She had met her match. Our cat never chased waterfowl again.

After that, there was a dry spell. Blackjack took a hunting hiatus. A full month passed. Then one morning she jumped up on the bed with an exciting new gift.

"What's that in Blackjack's mouth?" my wife asked, half-asleep. At that moment, a large rat plopped down onto the sheets and scampered beneath the covers.

We both leaped up, screaming like terrorized citizens in a Japanese monster film. It was, as they say, a pants-wetting experience.

Blackjack had a look on her face like "I think I made a mistake." She pawed around, fished the rat out of our bed and dashed outside with it. I was in Emily's room in seconds, explaining what had happened.

"That's a sign of affection," she replied. "Blackjack thought she was dropping a sack of money on your bed, not a rat."

Cats are known for delivering freshly caught gifts to their human companions. Some people believe it's a form of nurturing, much as other mammals and birds bring food to their offspring. Others say it's because they consider us part of their "pride" and want our approval. Some experts in feline behavior speculate that cats bring us gifts in order to train us. They want to "educate" their owners in the art of hunting.

While those explanations make sense, I'm convinced that Blackjack's motivation was different. I think she brought our family gifts because she wanted to repay us for saving her life.

~Timothy Martin

Reprinted by permission of www.offthemark.com

Fetch

Fun fact: Tortoiseshell describes a coat coloring found almost exclusively in female cats.

KC is a nine-pound, tortoiseshell cat with refined tastes, at least as far as toys are concerned. Most of the cat toys I bought for her lay untouched in a box or on the living room floor. After spending bunches of money on glitter balls, spongy golf balls, catnip-filled frogs made of denim, and other expensive cat baubles that she disdained, I finally hit upon something she actually played with — those three-for-ninety-nine-cents paper mice covered with a thin coat of fur — the ones with the tails made of fuzz-covered faux leather. They came in multiple colors. These three were orange, white, and black.

To my excitement, when I tossed one of the artificial creatures across the room, KC bounded after it. Unlike all the other toys that she sniffed and walked away from, this one she started batting around and pouncing on.

Soon, a game developed between the two of us. The first time it happened, I was watching TV. I felt her familiar head-bump against my shin. Like always, I bent down to scratch her back, but this time I noticed a neon orange mouse at my feet. I tossed it down the hall, and just like a dog, KC went tearing after it. After batting it around for a bit, she brought it back and laid it at my feet. Again I threw it. Again, she chased. My kitty had discovered the game of fetch.

The game soon progressed to another level. Normally when KC felt it was time for me to awaken, she would leap onto the bed and plant herself on my chest, making sure she was the first thing I saw when I opened my eyes. This particular morning, something was a bit different. She walked across my chest and sat next to me. When I sat up, I understood why. Falling from my chest onto my lap was a little white mouse with red felt eyes. KC stared at me expectantly as if I should be able to read her mind. I flung her toy out the bedroom door and down the hall. Digging her back claws into my leg, she used my lap as a springboard, narrowly missing what could have been quite a painful injury to me.

I plopped back onto the bed. Less than a minute later, she pranced back into the bedroom, her favorite toy in her jaws. She leapt onto the bed and dropped the folded paper with only a little fuzz remaining (it hardly resembled a critter anymore) onto my chest. Without sitting up this time, I again threw the orange mouse out the door. Again, she gave chase.

Like most cats, KC enjoys routine. After a week, our game of fetch had become a ritual. Some mornings, I'd wake up to find a mouse on my chest, around my feet or next to me. Sometimes, I'd have to do a little searching and find it in a fold of the bed sheets. Usually after the third round of toss-and-retrieve, she'd get lazy, and I'd find it on the floor next to the bed.

One morning, I was woken as usual by paws walking across my chest. As KC passed, she dropped her toy onto the bridge of my nose. In a semiconscious state, I picked up her toy, ready to fling it out the door, but something was off. This was a little bit heavier, and the fur felt way too soft. I opened my eyes, and realization struck. This was not a toy. Nor was it inert. A live mouse twitched in my fingers.

Normally, I am not all that squeamish, especially around mice, but the shock and surprise made me hurl that mouse harder and faster than any toy. Of course, KC tore after it.

As I sat on the edge of my bed, waiting for my heartbeat to return to something close to normal, KC pranced back in and dropped the mouse, now dead, at my feet. I didn't know if it was the cat that finally did it in, or my throw, but two things I knew for certain: One, I had mice in the house, and two, my little kitty was a darn good hunter.

~David Fingerman

86

An Embarrassment of Riches

Not-so-fun fact: Raptors, predatory birds, have been known to attack, injure, and even kill cats left outdoors unattended.

I cringed when I caught sight of Henry, my large-and-in-charge orange Tabby, emerging from the tall grass. He had something hairy, scary, and disturbingly rodent-like in his mouth. "Oh, goody," I grumbled to myself, bracing for the inevitable. It would seem that Henry was bringing me another of his gifts.

My magnanimous Henry was a pound cat for the first ten months of his life, but you'd never guess it from his imperious airs. He wasn't named after any historical monarch either, but he turned out to be a bit of a tyrant just the same. Henry is the king of the castle and ruler of all surrounding territories, which includes our back yard and the large, vermin-inhabited field just beyond it. The poor resident critters will forever rue the day that Henry moved in. Their feeble attempts to hide are no match for his sublime patience and stealth.

Through the kitchen window, I watched Henry prance toward the house with his glorious catch. Then he noticed the dog, Jed, and slowed his pace a bit. Changing course, he detoured past the dog, shamelessly flaunting the evidence of his superior hunting skills. He sashayed back and forth, his head held so high I wondered how he could see where he was going. The dog, for his part, actually seemed impressed. Instead of indulging in his customary game of chase-the-cat, Jed stood at attention and just let his feline friend strut his stuff.

Finally satisfied, Henry turned and headed for the house, big fuzzy rodent in full view. It was now my turn to step up and get what was coming to me… literally. But Henry's gift never made it that far.

Out of nowhere, a dark shadow appeared in the sky, rapidly gaining on the unsuspecting cat. An opportunistic raven had spotted a chance for an easy meal and, in true raven mode, he wasn't about to let this one slip away. He swooped in from behind, delivering a well-aimed smack to the head with one deft wing. *Thwap!* Henry didn't know what hit him! He yowled and jumped straight into the air, his legs pedaling wildly beneath him. The mouse tumbled from his gaping mouth and was instantly snatched up by the bird. Henry could only watch, dazed and confused, as the crook made off with his precious prize.

Poor Henry! He'd been burgled by a bird! Oh, the shame of it! And what was worse: the whole embarrassing thing had gone down right in front of the dog. If dogs could, Jed would have been laughing like a hyena. As it was, he certainly had one of the biggest doggie smiles I've ever seen. And what did the regal Henry do in his moment of mortification? Did he lose face, feel small, eat crow? Not Henry. He just plopped down on his roly-poly rump and started to groom himself. I guess he figured, if you're going to look bad, you might as well look good doing it.

~Emily Johnsen

87

The One That Got Away

*Fun fact: When it hunts, a cat's most highly refined
sense is its vision.*

Dawn had barely broken when sudden thumping noises, followed by shrill chirping, woke me from a deep sleep. Instinctively, my critter-radar engaged. I knew some creature that shouldn't be inside my house was huddled on the floor just beyond my husband's side of the bed. But early-rising Chuck had already left for work, leaving me to face the interloper on my own.

Gradually, as sporadic thumps and squeaks continued, my foggy brain detected the soft jingle of our male cat's bell-studded collar. After rescuing Hector from a farm as a kitten, we quickly discovered his hunting skills were top-notch. And, just as quickly, we invested in colorful, snap-on, jingle-bell collars to give the woodland varmints and birds a fighting chance.

"He's a herder," our neighbor informed me when I complained of Hector's propensity for nudging an animal long distances before taking its life. Our neighbor promptly nicknamed him Killer. Much as I detested Hector's pastime, I grudgingly admitted that the moniker fit.

Over time, our savvy kitten learned to stalk his prey in silent, snakelike fashion. But that particular morning in my bedroom, Hector's enthusiasm for the game obviously overrode his desire for stealth. Although I couldn't identify the victim by its chirp, its unnervingly high-pitched squeal led me to suspect the critter was very small. Peering over the edge of the bed, I tried to see what it was. But the room was dark, my vision was blurry, and my glasses were downstairs on a kitchen windowsill. Squinting, I barely made out a tiny glob on the rug. A baby mouse, perhaps? A giant bug?

Groaning, I rolled back in bed to consider my options. I knew how this game played out. At the moment, Hector was reveling in the fact that he was worrying the critter right under my nose. But the minute I made a move to rescue it, he'd clamp down hard and run away, ending its fragile life in an instant. I was surprised the creature wasn't history already. With deep regret, I decided to let nature take its course. The poor little guy was probably half-dead. Surely the chirping would soon cease.

It did not.

Finally, I took another tack. Rolling off my side of the mattress, I grabbed a book from the nightstand and warily crept around the bed toward my cat and his prey. Hector, of course, knew exactly what was going down, having seen this ridiculous maneuver countless times in the past. But this time, in his cockiness, he delayed a split second too long before lunging for his prey. And in that split second, I threw the book at his flank, successfully knocking him a few steps sideways, and affording me just enough time to come between him and his quarry. Miffed at his game's interruption, Hector glowered at me from the doorway as I surveyed the tiny brown spot lying, unmoving, on the carpet.

"I should probably just end your suffering," I murmured sadly.

Much as I hated the thought of smooshing it, I also hated the thought of it scurrying off to die somewhere secluded indoors. I'd had enough mice expire in the walls of a prior home to realize that even tiny critters, once defunct, emit a powerful stench.

Still bleary-eyed, I crouched down and retrieved my book. But having never heard this particular kind of chirp before, I was curious to see the strange creature up close before eradicating it. Book in hand, I edged steadily nearer, prepared to strike if it made a run for it. Inches from my target, my eyeballs finally adjusted — and recognition dawned.

"HECTOR HOBDAY HAUGH!" I shrieked, jumping to my feet

and chasing my cat down the hall. "BAD BOY!"

As Killer frantically dove for the stairs, I flew back to my bedroom, flicked on the overhead light, and emitted an exasperated wail. There at my feet lay not a tiny mouse or a giant bug, but one of my son's $2,000 hearing aids.

Apparently, Josh had forgotten to turn his pricey micro-machine off at bedtime. As a result, it sat on a shelf all night, emitting just enough of an intermittent high-pitched squeal to attract the interest of our farm-bred feline. Knocking the hearing aid to the floor, Hector herded it as he would any small animal the full length of the hallway connecting our two bedrooms, eager to show off his latest acquisition.

Although the hearing aid was damaged and required repair, I found it hard to hold a grudge. Hector was just doing what he'd been born to do. Besides, he wasn't the only seasoned hunter on the prowl that morning. Between my cat's sharp ears and my own dull vision, we'd both come dangerously close to destroying the device. Fortunately, the same innate curiosity that drove Hector to stalk that chirp in the first place ultimately compelled me to take an up-close look at the tiny thing before smashing it with my book.

~Wendy Hobday Haugh

Foxy

Chapter 9

My Very Good, Very Bad Cat

My Nanny Cat

Fun fact: Whether you're a "dog person" or a "cat person" usually depends on which pet you had when you were growing up.

88

Worst Cat Ever

Fun fact: Cats love to sleep on their humans' beds and
clothes because they smell like their
favorite people.

"I hate that cat! Elvis peed on my bed!" my son Logan screamed. He stormed into the family room — a stained pillow in one hand, a bunched blanket in the other. The unmistakable stench of cat urine permeated the room.

"Don't say that! He's the best cat ever!" my daughter, Kaitlin, snapped back. She scooped up Elvis, cuddling him against her, his head resting on her shoulder.

I glanced at Kaitlin and sighed. Seriously? I was firmly on Team Logan with this one — that cat was so naughty. But piddling on someone's bed was outrageously wicked — even for Elvis.

"More like the worst cat ever! He's on a pee-spree," taunted Logan.

"Hey, guys, enough. Everybody calm down," I intervened.

"Why does he do that?" demanded Logan.

I could only shrug.

Who knew?

The truth was, we knew very little about Elvis. A year ago, Kaitlin had pleaded, "Can we get him? He's so sweet!" cuddling the large brown Tabby cat snuggled in her arms.

I remembered the Humane Society lady saying sadly, "That's Elvis. He's an 'owner surrender' — they had a new baby, and he wasn't getting along with it."

In my naiveté, I had responded, "That's too bad," looking at my three kids and wondering how anyone could get rid of the family cat just because they had a new baby. Wasn't there enough love for both?

Well, my question was answered shortly after Elvis arrived home with his two cat companions, Mack and Twix. I was certain we had absolutely, without-a-doubt, positively chosen the three most wonderful cats in the world — they were perfect in every way.

For two weeks anyway.

Then the piddle problems began. Mysterious, ghastly-smelling puddles started popping up all over the house with alarming frequency. Initially, it was a mystery who the culprit was, but before long Elvis was caught tinkling on Logan's duffel bag.

I was at my breaking point.

I spent one morning scrubbing all three litter boxes, completely changing out the litter and spraying them with a special, no-odor, cat-loving, end-all-piddle-problems spray. I aired them in the sun. I put fresh mats under the litter boxes. I added a fourth litter box to our collection. And I was almost done. I could practically taste the cup of tea and see the first sentence of my book — a well-deserved break.

"Mom! Elvis peed in my beanbag!" Logan's angry voice ricocheted across the house.

My break vanished — the daydream abruptly ended by the errant bladder of a truly naughty cat.

"No, this cannot be happening — again — still — whatever!" I silently fumed. "Kaitlin! Now I know why Elvis was really at the Humane Society! Problem with the new baby? I'm sure there was — he was probably peeing all over the new baby!" I ranted.

I stalked off to clean Logan's room.

"That cat is never coming in my room again!" Logan proclaimed vehemently.

"Hey, Logan, I have an idea," I said quickly, hoping to defuse Logan's frustration before he erupted.

Logan watched me spread one of Kaitlin's quilts on his bed.

"No way, Mom! A girl quilt — on my bed? That's just wrong!" He was horrified.

"I know, I know." I held up my hand against his protests. "It won't be forever, but maybe, just maybe, it will smell enough like Kaitlin that Elvis will stop targeting your room," I explained.

"Oh, man," Logan groaned, mortified by the bright pink-and-yellow quilt.

"Let's just try it," I suggested, crossing my fingers he'd agree.

It didn't work.

Two years have passed and nothing has worked. I've tried sprays, vinegars, special reach-down-to-the-molecular-level solutions, plastic bags, deterrent fabrics, removing targeted items and, my personal favorite, numerous "there's nothing medically wrong, must be behavioral" vet visits.

But when I am at my wit's end, all I have to do is peek in my daughter's room at night. When I see Elvis curled up tight against her side, on the pink blanket she spreads out just for him, I am reminded of all that really matters.

Honestly, piddle problems, in the grand scheme of life, don't really matter.

Love matters.

Seeing the unconditional love and loyalty shared between that girl and her cat reminds me that love endures far beyond frustrations, anger, and even sheer naughtiness.

Of course, I am still shocked at how incredibly naughty Elvis is — continually.

But I am also shocked at how tremendously devoted and completely inseparable he and Kaitlin are.

Elvis may be the worst cat ever, but I feel truly blessed to have him — some days just not as much as others.

~Elizabeth A. Pickart

89

Chicken Soup
for the Soul.

Co-Parenting

*Fun fact: Some cats have very strong maternal feelings
and will adopt other kittens or even other infant
animal species as their own.*

For what seemed to be the millionth time, my two-year-old ran through the house, crying, "Rosie, Rosie!" Only this time, he added something to it: "Give that back, Rosie!" I peeked out of the kitchen to ask him what was going on, and he told me his kitty had stolen his toy soldier. I found her hiding behind a piece of furniture, quite calmly playing with his soldier and waiting expectantly for him to find her again, for that was what Rosie did. When she wasn't busy trying to convince (in no uncertain terms) her grown kitten to leave the nest, or spending time with her brother, she was taking care of her new kitten, which happened to be my son.

Now, you must understand something: When I say that our cat Rosie officially adopted my son as her new kitten, I mean that she literally and quite effectively adopted him. From the moment my son was brought home from the hospital, Rosie kicked her old kitten to the curb (he was nearly grown) and declared herself surrogate mom to the fascinating newborn. She would attempt to lick him clean, becoming disgruntled and pout when I wouldn't let her; she would jump up to wherever he was when he started crying, checking him over to see what was wrong, then meowing to get my attention if she thought I wasn't being fast enough to take care of her baby; and, as he grew old enough to walk and play, she would spend countless hours trying to coerce him into playing with her, trying to get his attention, or just simply babysitting him when she felt it was needed. I got quite used to such moments as the "stolen soldier" because she would do anything to get him to spend time with her, and she was quite shameless in her attempts.

However, I never fully realized just how much she had laid claim to my son until he was around four years old. My son was going through what some might delicately term the "Ferocious Fours." I forget exactly what it was he had done that day, but I do remember being frustrated and exhausted. He had continued to act out all day, and finally I was forced to grab him by his shoulders and explain to him sternly that he needed to stop or he would get punished. He, of course, was crying, more from the fact that I wasn't going to allow him to continue doing what he wanted than from the fact that I was mad at him.

That wasn't how Rosie interpreted it, though. I could see her out of the corner of my eye begin to pace back and forth, getting closer and closer. She even started meowing. She nearly always meowed when he cried, so I ignored it since I had bigger issues to deal with at the time, namely a wriggling, squirming, rambunctious little boy who wanted to continue creating havoc. As I continued to attempt disciplining my son, she grew closer. Then she did something that I had never known her to do in the six years I'd had her. She darted in and bit me on the arm, then grabbed my sleeve and tried to pull me away from her boy! I yelled out in shock, scaring her enough that she darted away to hide under the table. But it wasn't more than a few seconds before she bravely crept back, meowing and shrinking down to get closer. She needed to check on her crying kitten, and she wasn't about to let me get in the way of that! Sure enough, she finally drew close enough to sniff him all over and lick his face and rub up next to him.

Despite the irritation of having my parenting skills so blatantly questioned, I decided that my "punishment" was probably going to be over for the day, since Rosie had already transitioned my son into giggles and grins with her antics. And she was obviously so upset over her distraught "kitten" that I didn't have the heart to separate the two.

Apparently Rosie's parenting strategy was to never let your kitten cry. Scolding her when she acted that way never did any good because her first and foremost duty was to take care of her kitten, even when she had to risk bad consequences in order to do so. Rosie helped me calm down and gain a different perspective on the situation. So, despite having my own cat bite me and try to yank me away from my son, at the same time she proved just what a good "mom" she was. We started calling Rosie my son's "other mom" after that, for Mom was what she certainly was.

~May Hutchings

90

The Zen of Travel

Fun fact: Cats aren't native to the United States. It's believed that they came to the U.S. in ships hundreds of years ago along with the Europeans who were immigrating.

One spring day, I was cleaning out the garage when I came across my son's old pull-behind bike cart. My heart sank as I glanced over at my five-year-old, who was just on the cusp of outgrowing it. Technically, he could still fit in it, but he was a "big boy" now and much preferred pedaling alongside the family rather than rolling behind as a passenger.

Though it tugged on my mommy heartstrings to part with baby gear and the history that went with it, I told my husband, "Put it in the Goodwill pile... unless," I added with a chuckle, "Barney wants to take a ride in it."

My sons' ears perked up at my silly comment. Barney was our fourteen-pound, long-haired orange Tabby, who had a taste for adventure. Every other kitty I'd ever owned was not what you'd call a thrill seeker. They ran for cover whenever I hauled out the dreaded pet taxi because they knew what that meant — vet or vacation — and they detested both. Not Barney. He was up for going anywhere and doing anything. In fact, I would sometimes find him perched on top of our pink pet carrier, almost as if he were asking us to take him somewhere. And any time we dragged out suitcases, Barney would either crawl inside the luggage or stretch his body on top of it to send a clear message:

"Take me or I'll apply fur to all your outfits, man."

He was a "go kitty" so the boys were convinced he'd like to go biking.

"I'll go get him!" my older son Kyler shrieked.

"I'll help!" my younger son Trevyn said.

"Now, hold on just a second," I said, thinking this through. "A car ride is one thing. He's enclosed and not exposed to loud noises. But biking's a different story."

With so many sounds, smells, and sights to take in, I wondered if he'd feel overwhelmed.

"No, Mom, I promise he'll like this," Kyler said. "Trust me."

The boys ran off and returned to the garage moments later with Barney draped over Kyler's arm. Trevyn unzipped the carrier, and Kyler placed Barney inside. He circled twice the way cats do, then tucked his paws beneath his body. I had to admit, he looked right at home. It was as if this bike carrier was his own personal feline lounge chair.

Trevyn fastened his helmet, climbed on the bicycle, and started pedaling Barney down the road.

I watched from behind and noticed the huge sag on the bottom of the carrier where Barney was lying. Since he had positioned himself on the floor rather than on the seat, there was nothing to support his weight. Given that the material was thin and translucent, sort of like parachute cloth, Barney's bulging body hovered just millimeters from the asphalt.

"Hold up a sec," I hollered to Trevyn. My husband grabbed a board and placed it on the floor of the carrier, providing Barney with a much more comfortable ride.

I got on my bike and rode up alongside Barney to peek inside. I couldn't get over the Zen vibe he was emitting. His eyes half-closed, his head steady, the breeze gently tickling his white whiskers — it was as if he was enjoying a day at the spa.

A few months later, our family headed to our lake cabin in northern Michigan. Of course, Barney joined us. Not surprisingly, the kids decided that their fearless feline was ready for his next outdoor adventure: boating!

I wasn't so sure Barney would be up for this one. The roar of the boat's motor, not to mention other lake noise such as splashing kids, revving jet skis, and quacking ducks, might just be enough to send him over the edge.

"We can try it," I agreed. "But he has to stay in his pet taxi."

Barney's green eyes were bright and wide as he took in the sounds of the seagulls cawing overhead and the waves lapping the shoreline. He quickly turned his head when a neighbor revved his lawnmower. His little pink freckled nostrils went into overdrive when he caught a whiff of campfire smoke.

After situating Barney in his carrier, we flipped on the blower and lowered the boat into the water. Barney's ears momentarily flattened when we started the engine, but the second we backed off the hoist and began bobbing fluidly on the water, he relaxed.

We slowly toured the cove as the boys kept a close eye on their purring passenger. "What do you think, Barns?" they asked.

He offered up two sniffs, a yawn, and a gentle meow before dozing off.

"He likes it!" Trevyn announced.

"Well, of course," Kyler said with a gleam in his eye. "He loves exploring."

I had a hunch that a new question was forming.

"Mom, do we still have that baby backpack we used to carry Trevyn in?" Kyler asked. "Because I have an idea for tomorrow."

~Christy Heitger-Ewing

91

The Cat and His Boy

*Fun fact: A tower in Scotland is named after a cat
named Towser that killed 30,000 mice during
its lifetime.*

My husband rescued our cat, Pete, from the animal shelter and put him in our barn to control the mouse population. Pete stayed there for about fifteen minutes and then walked out of the barn, across the field, under the fence, through the yard and up the steps to our house. He took his place on our front porch, where he would live for the next seventeen years. He would not be told where to sleep or given parameters in which to roam. He could not be contained by the walls of the barn, although my husband tried several times to keep him there.

Pete did not believe he was with us to clear our barn of rodents. Pete had come to reign over our farm from his seat on the welcome mat at our front door.

Being allergic to cats, I kept a distance from Pete. That was fine with him. He was not born to be a lady's lap-sitter. He was a hunter and a protector. Too proud to eat our packaged cat food, Pete hunted his own food.

To prove to us his hunting prowess, he left the spoils of his nightly raids, the hearts and kidneys of our mice and mole enemies, on the welcome mat for us to find in the mornings. It was his way of saying, "I am on the job. No need to worry about things today. I will be watching over the farm while you are out."

From the day Pete joined us, the other animals knew he ruled our place. If they questioned his authority, a quick flick of a claw put them in their places. Pete bowed to only one, our four-year-old son, Peter. (I realize that to name a child Peter and an animal Pete may seem odd, but being lovers of good stories, my husband and I named our son for a character in *The Chronicles of Narnia* and our cat after the barn cat in the *Hank the Cowdog* books.)

It took Cat Pete about a day and a half to realize that if Human Peter was to live to manhood, he needed more than his father and me looking out for him. We had three older children, and Peter tended to get lost in the shuffle. With commiseration and a bit of pity in his eyes, Pete gave me a nod that said, "You've got your hands full. I'll take care of this one." And he stepped in to become Peter's companion.

They developed an unusual friendship. That cat let our young son mistreat him terribly. Any other animal of Pete's nobility would have fled. But with fortitude and indulgence, Pete allowed himself to be caught when Peter chased him around the yard. After getting his hands on the cat, Peter would pick him up by the tail, hang him upside-down by his back legs, and carry him around the yard with his front paws dragging the ground.

Pete never squirmed, fought or clawed his way out of Peter's arms. He just hung there in discomfort, wondering, I'm sure, how many years it would be before Peter outgrew the game. Occasionally, the cat would mew a little. It didn't seem to be a protest aimed at Peter. I felt it was more of a reassurance for me: "It's okay. Don't worry about me. I've got this. Really, I do."

One day, a few months after Pete arrived, I returned home from the grocery store to find our two oldest boys playing basketball in the driveway and Peter watching from the yard. I knew without asking that his brothers had said he could not play with them. Peter followed me onto the front porch and slumped into a rocking chair with a sigh that conveyed a magnitude of four-year-old sadness. Pete jumped into his lap to join him.

I left the two of them there and went inside with my groceries. In just a bit, I began to hear sounds coming from the porch. The pounding of small feet scurrying across the porch was followed by little-boy giggles. Peter was happy again.

The front door flew open, and Peter ran in. "Mama, Mama, come watch me play basketball! Pete and I are playing basketball, Mama!" Peter had gone from mournful to merry in two shakes of a cat's tail. (I feel sure Peter had done the actual tail shaking.) I could have kissed that cat, allergic or not.

I followed Peter out the door, entering into his imaginary basketball game. "Is Pete playing for the other team?" I asked. "Who is winning? You or Pete?"

I expected to see my son chase his cat around the porch with a ball in his hands. Instead, Peter walked to the top of the porch steps, picked up Pete and said, "He isn't on the other team."

"Is he on your team?"

"No, he's not on my team either."

"Then how are you and Pete playing basketball together?"

Hanging upside-down, Pete gave me an indignant glare that said, "You are going to owe me big time for this one!"

"Pete isn't a ball player, Mom," my son said with a big smile. "He's the ball!" Then, as I watched in amazement, that regal, proud, fierce, wonderful cat closed his eyes and let my son roll his body into a ball and pitch him off the porch.

~Leigh Ann Northcutt

92

Mother's Helper

Fun fact: Polydactyl cats, most commonly found in eastern North America and the UK, have up to eight toes on each paw versus five on front paws and four on hind paws.

Kiki the cat only had to yowl once for me to know the kittens must be on their way. Missy, my Border Collie-Greyhound mix, followed us into the tiny, downstairs bathroom where I'd prepared a box for the blessed event. Being Kiki's first litter, I expected her to be nervous. What I didn't expect was Missy's furious whining and tail wagging.

When the kittens finally started coming, the dog calmed down. Missy and I just sat there marveling at the miracle of birth. The dog appeared mesmerized by the six tiny fur balls. And her fascination didn't end there.

The following morning I awoke to something warm and sticky on my neck. Missy had brought the kittens upstairs to me. Kiki hovered nearby, but didn't seem to object. That wasn't the last time Missy transferred the kittens to my bed. She wouldn't leave those babies alone! And, of course, she always snatched them up when I wasn't looking. "Bad dog!" I kept saying. But she didn't care.

When the kittens were a little older, all six of them, Kiki, Missy, my husband and I sloshed around on our waterbed every night. During the day, Missy continued carrying the kittens around by the nape of the neck, often hiding them behind the couch. Sometimes she'd deposit them near the sliding doors in the sun so they'd be warm and cozy. And, of course, she kept placing them on the bed for the afternoon nap she took with them.

Then Missy did the unthinkable. She stretched out on the living room carpet more than once, and then nosed the kittens into her belly. She made believe they were nursing! She did this time and again, always panting as if nursing was hard work. Apparently, Missy felt the kittens belonged to her. And they might as well have! She continuously snatched them from their bewildered mom. We sometimes feared she might hurt them, but she never did.

Missy was a loving dog in other ways too. She was a real nurturer, tuned in emotionally to anyone around her. A grief group convened at my home regularly and Missy got to know the women well. Once, when one of them burst into tears, Missy quickly reached her side, and licked her tears away. She then put her head in the woman's lap.

Eventually, we found homes for all but one kitten, Missy's favorite, whose name was Paws. He was a polydactyl like his mother. Missy continued to carry Paws around in her mouth even as he grew larger.

When Paws disappeared, we looked everywhere. During the first few days of his absence, Missy whined and spent her time in the tiny, downstairs bathroom where she'd watched Paws come into the world. But when he didn't turn up, she eventually dealt with her grief and re-directed her efforts toward terrorizing Kiki.

We never had more kittens, but sometimes I asked my husband, "Do you think we should let Missy have her own litter?"

"No. I think this was her first and last mothering experience!" was his response.

And so it was. But it endeared her that much more to me.

~Jill Davis

93

Foster Cats

*Fun fact: Persian cats may have originated in Persia
(Iran), living in mountainous areas. Their signature
long hair is natural, while their flat faces are the result
of selective breeding.*

It all started with a dramatic change in our kitty litter's quality. The litter no longer "hid" the cats' urine smell, not even for a day. The smell knocked us over! Also, we were concerned that one or several of our five cats had a bad bladder infection, so we were giving them all a homeopathic remedy for irritable bladders. No matter how much we tried to help the cats, though, the litter continued to admit a noxious odor.

Then the house rule was broken: urine was showing up, mysteriously, anonymously, on the floor beside the litter. We thought that the cats must hate the litter odor as much as we did, so they were protesting on the floor, or that the infection had advanced and the sick cat or cats were trying to show us the problem. We could not pinpoint the offender, though, so we were talking about purchasing a motion detector camera to catch them in the act.

We changed litter. We even bit the bullet and bought a more expensive brand. But it, too, almost immediately took on the disgusting overwhelming odor that consumed an entire room.

We had been doing just fine with our five cats despite the fact that they were on the older side. Miss Wings, a Shaded Silver Persian and her eleven-year-old triplets, Nymbus, Myster E., and Whyspurr, had never had urinary problems before. Even our newest rescue, a senior Himalayan named Mini Purrl, was doing fine.

The mystery remained unsolved, until one day, while I was quietly watching TV. Myster E. casually approached the TV, sat in front of the glass unit that houses the DVD player, and calmly peered into it like he was enjoying a TV show.

"How cute," I thought. "He must see his mother hiding in there looking back out at him." Because it was a hot day, I did not want her to get to hot sitting on the components, so I opened the glass doors to retrieve her from her now not-so-secret hiding place.

What happened next sent me screaming out of the room! As I peered, without my glasses, into the dark space I wondered why Miss Wings' eyes were so small. Persians are known for their large eyes, and hers are huge. Then I looked at her nose. Persians' faces and noses are much flatter than most cats. So, why was her face suddenly elongated like a Siamese? The moment was surreal, like when Little Red Riding Hood says to the wolf, "My what a long nose you have," not realizing it was not her grandmother.

My brain came into focus! I was not looking at a little white cat. I was face-to-face with an unblinking, beady-eyed, white baby opossum, and he was staring back at me! I am not sure which of us was more scared!

Maybe it was me, because while the visitor remained snuggled on top of the DVD player, I ran from the room hollering for my husband. He thought I was nuts when I said (rather hysterically), "There is an opossum under the TV." It takes a while for the brain to process that.

We cordoned off the living room with boxes, making a direct pathway out the front door. Then my hero "helped" the unwelcome houseguest flee our home.

Now the kitty litter smell was making sense! We had been blaming the litter's quality and our innocent kitties! Apparently, the cats had not been breaking our much coveted house rule by tinkling on the floor. This hapless rodent had taken up residence here for several weeks and had been using the cat litter for most of the time.

The best we can surmise was the opossum was feasting on the

fallen apples off the backyard tree, and because of his small size he was able to squeeze through the Cat Castle (outside enclosure) wire and enter our home through the cat door. Our five cats, thinking this poor new albino baby "thing", with no fur on its long-skinny tail, was another one of our many fosters, gave him a royal welcome. They didn't chase it, hunt it, or even meow at it. It was only by Myster E. sitting placidly and silently in front of the glass doors watching it that we were alerted to the "new friend."

We had falsely blamed our cats, who were just doing their own kind of fostering, following our example. That night we served them their favorite homemade chicken stew. And we never had an "unusual" smell in the house again.

~Mary Ellen Angelscribe

Smokey the Sheriff

Fun fact: Cats do respond to training! In fact one of the
first scientific studies highlighting the importance of
reinforcement in animal behavior was done with cats.

"Smokey, whatever it is you want will have to wait — I've got to put these groceries away before the ice cream melts!" But Smokey continued yowling. Knowing I'd have no peace until I investigated his concerns, I quickly stashed the last of the frozen foods into the freezer, pushed the other groceries to the side on the counter, and rushed toward the front entryway where Smokey stood at attention at the foot of the stairs.

Viewing the chaotic scene, I laughed and said, "This is your emergency? Don't you think I would have discovered this when I walked upstairs?" Before returning to the kitchen I added, "And, don't be such a tattle-tale!"

Single, our North American Short-haired black-and-white feline trouble-maker, had a fetish for lingerie. Each time I left the house, he'd dash upstairs to check if I had left the drawer open. If I had, he would stand on his hind legs, pull the drawer open wider, then patiently fish out, one by one, anything he could reach. When I returned home I'd likely see bras, panties, silk nightgowns, and slips strewn up and down the curved stairwell — the focal point for guests who came in the front door.

Smokey had been king of the household for years until we rescued this eight-week-old bundle of trouble. What older cat wouldn't be upset by the intrusion of a young upstart kitten who immediately began siphoning off the family's coveted attention? But Single was especially irksome because he was born without good manners.

Single and his siblings, one female and one male, were found in the attic above my husband's commercial-glass contracting office. After his secretary and bookkeeper kept insisting they heard kitten mews overhead, Jerry and our son David reluctantly climbed up to investigate. During their ascent, Jerry muttered, "We've got to give those ladies some time off!"

When they poked their heads into the attic, all was quiet. But when their eyes adjusted to the darkness, they saw three pairs of bright glowing eyes from a corner where the abandoned kittens huddled quietly together. Once the kittens were rescued and brought out into the light, Jerry said it was love at first sight when his eyes locked with Single's.

"This one's mine!" he announced.

I wasn't convinced that we needed another cat, especially this sickly runt of the litter, nor was I happy with its name — Single Strength. When I finally gave in, I questioned the name, but Jerry was adamant.

"We named each kitten after the three types of glass in our business — Crystal, Plate — and this one was named Single Strength because that's the most fragile glass."

Fortunately, for convenience, we ended up calling him Single. Except for the times when I took full advantage of his full name — "Single Strength Chappell! Get off that counter!"

Our hearts were quickly captured by this rambunctious, inquisitive, risk-oriented creature. Smokey, however, was not impressed. Not even when Single started fetching wadded up paper balls. No matter how far or where they were thrown, he never tired of retrieving them and proudly dropping them at the feet of the thrower — much to the delight of our family and guests.

Smokey disdainfully tolerated this ruffian who had little respect for house rules. He decided it was his duty to monitor his every movement and make certain he followed all rules.

It was true that Smokey had challenged us with his own rebellious moments as a youngster, but he had quickly developed a respect for rules: No jumping on the sofa, no sitting in the chairs unless invited onto someone's lap, no jumping onto the kitchen counter, and definitely no jumping onto the dining room table — which was exactly what Single did one particular afternoon.

I had just entered the room when I saw Single leap into the middle of the table, barely missing the centerpiece. Smokey, dozing on the floor a few feet away, opened his eyes wide in shock and raised his head. He fixed a long hard stare on Single, then looked in my direction as if to ask, "Well, what are you going to do about that?"

"That is no!" I said sharply to Single.

Single had heard the word "no" before, but he suddenly developed a case of deafness. I loudly repeated the word — with more authority — expecting immediate obedience. Instead, Single began to bathe himself. Smokey now sat at full attention. He knew Single had broken the rules and eagerly waited to see some serious consequences to his behavior.

I swatted the table with a rolled-up newspaper, but Single simply moved over a few inches and resumed primping. Smokey was almost in cardiac arrest.

Swatting him lightly on the behind with the paper, I said sharply "Single, no!"

Finally, in slow motion, Single sauntered across the table and jumped down.

Smokey glared at Single, and then looked at me as if to ask, "That's it? That's all you're going to do?"

As Single strolled past him, Smokey gave me one last inquiring look. Apparently dissatisfied with my disciplinary action, or lack thereof, Smokey suddenly whacked Single on the side of the head with his big paw, bowling him over. Though Single was unscathed, Smokey walked from the room with head and tail high, satisfied at having taken matters into his own paws.

With time, Smokey and Single became close friends, the good traits of each rubbing off onto the other. Single learned to respect rules (for the most part) and Smokey took more risks by chasing birds in the back yard — a first for him. Smokey never fetched, however — he left that to the young upstart.

~Kitty Chappell

Cookie

My Very Good, Very Bad Cat

My Heroic Cat

Fun fact: Society for the Prevention of Cruelty to Animals Los Angeles (spcaLA) broke from tradition and presented its 33rd Annual National Hero Dog Award™ to a cat named Tara in 2014 after she saved her boy from a marauding dog.

95

A Lesson in Strength

Fun fact: People in ancient Egypt would shave off their
eyebrows when grieving for the family cat that died.

"Hi, my name is Stevie, and I'm an addict."

"Hi, Stevie," the room replied.

I inhaled deeply, and from the podium in the most matter-of-fact voice I could muster, I explained, "I started shooting heroin when I was twenty-one because my cat Spencer died."

The room burst into hysterical laughter. I did not expect that. This wasn't a joke any more than the tracks on my arms were.

At thirty days clean after a brutal five-year addiction, I was too raw to appreciate how hilarious this was to a room full of veteran ex-addicts who knew, even if I didn't, that shooting heroin because a cat dies isn't what "normal" people do. According to the unspoken wisdom of the room, I shot heroin because I suffered from the disease of addiction — and that's just what addicts do.

What the good people in the room were missing, however, was that Spencer had everything to do with why I shot heroin. Spencer was my hero, and the love she showed me was unconditional. Looking out from the eyes of my small self, she was who I wanted to be when I grew up: brave, defiant, tender, loving and wild.

On the way home from the pound where we adopted Spencer, Mom held the new kitty on her lap and told my sister and me that in a past life, when she was Cleopatra, Spencer had been her cat. As Mom regaled us with the details of her and Spencer's shared history of nobility and power, the two-pound, flea-ridden fur ball peed all over Her Majesty's lap. My sister and I didn't dare laugh but, inside, a deep admiration swelled in our hearts.

In the years to come, when either Mom or Dad hit Spencer or flung her off the deck so that her tiny body slammed against the side yard fence and slithered down into the trash cans, she didn't run away and abandon me, as I often feared she would. Instead, she would sneak back in the house later that evening to poop in Dad's shoe or pee on Mom's pillow, before slinking into my room to sleep. Unlike me, Spencer wasn't diminished by the abuse. She never cowered or played nice to win their love. It was as if my parents' rage was something that occasionally spilled over into her world, in which case she'd promptly exact revenge, but then carry on with her daily routine.

Spencer wasn't defined by the bad things that happened to her.

I wished that I could be brazen and fierce like her — that when I was smacked or slammed or choked, I too would retaliate and fight back like a person who wasn't afraid, ashamed, and secretly longing for acceptance. But I didn't even raise a hand in my own defense.

I was pathetic; Spencer was strong.

And yet, at night, once tucked into the safety of my bed, she nursed on my baby blanky well into adulthood, belying her toughness with a vulnerability which made me love her even more.

On my eighteenth birthday, as I moved out of my parents' house with a black eye and some matching trash bags full of clothes, Spencer moved out, too. Unbeknownst to me, when I failed to come home that night, she saw no reason to return either. Two months later, my mother left a message on my answering machine saying my cat was dead.

Devastated, I drove to my parents' street at a time when I knew they wouldn't be home and parked in the cul-de-sac in front of the baseball field where Spencer liked to hunt. I stood outside the car with my face pressed against the tall, chain-link fence and cried a blur of hot tears while making the kissing sounds I hoped would beckon her soul. After five minutes, ever cognizant of my parents' house a half-block away, I turned to go home.

Just before I got into my car, however, I looked back one last time to pucker a final farewell.

And then I saw it: a tiny brown speck streaking across the field. I couldn't believe my eyes. It was Spencer! She climbed through the fence where I'd stood just a minute before. Then, from a solid eight feet away, she leapt directly onto my chest, landing with a deafening purr.

I felt loved beyond measure.

I took Spencer home to my new house, where she settled in perfectly. I worried she'd miss hunting in the fields by my parents' house, but she didn't seem to mind the sedentary life of living with a college student who studied and worked all the time. The formerly lithe huntress even put on a few pounds, lending her a more matronly gait as she sauntered about the house.

Now if the story ended here — happily-ever-after — I don't know if I'd still be a brave, defiant, tender, loving and wild woman. I don't know if I would have been standing on a podium at age twenty-six, sharing my story with a room full of strangers.

I explained to the good people of the room that while I raced for three years between college, work, and home, doing my best to be perfect in every way, and while Spencer stretched out on the couch, undoubtedly doing her best to be perfect in every way, dark secrets were festering inside us both.

In Spencer, cancer was slowly eating her alive; in me, it was resentment.

As I waited for the vet to come back with the results, Spencer, all fur and bones, hid behind my neck and beneath my hair. My hero was terrified.

"Her insides are riddled with disease. I'll have to do an exploratory to see if there's anything we can do," he said.

Spencer never made it off the operating table, and I wasn't there to scratch beneath her chin and make the kissing sounds she liked.

When the vet told me she was dead, the already thin thread that tethered me to my better self broke.

I couldn't save her — my hero — ravaged, hiding in my hair, terrified and gone forever. I was writhing in pain, unable to sit with it — unable to be alone with it. I needed out of my skin! I wanted so badly to be strong like her, and I tried, but the harder I raged, the farther I fell down the rabbit hole.

"And now I'm here," I said as I stepped off the podium, exhausted.

As I walked back to my seat, the room clapped as loudly as they'd laughed, and voices from all over said, "Welcome."

One woman pulled me close to her chest.

"Honey," she said, "Spencer was strong because she had you to come home to. And now you have us."

~Stevie Trujillo

96

The Guardian and Her Boy

Fun fact: Cats sleep up to sixteen hours a day, but their brains still alert them to sounds and smells most of the time they're asleep to warn them of danger.

We met at the Leeds Grenville SPCA. From the moment my family walked through the door, the brown Tabby watched us calmly but intently with her hazel eyes. The fur around her face was fluffed almost imperceptibly, giving her a kitten-like appearance, and her front paws were extended in our direction. They stopped just short of the door of her cage, as if she didn't want to seem too eager.

There were other cats that were less concerned about seeming needy. Many rose to their feet as we entered the small section of the Leeds Grenville SPCA, meowing in every pitch imaginable.

More than one cat strained a lean furry arm in our direction as we passed, hoping to loop the tips of his claws into a sleeve or arm to capture our attention. My husband and I stayed just out of reach, not out of cruelty, but because our hearts are too easily swayed. We were here to find the best fit for our little family of three.

In my heart, however, I think I already knew which one was the right cat.

Portia was quiet. She watched us with partially closed eyes, as if she had already staked her claim.

"Take your time," her expression seemed to say. "In the end, I know it's going to be me."

As I neared her cage, one paw extended. There was no desperation, no ulterior motive, only a gesture that seemed to say, "Hello, at last."

That appendage quickly retracted when the silver Tabby housed below reached up and swatted her. Portia pulled back, giving me what looked like a hurt expression while still relaying that she knew she was "The One."

"Aw, that was sad," my husband said.

"I know!" I exclaimed. "You should pick her up and make her feel better."

Portia slid into his arms. As he pulled her close to his chest, she maneuvered so that her belly was exposed. Craning her neck, she touched her nose to his.

My husband was smitten. We were bringing home a cat that day.

After a day or two of settling in, Portia became a sort of small and fluffy nanny to my toddler. She would travel from room to room with us during the day, usually staying closest to my son. She wanted to sit where he sat, look out the windows from which he peered, and make valiant attempts to share (steal) whatever he was eating. At night, she would sprawl onto his lap during story time. We dubbed her "Guardian Kitten" for the way she always wanted to be where he was, watching over him as if he were her own.

Then, one day, she saved his life.

I was raking leaves while my child delighted in disturbing the piles. Portia was dozing on the porch, the tip of her tail periodically twitching, and her ears sometimes shifting toward the sound of our voices. Aside from these, she seemed gone to the world, lost in the lazy, dreamy repose that is best achieved on a fall day that is closer to the end of summer than the beginning of winter.

From down the street, a frantic voice cried, "No! Come back here!"

The phrase was repeated and the volume increased as the speaker drew closer. The Golden Retriever reached my property first.

It wasn't a bad dog. In the split second that it reached and then leaped over the low fence surrounding the front yard, I ascertained that it was a young one, and not well-trained. It veered toward my son with boundless energy and body language that expressed that it wanted to play.

"Puppy!" my son exclaimed, spreading his arms apart in a welcoming gesture. Unlike me, he was oblivious to the fact that this dog would, at the very least, knock him down with its uncontained enthusiasm.

And I wasn't going to be able to close the space between us in time.

A demonic scream erupted behind me, as Portia flew from the porch in a blur of brown and black stripes, landing between the dog and child. Compared to the fully grown dog, Portia was tiny, but her outrage overcompensated for that. Every hair on her body was raised. Her back was arched and her lips were drawn back to reveal sharp teeth.

She yowled again, claws extended as one paw exploded outward and struck the dog's nose. It yelped and took a step back. Once more she closed the gap, claws ready to slice. Hissing, growling, and striking, she drove the Retriever out of the yard. It gave me time to step in front of my child and contemplate how to protect both him and Portia should the dog retaliate.

It didn't. The owners arrived and apologized profusely while taking hold of their errant pet's collar before returning home. Portia watched with disdainful eyes until they rounded another corner and disappeared. With a bored glance in my direction, she returned to napping on the porch.

I still think often and fondly of the Guardian Kitten. Her certainty toward us and the seamless way she became a part of our family encouraged me to feel as if there is a kind of destiny to this existence. She was definitely beyond compare.

~Ligaya Flor

97

Chicken Soup for the Soul

Who Rescued Whom?

Fun fact: A cat can rotate its ears one hundred and eighty degrees.

I found Tiger and his sister Tigger on the highway in front of my home one summer afternoon. They were about six weeks old and scared. I brought them in with no intention of keeping them. I had a cat who didn't get along with other cats and had just turned eighteen. He was also in end stage kidney failure, and I had resolved that I would have no more feline companions. It hurt too much to lose them when it was their time to go.

The kittens endeared themselves to my older cat, Quackers. More than once I would come home from work to see the three of them curled up sleeping on my bed.

After a couple of months Quackers succumbed to his disease and passed on. I bought my first home and was busily moving boxes and furniture. I was single and so with working full-time, unpacking became a slow luxury. As a result, I found myself sleeping on the couch since I had not found time to set up my bed.

One night, around two a.m., Tiger came bounding in and jumped on my chest. He began pawing my face, which he had never done before. I placed him back on the carpeting and rolled over. I was too tired to play. But he was relentless and repeated his earlier actions. This time he added a growl sound to his frantic motions. When I finally sat up, he ran to the kitchen. Thinking that maybe he wanted a treat, I decided to give him one if it would allow me another couple of hours sleep.

I made my way to the kitchen and was surprised to see him sitting in front of the back door. Instead of heading to his bowl or the treat cupboard, he placed himself there like a soldier on duty. When he saw I was near, he began to meow louder than before and then paw at the door. Since he was an indoor cat, I couldn't figure out his actions. Then I saw it. The doorknob was moving. Someone was trying to get in.

I immediately turned on the lights and dialed 911. Unfortunately, by the time the police arrived, the intruder had fled. I would later find out that there had been a series of break-ins in the area.

Needless to say, Tiger and Tigger both got treats galore that morning!

So while I took in two helpless kittens just a few months before, I lay the question before you: Who really saved whom?

~Pastor Wanda Christy-Shaner

98

The Guardian

Fun fact: The blue-eyed Siamese cat is one of the oldest breeds, treasured members of the Thai royal family, seen in ancient manuscripts as far back as 1350.

Long ago I lived in Vancouver with a Doberman named Sasha and a Siamese cat named Paxton. Now, Paxton was a great cat, tolerant of people in general and kids in particular, but he hated dogs. All dogs, any dogs, he made no distinction. The day we moved into our new home I remember a black Lab wandering across our front yard and hearing, later, some high pitched, dog-type yips. Shortly after a very irate dog owner showed up claiming my cat had chased his dog down the street and swiped its snout, which now sported some (relatively) minor gashes. Pax loved sitting at the end of our driveway hissing at the dogs walking by on leash. He didn't discriminate: large or small, pure bred or mutt, if you were canine he hated you.

The only dog he tolerated was our Doberman Sasha, probably because she had been there first. He completely ignored her attempts at friendship, but they coexisted more or less peacefully. At least Sasha never turned up with her nose in shreds.

As Sasha aged she started to have trouble walking and controlling her bladder. I took her to a specialist. We learned she had a tumour wrapped around her spine. There was no treatment that would work so we just brought her home to let nature take its course.

Sasha deteriorated gradually, to the point that she became unsteady and sometimes had to be helped to stand. But it was summertime in Vancouver, which allowed for Sasha to be outside most of the day, slowly making the rounds of the back yard or basking in the shade. It was a good summer.

Toward the end of July I had left Sasha in the back yard and gone with the kids for the weekly grocery shop. I noticed, coming back to the driveway, that there seemed to be an inordinate number of ravens sitting on top of the fence that surrounded the yard, hopping on and off and calling incessantly. I knew instantly they were after Sasha.

My heart pounding, I ran to the back yard, but something beige whizzed past and beat me to it. There was Sasha, unable to get up, surrounded by a mob of ravens edging ever closer. The ravens, sensing an easy target, had gathered to defeat her by numbers. But the real action was happening a few feet away. Paxton literally had one raven by the leg, another by a wing, and was going for a third. They were attacking him but he wasn't giving up.

Paxton drove the ravens off and they retreated to the top of the fence. The cat remained crouched, every hair on end, spitting and yowling in a way that would have made a wolf think twice. I'd never heard anything like it. After a couple of minutes the ravens dispersed.

Amazingly, neither Sasha nor Pax was really injured. Given the number of black feathers littering the yard I'm not sure the same could be said for the ravens.

Summer passed into a long, uncharacteristically warm and dry fall. I never again let Sasha into the yard unless I was home. But she loved lying in the grass, watching the bees and smelling the earth, so I did let her enjoy long periods of time outside. And ever after that day, she had a guardian. No matter where he was, within a few minutes of Sasha going outside, Pax would appear, sitting on the fence above wherever she lay, sharing the last warm rays of the season. Sometimes they would sleep together, dog on the grass, cat on the fence above, but the cat was always there. The dog was never alone again.

As the fall grew colder, Sasha reached the point where life was more pain than joy, and I let her go.

Some may say Pax was being territorial, defending what he saw as his own. Some may say he just figured Sasha was the best bird bait the cat goddess ever made. But after I put Sasha down, that cat sat on her bed for three days and, other than to relieve himself, did not move. So judge as you will.

Paxton lived to tolerate another dog in our family, a German Shepherd named Kia. As with Sasha, Pax seemed to barely stand her and spent a lot of time glaring at her down his very long Siamese nose. But he didn't fool me, not for one second!

~Trish Featherstone

Lion and the Uncouth Bear

*Fun fact: At the Berlin Zoo, a cat named Muschi
voluntarily shares a cage with his best friend,
a black bear.*

My full name is Richard the Lionhearted but, for their ease and convenience, I grant my staff permission to call me Lion most of the time. If any soul troubled itself enough to inquire, my staff would readily concur that I have full membership status in the Association known to you as Very Good Cat.

Although it pains me to admit this, it hasn't always been so. Allow me, if I may, to elucidate for you my proof of this somewhat disagreeable truth.

I was born to a charming and respectable family, but as is the wont of foolhardy and recalcitrant youths, I found that way of life much too staid and circumspect for an intrepid and adventurous swashbuckler such as I. One day, I gathered my inner fortitude around me and escaped the confines of family and friends to courageously make my own way in the world.

The Montana mountains are a treacherous place for an unsophisticated and untried young cat such as myself, and I rapidly blew through several of my allotted lifetimes. One day, cold and weak with hunger, I came upon an old truck bed filled to overflowing with kitchen refuse

Oh my… Oh my… Oh my. This was going to be a heavenly treat.

Soon, I was industriously consuming the most delectable comestibles I could ever recall devouring. Indeed, I was so preoccupied with enjoying this fine repast that I neither saw nor heard The Bear.

You, dear readers, may not be aware that the Yellowstone National Park officials had recently decided that there was a superfluity of bears in the Park, nor that they devised some nonsensical plan to capture said bears and relocate them to the wilds of Canada. I must say, to this day I consider that to have been quite rude and presumptuous on the part of the officials. It was disrespectful to the bears and, more importantly, nearly cost me… well, I'm getting ahead of myself.

Now, this truck filled with a garbage buffet and the house it belonged to, lay directly in the path the deported bears had to take as they made their laborious journey home from Canada to the Park, where they preferred living. This fine morning, as the sun rose over the mountains and warmed my happy little back, I filled my happy little stomach.

But not for long.

Suddenly, sensing that the feaster was about to become the feast, I whirled around and came nose to snout with an excessively ill-humored bear. He was, no doubt, as tired and hungry as I was. Unlike me, though, it was through no choice of his own that he now found himself in this sad situation. I'm ashamed to admit that his feelings, however, never entered my mind at the time. Like any callow youth, I thought only of myself.

Quite naturally, I yowled my protests and leaped out of the truck-bed, forgetting entirely about my half-finished breakfast. I saw that the back door of the house was open and, at a loss for a better plan, I took a chance that I could find a hiding place before that uncouth and pestilential bear could make use of my skinny body to break his fast.

Good lord, that bear was fast! There was no time to make the hard right turn into the kitchen, so I plunged down the stairs into the dirt basement instead, with the bear, as they say, hot on my tail. Round and round we went in that tiny dirt room. I could feel his noxious breath and the whoosh of air as his great claws slashed the air by my rump.

Somewhere above us, I heard the welcome screeching and roaring of agitated human creatures. I sincerely hoped they would get to me in time. I was fast losing steam. The Bear apparently registered human activity, too, because he seemed instantly to lose interest in me as he skidded to a halt and gazed around wildly for the exit. Indeed, I managed to make two more laps around the room before I realized he was no longer paying the least attention to me. Instead, up the stairs he charged, quite possibly even faster than he had come down. Moments later, I heard a gunshot.

Wisely, I remained concealed in that dark hole under the house till evening. Nothing and no one could convince me to emerge any sooner. Finally, I stealthily tiptoed, in slow motion, up the stairs and out into the woods, peering warily in all directions as I went. There was no bear to be found, and I must admit I was glad, since it was my own guidance that led him into that basement. The old chap must've got away after all. He likely even told his grandcubs the story of how he almost had fresh young cat for breakfast one morning on his Long Journey Home.

~Loral Lee Portenier

We Rescued Each Other

Fun fact: Studies have found that pets can help develop positive social behaviors in autistic children.

"Why can't you be like everyone else? You're weird. I don't want to talk to you." Those statements had been ingrained in my mind for so long that I just accepted them as part of the daily life of someone who has Asperger's. As I entered high school and college, I could feel the eyes of strangers intently locked on me, waiting for me to make that one awkward expression or statement that made absolutely no sense. At home, it wasn't much better. I went to bed confused, even frightened, by this condition that had taken hold of me and had no intention of ever leaving.

In August 2011, my life forever changed when I was offered a position with the federal government. It was the chance of a lifetime, one I had imagined for so long when I was a student. I was fascinated by the history of our country and the workings of Congress. Whenever I pictured the heartbeat of our democracy, one city came to the fore-front — Washington, D.C. I closed my eyes and visualized what it must have been like to be part of the Continental Congress, to have your name called as you were asked to sign what would become the greatest and most important document ever created. In my eyes, it was not a privilege, but an honor to be living and working in one of the most special cities anywhere.

The first day I found myself on the Metro, traveling to the office,

I could hardly believe it was happening! In the crowd of well-dressed commuters, I was one of them. However, I began to face the frustrations of being an "Aspie" more each day. I attended social events such as speed dating and black-tie galas, only to discover that instead of fitting in I was standing out in all the wrong ways. I'd return home feeling bitterly disappointed and tormented, asking why I had to be different. I made small talk at work, but still found it a challenge to maintain a steady conversation — until the day one of my co-workers posed a question: "Have you considered adopting a pet?"

It was like a thunderbolt out of a clear blue sky. When I was growing up on Long Island, we had tried to welcome pets into our household, but failed miserably twice. The first time was with a gray Labrador named Jason, who loved my brother and me, but not my parents — so he was given away. The tears I cried that day could have filled the Chesapeake Bay. Three years later, we adopted a Basset Hound named Barney with the cutest floppy ears and a sad expression. When we were eating, he'd put his jaw on our knees and stare at us with droopy eyes. How could we not love him? But one night, my grandmother came over, and Barney decided to eat her pink slippers for dinner. Two days later, he was returned to the shelter.

I knew that animals were excellent for "pet therapy," but I just wasn't sure if I was ready for the challenge of ownership. What I did know, though, is that I was hurting and alone, with little social options, and feeling like the color in my world was slowly being erased each day. On a spur of the moment, I called home and announced my intentions. After being told "good luck and do your research," I was off and running.

I didn't know what type of cat I wanted, but I did know I wanted a black cat, for a number of reasons. First, being a person who has Asperger's and a stutter, I had known all my life what it was like to be an outcast and feel unwanted. In our culture, people often feel black cats bring bad luck, so the odds of them being adopted are lower. Many shelters even offer incentives for adopting them. Many people also consider black cats to be ugly, and I had had more than my fair share of days feeling that way.

When I walked into the animal shelter, an associate's eyes lit up when I said I wanted a black cat. She took me in the back to meet two: Frederica and Abracadabra. Frederica seemed very disinterested and did not like being petted, which automatically eliminated her. But there was something about Abracadabra — his eyes were hypnotizing, and as soon as he walked out of the cage, he spent three minutes rubbing my leg. I knew he was the one.

After my references were checked I was able to bring him home. I was so excited that I even put up a "Welcome Home" banner, even though he was completely oblivious. I changed Abracadabra's name to Lucky. Over the next few days, I began to notice that my personality was changing. I became more outgoing. I would ask for what I wanted instead of settling for things. My stuttering became less severe, and I didn't care about it as often as I once did. I learned that I am okay, and so are others. Although I found out later that my cat had crystals in his urine and would need a special diet the rest of his life, it was a small price to pay for what he was giving me.

Lucky tested my patience, as all cats do. He'd jump on the television and the kitchen table, and chew the blinds, which led to him being the recipient of some squirts from my water gun. One day, though, when the perfect storm came together, everything was brought into perspective. I couldn't speak coherently, and I was having the worst day relating to people. I came home and went to bed early. As I drifted off to dreamland, I felt Lucky jump on my back and close his eyes, purring gently. He loved me, and I knew things would work out.

I've been asked if I rescued my cat. The truth is, we rescued each other.

~Steven M. Kaufman

Hero in the Making

Fun fact: Eighty percent of ginger cats are male.

t was finally spring and my husband and I planned to take advantage of it. The front door stood wide open, making the porch of our century-old home even more inviting. Clean outdoor scents would replace the mustiness inside.

I rubbed my lower back and surveyed the flowerbed. Where weeds hadn't overrun the plantings, slugs had done their damage. The greenery was as lacey as a grandmother's doily. It certainly wasn't the sturdy ground cover I'd expected. It would take many more hours on my knees to bring this area back to life after our long winter.

"Do you want to break for a few minutes?" My husband stood across the entry path, attacking another area of the yard with well-worn clippers. A few stray twigs and leaves clung to his jeans.

I squinted up at the sun, its rays beating down on us, clear and bright.

Why not? I rose and stretched, my spine shouting in appreciation as I breathed in the fresh spring air. A cup of coffee or a soda on the porch would suit me fine. "Sure. I'll grab us something."

Just then, out of the corner of my eye, I sensed movement. I turned to see a dog at the end of the street, moving at a steady clip in our direction. I glanced at my husband and shrugged. Another mutt running loose in our town would never make the news.

"Let me get it this time." David headed for the steps to the porch.

The dog, a young Pit Bull, came nearer, his pace never slowing.

Fur the color of caramel covered his rippling muscles.

I've met several dogs of that breed, sweet as honey, but something about this one made the hair at the nape of my neck stand on end. He was aching for a scuffle. I could almost taste his aggression.

He passed the next-door neighbor's house, as if on a mission, his hackles raised.

Dave had reached the top of the concrete steps leading to our front door. His relaxed posture told me he had no idea what was going on.

My breath caught in my throat, strangling any warning I could have offered.

Two seconds later, the beast scaled our stairs as if he owned the place, confidence and power exuding from his frame like a boxer in the ring.

I screamed, a terrified yell, which caught Dave's attention. He stood frozen at the open doorway as the dog rushed past.

The last time I'd checked, our cat Johnny, who we had rescued from a litter of kittens dumped in our neighborhood, was resting in a quiet corner of the sitting room, near the fireplace. He was dozing in his favorite overstuffed chair, shedding tufts of vivid orange fur on the white upholstery. I'd long ago given up on protecting that piece of furniture from cat hair.

I raced to Dave's side, eager to protect sweet, strong, not-terribly-bright Johnny. But we were too late. The dog stood stock-still now, just within the entry, a low growl rumbling from deep within its chest.

From the overstuffed chair, I heard fast movement, like a soldier snapping to attention. And a moment later, there he was—Johnny! He hesitated for a long moment and then hissed from the seat's edge, his arched back making him appear half a foot taller.

Before I could blink, he'd dropped to the carpet, a snarling, moaning sidewinder of four-legged trouble.

My heart skipped a beat as he sidled up to the stray dog, whose expression changed in a flash. This aggressor now resembled a frightened puppy.

My gaze met my husband's. His raised brows said it all. We weren't going to get into the middle of this mess. We'd clean up the aftermath, if need be, but only a fool would try to break up a battle of this sort.

Still in full attack position, Johnny advanced, each slinking step slow and deliberate. His eyes were slit like Clint Eastwood's in *Dirty Harry*, I'm convinced he transmitted a thought to the mutt: "Go ahead, punk, make my day."

Without warning, Johnny sped faster than I'd ever witnessed in the direction of the dog, whose cocked head and dropped jaw registered deep concern. Wide-eyed, the dog spun on his heels, tail tucked between his legs. He raced out the entry doorway and skipped the top stair, airborne. Landing on the walkway, his feet didn't miss a beat, tearing up the lawn as he crossed.

Johnny gave chase in hot pursuit of the invader. At the edge of our property, he stopped and sat, glancing back at us.

The Pit Bull continued running until he was out of sight. We never spotted him again.

Johnny straightened his back and swaggered into the house, reclaiming the cozy spot on his chair. Like a gunslinger in an old-time western, I half-expected to see him blow smoke from a pistol's barrel and tuck it back into its holster.

I sighed. It was over. Dave nodded. "Until the next exciting episode. Right, Johnny?"

Johnny gazed at us and blinked once, slowly. A few seconds later, he tucked his head beneath a paw and curled up for a well-earned nap. Our little toughie.

He's small and has no superpowers to speak of, but he gets the job done when it comes to protecting us. Dave and I have a new hero.

~Heidi Gaul

Meet Our Contributors

Ruth Acers-Smith was born in Missouri, raised in Golden, CO, and now lives in Bakersfield, CA. In addition to being the mother of three and the grandmother of seven, she also is the great-grandmother of seven with the eighth due in January 2016. Bam Bam lived to be seventeen.

Mary Ellen Angelscribe is author of *Expect Miracles* and *A Christmas Filled with Miracles*, and an international pet columnist. Animal Planet's *Must Love Cats* featured her cats doing the "kitty paddle!" Her stories and cat videos can be seen on Facebook under Angel Scribe and Pet Tips 'n' Tales. Learn more at www.AngelScribe.com.

Elizabeth Atwater started writing almost as soon as she was able to grasp a pencil in her hand. The only thing she is more passionate about is her terrific husband, Joe. She also finds joy in reading, gardening, and doing volunteer work through senior services and hospice. She lives in a very small town in North Carolina.

Anita Aurit is an entrepreneur, eclectic writer and speaker who has been published in magazines and book compilations. She is currently working on a novel and enjoys writing from a feline point of view in her blog, *Feline Fine*, at www.felineopines.wordpress.com.

Tori Bailey is the author of the *Coming Home* series. She is a contributing writer for *Georgia Connector* magazine and *Georgia Home and Life* blog. Her short stories have appeared on several blogs and in *A Cup* *of Christmas*. An avid cat lover, Tori shares her home with six rescue cats and her husband.

Catherine Barry was born in Dublin in 1963 and is a poet, short story writer, journalist, playwright and published author. Her first novel, *The House That Jack Built*, was published in 2001, her second, *Null & Void*, in 2002 and her third, *Skin Deep*, in 2004. Her fourth book, *Charlie & Me*, a factual story, was published in 2011.

Elizabeth Batman is a fourth year nursing student at UCLA with plans to become a geriatric RN. She will graduate in June 2016 and is very excited about the start of her career. Elizabeth enjoys reading, writing, embroidering, and spending time with friends. She plans to continue writing while working as a nurse.

Diane Ganzer Baum has been writing professionally since 2004, beginning with her book titled *Patrick the Wayward Setter*. She has since been writing fiction for all ages as well as nonfiction. It is her hope that over the years she will have written something that interests readers!

Garrett Bauman is the author of two college textbooks and stories in *Yankee*, *The New York Times*, *Sierra*, *The Chronicle of Higher Education* and a dozen *Chicken Soup for the Soul* books. He and his wife have adopted twenty strays over the years and will not run out of cat stories any time soon.

Valerie D. Benko writes creative nonfiction from her home in Pennsylvania. She has more than two-dozen essays and short stories published in the U.S. and Canada, encompassing themes such as kayaking, cats, health and family. Visit her online at www.valeriebenko.weebly.com.

Clara Blake, a writer and a self-defined Crazy Cat Lady, holds a degree in zoology and often works as an environmental consultant when she is not researching. She currently lives in New York City with her husband and their three adopted cats.

Laura Boldin-Fournier is a previous contributor to the *Chicken Soup for the Soul* book series. She has degrees from Arizona State University and C.W. Post. Laura has worked as a teacher and a librarian in New York. Today she lives in Florida and enjoys reading, writing and traveling. Learn more at www.lauraboldin.com.

Books one and two of **Jan Bono's** new cozy mystery series are now available! She's also published five collections of humorous personal experiences, two poetry chapbooks, nine one-act plays, a dinner theater play, and has written for magazines ranging from *Guideposts* to *Woman's World*. Learn more at www.JanBonoBooks.com.

Lois Bradley is an illustrator and author, graphic designer, and visual artist with a BFA in Studio Art from the University of New Mexico. Lois is a Published and Listed member of the Society of Children's Book Writers and Illustrators and loves writing for children. She is the proud kitty-mama to four fuzzy felines. Visit her at www.bobbycatandcompany.com.

Dylan Brody is a humorist and storyteller. He won the 2005 Stanley Drama Award for playwriting and opens for David Sedaris sometimes when he is on the West Coast. He has released five CDs through Stand Up! Records, and two full-length digital downloads through Rooftop Comedy. He feels frequent self-loathing.

Jill Burns lives in the mountains of West Virginia with her wonderful family. She's a retired piano teacher and performer. She enjoys writing, music, gardening, nature, and spending time with her grandchildren.

Dan C. is a freelance writer and aspiring author with degrees in sociology and art. He has many interests, including writing, reading, social science, art, philosophy, bike rides, and learning new facts. He cherishes his family and Frankie, a spunky female Terrier he adopted at a local pet shelter.

Emily Canning-Dean graduated with a bachelor's degree in English from The University of Akron. She is a reporter for *The Post Newspapers* and lives in Ohio with her husband Eric and their fur babies.

Eva Carter enjoys writing, photography and travel. She has worked in finance and has created greeting cards for Hallmark. She and her husband Larry live in Dallas, TX with a kitten named Ollie, who hopes to be featured in a future *Chicken Soup for the Soul* story — as soon as he does something noteworthy. E-mail her at evacarter@sbcglobal.net.

Founded in the UK, but representing artists all over the world, **CartoonStock** is a searchable database of over 500,000 humorous and political cartoons, cartoon pictures and illustrations by more than 1,000 of the world's top cartoonists, all available for instant licensing and download.

Paige Cerulli is a freelance writer who specializes in writing on pet and equestrian topics. She lives in the Berkshires with her two cats, Dylan and Cara, and her Thoroughbred mare, Whisper. Paige loves to write poetry and fiction, and hopes to one day publish a novel.

Award-winning author **Lynette Chambers** enjoys touching hearts with her stories. She and her husband Jim live on top of a small mountain in the Ozarks, near where she grew up. When not traveling, they enjoy visits from their children and grandchildren. Learn more at www.lynettechambers.com.

Radio and television guest **Kitty Chappell** is an international speaker and award-winning nonfiction author of articles, poetry and three books. Her latest release is *Friendship: When It's Easy and When It's Not*. Kitty welcomes your comments at www.kittychappell.com.

As a minister **Wanda Christy-Shaner** has been honing her writing skills all her life. As an avid reader and collector of *Chicken Soup for the Soul* books, she is honored to be a part of this wonderful publication.

E-mail Pastor Wanda Christy-Shaner at seekingtruth65@yahoo.com.

Connie Cook is a Registered Nurse. She spent ten years of her forty-year career working in mental health and thought she had a good handle on behaviors. But then she met George. Bottom line, the story is all true.

Harriet Cooper writes essays, humor, creative nonfiction and health articles for newspapers, newsletters, anthologies and magazines. She's a frequent contributor to the *Chicken Soup for the Soul* book series. She writes about family, relationships, health, food, cats, writing and daily life. E-mail her at shewrites@live.ca.

By day **Sean V. Cronin** is a manager with several veterinary practices near D.C., but by night he's a father, husband, and writer. Sean is working on a series of fantasy novels and is a contributor to a new podcast called *Nerd Turtle*. You can check out some of his work at nerdturtleblog.wordpress.com or e-mail him at seanvcronin@gmail.com.

Jill Davis lives with her husband Gary in Florida.

Beth DiCola self-published *Homeseekers: Flight to the Mountain* under her maiden name, S.B. Broshar. She is sixty-eight years old and discovering a different life through writing. She is currently working on the continuing story in her second novel and is a member of a local writers' group. E-mail her at diuncola@gmail.com.

Kevin Dobson received his B.A., with honors, and B.Ed. degrees from Queen's University and his Master's of Education, in the Arts, from U of T. He then went on to have an extremely rewarding thirty-year career in education, as both a teacher and an administrator. He is now in the next phase of his journey, looking for new challenges.

Rhonda Dragomir is a pastor's wife, Bible teacher, and professional communicator. She received her Bachelor of Arts degree, with honors, from Asbury University. Actively involved in ministry for more than thirty-five years, Rhonda is a flutist, artist, writer, and speaker with a special passion for encouraging women.

Rita Durrett teaches in northern Oklahoma. She is a mother of two sons and grandmother to four boys and a girl. She belonged to the now deceased cat, Mousey, described in her story, and two big attack dogs that might lick an intruder to death but, she admits, wouldn't bite unless someone came between them and their food.

Tanya Estes is a writer, blogger, photographer and mother. She graduated from The University of Texas with a Bachelor of Fine Arts in Art History and a Master of Science in Library and Information Science. After many years as a librarian, she decided to write in the hopes of one day leaving a literary legacy for her son.

Trish Featherstone is a retired RN living in the Interior of British Columbia. Her nom de plume is an acknowledgement to her mother, who gave her the gift of loving books.

After more than twenty years working in the Hennepin County court system, **David Fingerman** now spends his days writing and bowing to the whims of his cat, KC.

Ligaya Flor grew up in a large, loving family whose practical jokes continue to inspire much of her writing. She is currently writing a young adult fantasy novel and fighting writer's block by training for the San Francisco Marathon.

Jennifer Froelich is the author of two novels, *Dream of Me* and *A Place Between Breaths*, and is currently writing a trilogy for young adults. She graduated from the Walter Cronkite School of Journalism at Arizona State University and now lives in Idaho with her husband, two children and cat, Katniss.

Heidi Gaul's writing appears in several *Chicken Soup for the Soul* books.

In addition to her love for cats, she is an avid traveler, be it around the block or the world. Visit her at www.HeidiGaul.com or reach her via e-mail at dhgaul@aol.com.

Jessica Goody writes for *SunSations* magazine and *The Bluffton Sun*. Her work has appeared in more than two-dozen magazines and anthologies. She was awarded second place in the 2015 Reader's Digest Poetry Contest. Her poetry collection *Defense Mechanisms* will be published by Autonomous Press in 2016.

Kristine Groskaufmanis has been writing in her journal since she was eleven years old. She lives in Toronto with her husband and their dog Bella, who they are convinced is half Muppet. She is a big fan of staying at home in her pajamas and watching too much TV.

Leslie Gulvas is a mild mannered high school science teacher, freelance writer, and former scientific researcher. She travels whenever possible and writes novels. When not wandering, she lives on a farm in Ohio with the world's cutest donkey and a very confused pig.

Rachel Lajunen Harnett is a teacher with a passion for writing short stories. She runs (often chasing her husband, two kids and Great Dane!), bikes and plays Ultimate Frisbee. Rachel is a graduate from Carleton University's journalism program. She lives in Toronto.

A freelance writer, piano teacher, mother of three and grandmother of two, **Wendy Hobday Haugh** lives in upstate New York with her husband Chuck and her two cats: Hector and Mousy.

Christy Heitger-Ewing is a freelance writer living in Avon, IN with her husband and two sons. She is a columnist for *Cabin Living* magazine and writes regularly for Christian magazines. Her book *Cabin Glory* (www.cabinglory.com) was a grand prize winner. Visit her website at www.christyheitger-ewing.com.

Eileen Melia Hession is a former teacher and publisher's representative whose writing has appeared in various publications. She has one daughter and enjoys running, yoga and ceramics. She believes there is a need for more levity in life and her writing reflects that belief.

Mary Hickey is a backgammon champion and teacher, and has co-authored a book on middle game strategy for that game. She is the author of *Arise and Call Her Blessed*, about Mary the mother of Jesus as we know her from the Bible, and is currently writing a book about the experience of moving from the city to the country.

David Hull is a retired teacher who shares his home with several rescue cats. He enjoys reading, gardening and spending time with his nieces and nephews. David writes every day — he has found it's cheaper than therapy! He has had stories published in other *Chicken Soup for the Soul* books and numerous magazines.

May Hutchings received her Associate of Arts degree, with honors, in 2009. She has one son and works as a freelance copywriter and editor. May enjoys animals of all types, the great outdoors, and traveling with her young son. She has won several awards for her creative fiction stories and plans to write young adult fiction books.

Cindy Hval is the author of *War Bonds: Love Stories from the Greatest Generation*. Fully illustrated with original photos, *War Bonds* tells the stories of thirty-six couples who met/married during or shortly after WWII. Her work has been included in seven *Chicken Soup for the Soul* books. She's mom to four sons and is owned by two cats. E-mail her at dchval@juno.com.

Emily Johnsen is a freelance writer, blogger, social media marketer, entrepreneur, wildlife rehabilitator, animal lover, wife, and mom… in no particular order. She currently resides in historic Fort Worth, TX with her husband and two inspiring tween-aged sons. Visit her at www.eljohnsen515.com.

Kay Johnson-Gentile received both her Ph.D. and master's degree in Education from the University at Buffalo. Family, teaching, music and writing are the loves of her life. She is now retired and writes short stories from the heart, as well as a weekly blog at www.drkayjg.com. E-mail her at kjohnsonge@gmail.com.

Ann Joseph received a B.A. degree in English and M.A. degree in Communication prior to a career in various medical research and administrative positions. As her children and career matured, she also started to write, publishing her first book, an allegory entitled *Across the Stream*. She plans to write much more in the years to come.

Steven M. Kaufman received his Bachelor of Fine Arts in Journalism, *magna cum laude*, from Long Island University–C.W. Post in 2002. He currently works in office administration for the National Institutes of Health (NIH). Steven lives in the Washington, D.C. suburbs and enjoys karaoke, traveling, and motivational speaking.

Ann Kenna is a poet and memoirist. Her work appears in anthologies, online journals, newspapers and magazines. This Long Island mother and former flower child draws inspiration from her family, friends, and her salty island life experiences. She is currently creating a new world in an ambitious work of fiction.

Deborah Kerr is a graduate of Queen's University Belfast with a B.A. degree, with honors, in English and Theology. She is married to Gareth and they have two small children. Deborah loves books, trying new recipes and going on adventures with her family. She writes (and drinks more tea than is good for her) on a daily basis.

Kathryn Kingsbury is a writer and editor living in the Upper Midwest. Having grown up with dogs, it took her a while to get used to the mysterious ways of cats. She blogs about food, thrift, and felines at www.seasonofplenty.com. Learn more at kathrynkingsbury.com.

Following his graduation from the Professional Writing program at Grant MacEwan University (Edmonton, AB), **Rick Lauber** has pursued freelance writing and has authored *Caregiver's Guide for Canadians* and *The Successful Caregiver's Guide*. Rick enjoys hiking, watching movies, listening to music, and playing pool. Learn more at www.ricklauber.com.

Mark Leiren-Young won the Leacock Medal for Humour for his memoir, *Never Shoot a Stampede Queen*. His latest comic memoir is *Free Magic Secrets Revealed*. Learn more at www.leiren-young.com or contact him via Twitter @leirenyoung.

Brenda Leppington currently works as an Information Manager within the health care system. Brenda enjoys traveling, riding horses, and sharing stories about the many animals that have been a part of her life.

Keri Lindenmuth is currently a college senior studying toward her English degree with a writing certification. Her nonfiction essays have won statewide and national awards and her poetry has appeared in several literary magazines. She resides in eastern Pennsylvania with her family.

Irene Maran, a mother of four and grandmother of five, is a retired high school administrator living at the Jersey Shore with her three cats and turtles. She writes two newspaper columns and is a professional storyteller. Irene shares her humorous stories with children and adults.

Joshua J. Mark is an editor/director and writer for the free online history site Ancient History Encyclopedia. His nonfiction has also appeared in *Celtic Guide* and *Timeless Travels* and his short fiction in *Litro* and *Writes for All* among others. He lives with his wife Betsy and daughter Emily in upstate New York.

Tim Martin is an opinion columnist for *Times-Standard*, and the author of *Rez Rock*, *Somewhere Down the Line: The Legend of Boomer Jack* and *Summer With Dad*. Tim has completed nine screenplays and is a contributing author to almost two-dozen *Chicken Soup for the Soul* books. E-mail him at tmartin@sitestar.net.

Tina Wagner Mattern is a Portland, OR writer. She and her husband have had many wonderful cats over the years, but Sam Hill was the best. Not a day goes by that they don't miss him. E-mail her at tinamattern@earthlink.net.

Most of the time you'll find **Beverly Stowe McClure** in front of her computer, typing stories that little voices whisper in her ear. To relax, she plays the piano. Her cats don't appreciate good music and hide when she tickles the ivories. Beverly has twelve novels for children and teens published.

Kelly L. McKenzie delights in blogging about her decidedly eccentric life. Widowed when her two children were mere tots, this quirk magnet is awash with material. Now that they're adults, she's run out of excuses and is finally writing a memoir about the decade she and her mother survived working together, selling antiques.

Lynn Maddalena Menna's young adult novel, *Piece of My Heart*, was *Seventeen* magazine's recommended book for summer 2013. Her song "(You Have) No Soul" is available on YouTube. She is a frequent contributor to the *Chicken Soup for the Soul* series. Lynn and Prospero live in New Jersey. E-mail her at prolynn@aol.com.

Courtney Mroch is the Ambassador of Dark and Paranormal Tourism for Haunt Jaunts, a travel site she created while battling cancer. She also writes fiction. Her latest novel is *The Ghost of Laurie Floyd*. When she's not writing or traveling, it's likely she's on a tennis court somewhere. She lives in Nashville, TN.

Allison Nastoff received her bachelor's of science degree in Communication from Carroll University. She is currently a case manager at a law firm, but enjoys writing as a hobby. In 2014, she self-published a book called *Paws that Changed My Life: A Diary About Training With My First Guide Dog*.

Leigh Ann Northcutt lives on a farm in Kentucky where she reared five children and one husband. Her family has shared their home with myriad animals, including Pete the barn cat. Leigh Ann spent many years gathering material for her family stories and now writes them in newspapers, magazines and at www.lanorthcutt.com.

Andrea Arthur Owan is still looking for another feline to capture her heart. Her work has appeared in *Guideposts*, *Chicken Soup for the Soul* books, love story anthologies, magazines, and newspapers. Her inspirational blog, *Broken Hearts, Redeemed*, helps families navigate grief and restore their joy following the loss of a baby.

PJ's sixty-eight years old, married to a great guy and mother to four girls: two engineers, one of whom is also a doctor, one ecologist and one Jane of All Trades. PJ writes a little, likes to create things and do a little household engineering, and plays *Scrabble* online to try to hang onto the old brainpower as long as possible.

Mark Parisi's "Off the Mark" comic panel appears in over 100 newspapers worldwide and is distributed by Universal Press Syndicate. Visit www. offthemark.com to view over 8,000 cartoons. Mark's cartoon feature has won best newspaper cartoon twice and best greeting card once by the National Cartoonists Society. Lynn, his wife/business partner, and their daughter, Jen, contribute with inspiration (as do four cats and a dog).

Denice Penrose has an MSc degree and is a freelance writer. She is cat mad, and owned by four furry tyrants: a pedigree Somali named Raider, Terri the Bengal and two moggy babies KC and Sooty. She has a lovely tolerant husband who puts up with the cats and the writing!

Elizabeth A. Pickart is a pediatric physical therapist at several schools in Wisconsin. She and her husband Bill enjoy their three children and three cats. Elizabeth loves reading, running and family time, and is currently writing a children's book. E-mail comments about "Worst Cat Ever" to pickart.liz@gmail.com.

Loral Lee Portenier, Ph.D., is a psychologist, depth coach, painter, and writer who currently lives in Kansas caring for her mother, two geriatric cats, and the feral cats across the street. She recently decided to start learning French.

Connie Kaseweter Pullen lives in rural Sandy, OR near her five children and several grandchildren. She earned her Bachelor of Arts degree at the University of Portland in 2006, with a double major in Psychology and Sociology. Connie enjoys writing, photography and exploring nature. E-mail her at MyGrandmaPullen@aol.com.

Yolanda Ridge is the author of *Trouble in the Trees* (Orca Book Publishers, 2011), *Road Block* (Orca Book Publishers, 2012) and *Inside Hudson Pickle* (Kids Can Press, 2017). When she's not writing books for young children, Yolanda likes to hike, bike and ski with her family in their small mountain town of Rossland, BC, Canada.

April Riser is an Instructional Coach who taught middle and high school for nineteen years in the U.S. and abroad. She loves to read, is passionate about animals, hiking and being outside, and yearns to wander the world whenever possible. She is currently working on a series of children's books.

Bruce Robinson is an award-winning internationally published cartoonist whose work has appeared in many magazines, including *National Enquirer*, *The Saturday Evening Post*, and *Woman's World*. He is also the author of the cartoon books *Good Medicine* and *Bow Wows & Meows*. Visit him at www.BowWowsAndMeows.net or e-mail him at CartoonsByBruceRobinson@hotmail.com.

Kassie Rubico's work has appeared in *Guide to Kulchur Creative Journal*, *InSight: Rivier Academic Journal*, and *River Muse: Tales of Lowell & the Merrimack Valley*. She holds an MFA degree in Creative Nonfiction from Solstice at Pine Manor College and teaches writing at Northern Essex Community College. She lives with her three daughters and loves to run.

Linda Sabourin makes her home in the Arkansas River Valley, where she lives with her brother Mike and their cats. She enjoys going to auctions and often lists her treasures on eBay. She loves writing stories about her life (and submitting them to Chicken Soup for the Soul!) and hopes to someday have her own cat rescue.

Lori Sciame received her B.A. degree from the University of Wisconsin–Whitewater, and an MFA degree from Bowling Green State University. She writes for PeKu Publications, and is a Senior Lecturer of English and a student advisor. She has had essays published in *Angels on Earth* and *Guideposts*. Lori has three children in college.

Laura Snell, her husband Dave and their dog Gus Gusterson live in Wasaga Beach, ON, where they operate their business GBSelect.com. Her son Ryan lives in Melbourne, Australia. E-mail her at laura@gbselect.com.

Cheryll Snow is a wife, mother, grandmother, author, and RN. This is her fifth piece published in the *Chicken Soup for the Soul* book series. She and her husband live just north of Chattanooga, TN in beautiful Sequatchie Valley. Besides writing, her other passions include gardening and travel. Contact her via her website at www.cheryllsnow.com.

Diane Stark is a wife and mother of five. She is a frequent contributor to the *Chicken Soup for the Soul* book series. She loves to write about the important things in life: her family and her faith. E-mail her at DianeStark19@yahoo.com.

John Stevens has a restless soul that has visited many parts of the world. He has worked in TV, as TD of Softball Canada, ED of the Canadian Association of Journalists, a computer instructor and supply teacher. He now teaches ESL and runs a B&B with his wife, cat and two dogs in St. Marys, ON. E-mail him at john.stevens@rogers.com.

Shirley K. Stevenson earned her B.Ed. from University of Alberta. She is a retired teacher and widow with two grown children. She is very active as a volunteer with seniors in care and in teaching and helping at senior centers in Edmonton, AB. Shirley enjoys writing up her own memories and helping others do so.

Deborah Sturgill and her husband Mike share a home with five beloved fat cats: Pippy, Little Kitty, Teddy, Benji, and Minnie. She's a small business owner with a passion for nature photography and writing. She's been published in three *Chicken Soup for the Soul* books, and is working on publishing Christian books. E-mail her at deborahsturgill1@gmail.com.

Stephen Taylor is a writer and graphic artist. He lives in the San Francisco Bay Area with his cat Maxi, volunteers at a local animal shelter, and does catsitting for several feline friends. His story "The Marks of a Lasting Love" appeared in *Chicken Soup for the Soul: The Cat Did What?* For more info, e-mail him at malchats@yahoo.com.

Carol Teed enjoys writing about her life's work as a veterinarian. She lives in Ontario, Canada with her husband, four children, two dogs and three cats. This is her second story published in the *Chicken Soup for the Soul* book series and she has also published a book entitled *Learning the Secret Language of Cats: A Vet's Translation*.

Stevie Trujillo is a writer and nomad slow-traveling the world with her family of three. They've driven through eighteen countries and counting! Follow her blog at www.nomadlyinlove.com where she writes about her travels, alternative-living, and personal transformation. She aims to make you laugh, cry, and live inspired.

Carol Weeks is a Christian humorist, author, speaker, Certified Laughter Leader and award-winning poet. She blogs each week at *Carol Weeks Speaks!* (www.CarolWeeks.blogspot.com). She and her husband are retired and love to go camping.

Kevin Wetmore is a writer, actor, director and comedian originally from Connecticut but now calling Los Angeles, CA home. He is the author or editor of over a dozen books and several dozen short stories, and a Professor at Loyola Marymount University. Learn more at www.somethingwetmorethiswaycomes.com.

Erika Whitmore started writing in the womb. Or not long thereafter. She developed an early love and respect for all animals, and has a uniquely "twisted" imagination. She graduated, with honors, from SFSU and was writing and directing TV spots by age nineteen. She now resides in Portland, OR with her beloved Snowshoe cat, Penelope.

Mary Z. Whitney has contributed stories to over twenty-five *Chicken Soup for the Soul* books. She also writes for *Angels on Earth* and *Guideposts*. Her children's book *Max's Morning Watch* is available through Amazon.com as well as *Life's A Symphony*, an adult inspirational fiction. Mary and husband John reside in Leavittsburg, OH.

Jeanne Zornes, of Washington State, has written hundreds of articles and seven books, including *When I Prayed for Patience… God Let Me Have It!* She has contributed to five other titles in the *Chicken Soup for the Soul* book series. She and her husband, a retired teacher, have two grown children. She writes weekly at www.jeannezornes.blogspot.com.

Chicken Soup for the **Soul.**

Meet Amy Newmark

About Robin Ganzert and
American Humane Association

Thank You

About Chicken Soup
for the Soul

Meet Amy Newmark

Amy Newmark was a writer, speaker, Wall Street analyst and business executive in the worlds of finance and telecommunications for thirty years. Today she is author, editor-in-chief and publisher of the *Chicken Soup for the Soul* book series. By curating and editing inspirational true stories from ordinary people who have had extraordinary experiences, Amy has kept the twenty-three-year-old Chicken Soup for the Soul brand fresh and relevant, and still part of the social zeitgeist.

Amy graduated *magna cum laude* from Harvard University where she majored in Portuguese and minored in French. She wrote her thesis about popular, spoken-word poetry in Brazil, which involved traveling throughout Brazil and meeting with poets and writers to collect their stories. She is delighted to have come full circle in her writing career — from collecting poetry "from the people" in Brazil as a twenty-year-old to, decades later, collecting stories and poems "from the people" for Chicken Soup for the Soul.

Amy is a frequent radio and TV guest, passing along the real-life lessons and useful tips she has picked up from reading and editing thousands of Chicken Soup for the Soul stories.

She and her husband are the proud parents of four grown children and in her limited spare time, Amy enjoys visiting them, hiking, and reading books that she did not have to edit.

Follow her on Twitter @amynewmark and @chickensoupsoul.

About Robin Ganzert and American Humane Association

Robin Ganzert has been president and CEO of the American Humane Association since late 2010, leading the nation's oldest organization dedicated to the protection of animals and children. Dr. Ganzert utilizes the insights she gained as deputy director of the prestigious Pew Charitable Trusts and, prior to that, as Wachovia's national director of philanthropic strategies, to bring visionary leadership and a renewed vibrancy to the 134-year-old American Humane Association.

Since 1877 the historic American Humane Association has been at the forefront of every major advancement in protecting children, pets and farm animals from abuse and neglect. AHA also leads the way in understanding human-animal interaction and its role in society. As the nation's voice for the protection of children and animals, American Humane Association reaches millions of people every day through groundbreaking research, education, training and services that span a wide network of organizations, agencies and businesses.

Under Dr. Ganzert's leadership, American Humane Association has been named a "Top-Rated Charity" by CharityWatch and achieved the prestigious "Gold Level" charity designation from GuideStar.

A familiar face to millions of Americans from her frequent TV appearances and the highly-watched Hallmark Channel's *American Humane Association Hero Dog Awards,* she also hosts her own radio show, *Be Humane™ with Dr. Robin Ganzert,* which mixes practical expert pet advice with guest appearances by some of America's best known pet lovers from the movies, music and sports.

She is the author of *Animal Stars: Behind the Scenes with Your Favorite Animal Actors.* She authored the foreword of *Animals and the Kids Who Love Them: Extraordinary True Stories of Hope, Healing and Compassion.*

Meanwhile, the Association's best known program, the "No Animals Were Harmed®" animals in entertainment certification, which appears during the end credits of films and TV shows, today monitors more than 1,000 productions yearly with over 3,400 production days with an outstanding safety record. American Humane Association's farm animal welfare program ensures the humane treatment of over a billion farm animals, the largest animal welfare program of its kind.

Most recently, Dr. Ganzert spearheaded a groundbreaking clinical trial that hopes to provide scientific substantiation for animal-assisted therapy (AAT) in the treatment of children with cancer and their families. The trial is now underway at five pediatric cancer hospitals across the nation.

A graduate of Wake Forest University with undergraduate degrees in business and accounting and a Masters in Business Administration, she served as Assistant Dean for Finance and Administration at the university's Babcock School of Business while pursuing her doctorate in higher education finance.

Robin has appeared on NBC's *Today*, *ABC World News Tonight*, *Fox & Friends*, *On The Record with Greta Van Susteren* as well as other local and national television programs. She has been a guest on *The Diane Rehm Show*, Sean Hannity's radio show and many other radio programs. Robin has written for or been quoted in *The New York Times*, *Chicago Tribune*, *Los Angeles Times*, Foxnews.com, *USA Today*, *Fast Company*, *The Boston Globe*, *The Tennessean* and other news outlets.

Robin and her husband Bart reside in North Carolina and are the proud parents of three human children. Fur children include dogs Gatsby, Daisy and Chas, as well as feline family members Rosebud, Poochie and Cedes. Robin is photographed above with decorated war hero Sgt. Matt Eversmann's family feline, Genghis Khan, of West Palm Beach, Florida. Genghis has his own special story. He and his siblings were found alongside the road with their mother, who had been killed by a car. Rescued and provided a fur-ever loving home by the Eversmann family, he inspires us all to give second chances by visiting a shelter or rescue group to meet our new best friends.

Thank You

We owe huge thanks to all of our contributors and fans, and to their fascinating felines. We loved your stories about your cats and how they enrich your lives. We could only publish a small percentage of the stories that were submitted, but we read every single one and even the ones that do not appear in the book had an influence on what went into the final manuscript.

We owe special thanks to Susan M. Heim, who read the thousands of stories submitted for this book, selected the finalists, and organized them into chapters. Susan also came up with the fabulous idea of including fun facts about cats at the beginning of each story instead of our normal quotations. She did an amazing job finding the facts and pairing them with the stories.

Chicken Soup for the Soul's VP and Assistant Publisher D'ette Corona worked with the contributors on any edits to their stories, and the whole publishing team deserves a hand, including editors Barbara LoMonaco and Kristiana Pastir, who proofread the final layout, our Director of Production, Victor Cataldo, and our graphic designer, Daniel Zaccari, who turned our manuscript into this beautiful book.

Sharing Happiness, Inspiration, and Wellness

R eal people sharing real stories, every day, all over the world. In 2007, *USA Today* named *Chicken Soup for the Soul* one of the five most memorable books in the last quarter-century. With over 100 million books sold to date in the U.S. and Canada alone, more than 200 titles in print, and translations into more than forty languages, "chicken soup for the soul" is one of the world's best-known phrases.

Today, twenty-three years after we first began sharing happiness, inspiration and wellness through our books, we continue to delight our readers with new titles, but have also evolved beyond the bookstore, with super premium pet food, a line of high quality soups, and a variety of licensed products and digital offerings, all inspired by stories. Chicken Soup for the Soul has recently expanded into visual storytelling through movies and television. Chicken Soup for the Soul is "changing the world one story at a time®." Thanks for reading!

Share with Us

We all have had Chicken Soup for the Soul moments in our lives. If you would like to share your story or poem with millions of people around the world, go to chickensoup.com and click on "Submit Your Story." You may be able to help another reader and become a published author at the same time. Some of our past contributors have launched writing and speaking careers from the publication of their stories in our books!

We only accept story submissions via our website. They are no longer accepted via mail or fax.

To contact us regarding other matters, please send us an e-mail through webmaster@chickensoupforthesoul.com, or fax or write us at:

Chicken Soup for the Soul
P.O. Box 700
Cos Cob, CT 06807-0700
Fax: 203-861-7194

One more note from your friends at Chicken Soup for the Soul: Occasionally, we receive an unsolicited book manuscript from one of our readers, and we would like to respectfully inform you that we do not accept unsolicited manuscripts and we must discard the ones that appear.

Chicken Soup for the Soul

Brand Pet Food ®

because Food is more than just Nutrition, it's also about Comfort, Love and Appreciation ™

We are inspired by the thousands of stories we receive about the love between pets and people. The stories are of moments... moments of love, gratitude, laughter and even heartache. So many of these stories revolve around food. That is why we developed our line of super premium, all-natural pet food more than ten years ago — to help you turn your own moments into stories.

We believe that all pets deserve to feel loved and appreciated so we proudly feature rescues on our packaging and encourage pet adoption nationwide.

Visit www.chickensoup.com/pets to learn more about our food and how your purchase helps shelter pets in need.

Chicken Soup for the Soul

for the Soul.

My Very Good, Very Bad Dog

101 Heartwarming Stories about Our
Happy, Heroic & Hilarious Pets

Amy Newmark
Foreword by Robin Ganzert
President and CEO, American Humane Association

Royalties from this book go to
AMERICAN HUMANE ASSOCIATION

Sometimes you can choose your family... by choosing to love a dog! But just because they're dogs, it doesn't mean they won't be as complex and individual as anyone else around. Our dogs can be so good, and then they can be not-so-good, but boy do they give us great stories! This collection of 101 funny, heartwarming, and sometimes mindboggling stories is all about all the very good, very bad, simply amazing things our dogs do.

978-1-61159-956-5

More Fun and Support for AHA

Chicken Soup for the Soul.
The Cat Did What?
101 Amazing Stories of Magical Moments, Miracles and... Mischief

Royalties from this book support the American Humane Association

Amy Newmark
foreword by Miranda Lambert

With a special emphasis on the benefits and joys of adopting abandoned and rescue cats, these loving stories will amaze you and put a smile on your face. Most of them will make you laugh out loud, some will make you tear up a little, and others will have you nodding your head in recognition, as you see your own cat in a new light.

978-1-61159-936-7

More Cat and Dog Tales

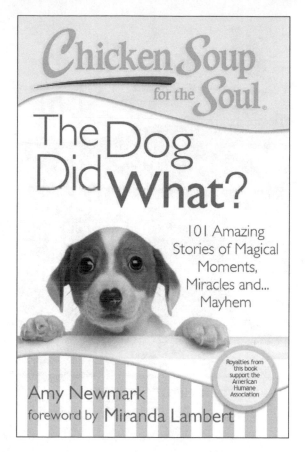

Chicken Soup for the Soul.

The Dog Did What?

101 Amazing Stories of Magical Moments, Miracles and... Mayhem

Royalties from this book support the American Humane Association

Amy Newmark

foreword by Miranda Lambert

With a special emphasis on the benefits and joys of adopting abandoned and rescue dogs, these loving stories will amaze you and put a smile on your face. Most of them will make you laugh out loud, some will make you tear up a little, and others will have you nodding your head in recognition, as you see your own dog in a new light.

978-1-61159-937-4

and Support for AHA

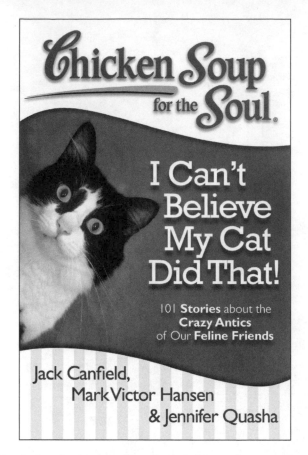

Chicken Soup for the Soul®

I Can't Believe My Cat Did That!

101 **Stories** about the **Crazy Antics** of Our **Feline Friends**

Jack Canfield,
Mark Victor Hansen
& Jennifer Quasha

We all rejoice in the simple absurdities, funny habits, and crazy antics of our cats. They make us smile every day, but sometimes they really outdo themselves. You will love reading all the heartwarming, inspirational, and entertaining stories in this book. We know after reading the stories you'll say, "I can't believe a cat did that!"

978-1-935096-92-4

Classics for Cat Lovers

Chicken Soup for the Soul®

What I Learned from the Dog

101 Stories about Life, Love, and Lessons

Jack Canfield,
Mark Victor Hansen & Amy Newmark

With a foreword by Wendy Diamond,
pet lifestyle expert as seen on *Today* and *Greatest American Dog*

An old dog might not be able to learn new tricks, but he might teach his owner a thing or two. Dog lovers will recognize themselves, or their dogs, in these 101 new tales from the owners of these lovable canines. Stories of learning how to be kinder, overcome adversity, say goodbye, love unconditionally, stay strong, and tales of loyalty, listening, and family will delight and inspire readers, and also cause some tears and some laughter.

978-1-935096-38-2

Classics for Dog Lovers

Chicken Soup
for the Soul

Changing lives one story at a time®

www.chickensoup.com